"A worthy mix of entertainment and introspection. Brown's descriptions are deft and his eye all-encompassing."
—*Publishers Weekly*

"An entertaining book that sheds some light onto the male animal . . . emphasis on the animal." —*San Mateo Times*

"Unexpected humor, wry observations, brilliant turns of phrase and effortlessly moving prose."
—*Globe and Mail* (Canada)

"A psycho-social walk across the landscape of American manhood." —*Roanoke Times & World News*

"With warmth, humor and often great style, he has put together his own highly original masculinity workshop. Best of all, it is open to both genders." —*Maclean's*

"Sparkles with gems." —*Entertainment Weekly*

IAN BROWN was born in Montreal. His magazine journalism has won many awards, and he is heard regularly on CBC Radio. He lives in Toronto with his wife and daughter.

MAN MEDIUM RARE

Sex, Guns, and Other Perversions of Masculinity

Ian Brown

A PLUME BOOK

PLUME
Published by the Penguin Group
Penguin Books USA Inc., 375 Hudson Street, New York, New York 10014, U.S.A.
Penguin Books Ltd, 27 Wrights Lane, London W8 5TZ, England
Penguin Books Australia Ltd, Ringwood, Victoria, Australia
Penguin Books Canada Ltd, 10 Alcorn Avenue, Toronto, Ontario, Canada M4V 3B2
Penguin Books (N.Z.) Ltd, 182–190 Wairau Road, Auckland 10, New Zealand

Penguin Books Ltd, Registered Offices: Harmondsworth, Middlesex, England

Published by Plume, an imprint of Dutton Signet, a division of Penguin Books
USA Inc. Previously published in a Dutton edition. Originally published in Canada
by Macfarlane Walter & Ross under the title *Man Overboard*.

First Plume Printing, June, 1995
10 9 8 7 6 5 4 3 2 1

 REGISTERED TRADEMARK—MARCA REGISTRADA

The Library of Congress has catalogued the Dutton edition as follows:
Brown, Ian.
    Man medium rare: sex, guns, and other perversions of masculinity/Ian Brown.
      p.   cm.
    ISBN 0-525-93825-7 (hc.)
        0-452-27449-4 (pbk.)
    1. Men—United States—Psychology.   2. Masculinity (Psychology)—
United States.   I. Title.
HQ1090.3.B76   1994
155.3'32—dc20   93–46982
                                          CIP

Printed in the United States of America
Original hardcover design by John Pylypczak

BOOKS ARE AVAILABLE AT QUANTITY DISCOUNTS WHEN USED TO PROMOTE
PRODUCTS OR SERVICES. FOR INFORMATION PLEASE WRITE TO PREMIUM
MARKETING DIVISION, PENGUIN BOOKS USA INC., 375 HUDSON STREET,
NEW YORK, NEW YORK 10014.

The male is completely egocentric, trapped inside himself, incapable of empathizing or identifying with others, of love, friendship, affection or tenderness. He is a completely isolated unit, incapable of rapport with anyone. His responses are entirely cerebral; his intelligence is a mere tool in the service of his drives and needs; he is incapable of mental passion, mental interaction; he can't relate to anything other than his own physical sensations. . . . Every man, deep down, knows he's a worthless piece of shit.

– Valerie Solanas, *S.C.U.M.*
(Society for Cutting Up Men) Manifesto, 1968

He had no particular theory on the subject; it had scarcely as yet become a necessity of self-defence to have a collection of theories.

– Henry James, *Washington Square*

Contents

Acknowledgments

I interviewed approximately two hundred men in the course of writing this book. Although I have changed names and identifying details in some chapters, they know who they are, and they should know I am grateful for their candor.

Several trusted friends read all or part of this book and offered valuable suggestions: Marni Jackson, Cathrin Bradbury, Zoë Huggins, Tom Teicholz, Brian Johnson, Tim Brown, and Frank Rioux. Phil Jackman of the *Globe and Mail* had his hand somewhere in this, as did Stephen Brunt, Ernest Hillen, Dr. Steven Frank, Dr. Philip Keddy, Anne Schneller, David Wilcox and Charlotte Pierce, Professor David D. Gilmore at the State University of New York at Stony Brook, Professor Peter Wood of Duke University, Stuart Brent (owner of the Stuart Brent Bookshop in Chicago), Alan Weinstein and Nina Barragan in Iowa City, Nancy Griffin, Murray Campbell, Douglas Bell, Richard Lewis, Gene Conti, Robert Souaid, The Dog Club, Jake and Joanne Green, and my father and mother, Peter and Veronica Brown.

I need to thank Laurence Andrews and Jack Laschever in particular. They were my first guides to California, and became good friends. Much of what they set in motion became part of this book.

Finally, I doubt I would have proceeded very far without Jan Walter's gentle encouragement, the advice of Joe Spieler and the late Peter Livingston, the copy editing of Wendy Thomas, or the talents of Arnold Dolin and Gary Ross, my editors, who convinced me more than once that I could and should write this book.

In the end, however, I owe it to Johanna, my wife, for it was she who gave me its heart and its story, and our daughter. There are no thanks that big.

Los Angeles
June 1993

I

The Couple Across the Street

In which the Author admits to various perversions –
Fears his wife's desires – And lays out other
preliminary considerations

There's a couple across my street who make love in their living room. I hear them in the evening, when I walk after dinner. I love the evenings in Los Angeles: it's the only bearable time of day in this circuit board that passes for a city. The heat drops away, the scent of gardenias and camellias expands in the air, spike palms and corners of buildings stand out against the lightly toasted sky. The loud hot day is over, the gray-haired, sirened night is yet to come.

From the sidewalk I can see cream walls, a mantle draped in animal hides, African carvings. The woman makes most of the noise: mid-range Ohs, a second apart, dropping like small crystal cups out of the open french windows of their flat. Passion, and disregard for the neighbors: a tremendous combination. The air stops moving around me.

Her cries arouse me. Is their sex better than my own? I wonder what she looks like when she's moaning. Does she love him—presuming it's a him, which I always do? Or is she there for the sex? I can never decide which would be more exciting. I imagine she's in her thirties, and that she has dark hair, an ordinary woman with ordinary chores whose passion is nonetheless excitingly unsuppressible in the evening. But which woman is it? Is the moaner the doctor who just had a baby, only now returning to sex? The Mexican girl who works out all the time at the gym? Or the Chinese caterer, the woman who drives the Volvo with Ohio license plates?

Her cries never last more than half a block. Walking back to my house, I usually have a few bent, embarrassed thoughts: you're a thirty-nine-year-old married man who stands in front of his house listening to an unseen couple make love. But I keep stepping out there, hoping to hear their little duet.

My wife wants to have a baby. And it's not just talk, or a plan she inherited at birth, or the fantasizing she used to practice with her girlfriends ("Well, I want to have four"). This is different, more insistent. "When would you like to start?" she said again this morning (third time in a week) as we read the newspaper over breakfast. The sun was already bearing down furiously at half past eight in the goddamn morning. I could hear the buzz of a weed-whacker next door.

"Any time you like," I said, not taking my eyes off the paper. There was news of war in South Africa, trouble in Yugoslavia, layoffs here in California. I refused to look up from the worldly details into which I slip every morning, hoping to be distracted from the list of my daily life. I didn't want to encourage her, because the truth is this: some days I'm for it, but when I'm not for it, I'm really not for it.

My wife's body has changed. Her body, overtaken by hormonal committee, is telling her to get on with its grandest physical purpose. I can see it in the slight post-marital widening of her hips—no less sexy than the originals, but still wider—when she lilts away from the bed at night to perform her ablutions; in her taste in clothes (she doesn't go any more for the sprayed-on Lycra skirts I used to buy her); even in her sexual habits. She has less interest in sex than she used to; she wants to make love for keeps. Pause here for sadness.

Last week, as if by magic, two baby books appeared in the pile on the floor on her side of the bed. At the bottom of the pile, but there they were. I walked into the bedroom, saw them like a promise I made long ago, and had to leave the house. I went to a matinee.

Don't misunderstand: it's not that I'm completely allergic to the idea. When I imagine our lives together without another being to build some traditions around, I hate its stretching emptiness. But when I imagine a wailing baby, the feedings, the sleeplessness, the shit-loaded diapers, the complete colonization of my mind, terror bubbles in my throat like heartburn: no time to read, no time to travel, the inevitable compromise of my dreams, whatever they are, or were. It's something she wants, an act of selfishness; for me, it's a sacrifice. I had plans to write a novel, see the world, take up surfing, run a marathon. Most of the time when I imagine a baby, I see the same set of rooms, the same corridor, stretching ahead of me like an apartment I long ago began to despise for its lack of a view. To me it smells like compromise, a set piece, a twenty-year-long run of a Broadway musical, with the original cast long since retired.

Some time, years ago, we talked about it. She said she wanted kids, and the unstated premise of the ongoing fact of our lives together was that we'd have one someday. I missed my chance to put my foot down because I didn't want an argument, and in my frightened silence that desire—I can't call it her desire alone, but these days I want to think of it that way—became the fact of our lives. Gradually the notion became a promise and the promise became a deal, a ghost living with us. This baby has been around for a while, and we haven't even started. Before long it was understood, if never stated, that to decide otherwise would be a betrayal—not only of her age, of the shortening scope of her reproductive possibilities, but of our love.

Or maybe I just began to need her, and the condition of my need was that we have a child.

When did all that happen? I can't remember anything. My confusion, vast on any issue, was intergalactic where the baby/commitment praxis was concerned . . . like the universe itself, without beginning or boundary. . . . The dates of our courtship, the countless touching things she claims I said—they're at best a blur to me, a fog of declarations. One day I was living my comfortable life, and the next she was living with me. On a bad day it makes me nervous to remember all this. On a bad day, when I think about the slow gelling of our togetherness, its gathering weight and formality, the muscle around my heart closes in, and my breath comes short, and I start to panic. I love her, but it's never clear, my love; it never shines out alone, unobstructed and pure, the way hers seems to.

One day she and I were dating, and then we were living together, and then we'd bought a house, and then we'd married, and then she wanted to have a baby—an escalator of commitments onto which I had apparently stepped. My friends were astonished; they said I wasn't the type to marry. A few of them had made bets against it. I told them I wanted "to find out what lay on the other side of boredom." I stole that line from an old girlfriend.

I thought I was an adventurer. And yet here I stand, in a well-trimmed front yard, surrounded by neighbors and swing sets and sport-utility vehicles, the movable monuments of domesticity, listening to a couple fuck.

Across the yards I see another man looking warily back at me, doing exactly the same thing.

I hadn't planned on being in Southern California in the first place. One day my wife came home and announced she'd been offered a job in Los

Angeles. Three months later we rented our house in Toronto and drove west.

I protested, but half-heartedly; she had moved from New York to live with me, after all, so I tossed a fairly robust fifteen-year career as a reporter into the deep-freeze to give my wife a chance to pursue the glories of professional life. It was a modern thing to do.

At first, of course, before the baby train pulled out of the station, our life in Los Angeles was tremendously exciting. I remember that. I remember excitement. I'm a man. The novelty was exciting. You could walk into a grocery store, say "How's it going?" to the giantess behind the counter, and be treated to a ten-minute discourse on the state of her gall bladder. But if you then asked if gall bladder trouble ran in her family, she'd look at you like you were some kind of sex pervert. "Not at all," she'd say. "Will there be anything else?" It was hard to tell where an American's sense of decency began and ended. Even that was exciting.

In Boise, Idaho, on our way out to California, I had walked into our motel room and found the maid leaning on the towel rack in the bathroom, moaning and holding a wet flannel to her head. "I feel bad," she said. "Really bad."

I sat on the bed and listened. Her husband was ill. Their lives were in turmoil, something to do with the rent. Her daughter was failing school. She reminded me of a duck caught in an oil spill. Eventually I said, "Could I use our bathroom?"

"Sure," she said, and sat on the bed. I closed the door. "The thing is," she began anew, "I usually never feel this lousy. . . ."

I was an alien—and not just in a foreign country, but among my own kind. I was waiting for my wife in the motel restaurant when the waitress asked me what I wanted for breakfast. "I'm tired of bacon and eggs," I said. "Do you have something like"—I didn't know how these concepts would go over in Idaho—"yogurt or granola?"

She looked at me, worried and yet dignified. I wondered if she thought I was a homosexual. "I think maybe we could fix you up a fruit bowl."

I almost wept with gratitude. Within minutes, I was eating a mountain of strawberries and cantaloupe covering another, a hidden mound of pineapple. It struck me that the pineapple was a secret message, from the waitress to me, the alien man! *I know what you're looking for.*

My wife and I didn't hike out on the Conception Trail right away; we wanted to wait, to see what life resembled in California. From what I could see, it lacked form. I was thirty-nine years old and living in Los Angeles with no prospects and a wife who wanted to become pregnant, and who in the meantime worked at a great job as the West Coast correspondent of a national magazine and was willing to pay all my bills.

I had a contract to write a book about men, about what it was like to be a man. Yes. An impossible project, but one that had grown like a rogue squash out of my own eighteen-acre patch of defensiveness: my pouting sense, as a man (not to mention a white, middle-class one) living at the end of the twentieth century amidst huge tectonic shifts, such as the "empowerment" of women, that the definition of masculinity had done a backward gainer off the high board. No more hunting and gathering! No more war! I couldn't do anything right. All around me people seemed to think the world and even their own lives were perfectible but for the presence of idiot guys like me. Half the time I agreed. Meanwhile men themselves were allegedly undergoing great changes, renouncing traditional manhood to become something called New Men. That sounded like a tight fit, plus the baby thing . . . I thought it was a lot of pressure. I desired many drinks.

But . . . at least I could do most of what I wanted, mostly when I wanted, wherever I wanted in the land of the free. That was our deal. Sometimes I did what I called work, and at a lot of other times I called Jerry and the Professor to goof off. We'd barbecue, or head down to the park to practice our putting, or attend gallery openings to look at bad art and pretty women. For a while I did nothing but get up early, read in the midday, and play golf or surf in the afternoon.

At other times I kissed my wife good-bye and climbed into my truck and followed the road for weeks on end to find some reliable, or at least presentable, definition of what it meant to be A Man. I discovered generalizations were for imbeciles, definitions were irrelevant, and that it didn't matter where I went: to be driving, engaged in the act of going somewhere, was enough—and the more unpredictable my destination, the better. Do you know why men don't like to ask for directions? Not because our egos insist we should know where we are at all times; we don't ask, because we don't *want* to know where we are. We like being lost and finding ourselves.

It was in the middle of nowhere, hanging out with a bunch of fools I barely knew, waiting to see what would happen, that I remembered what I had forgotten surrounded by the embroidered cushions of domestic life, by living rooms and a wide hot sea of houses.

2

Hackett's New Face

*The sudden popularity of cosmetic surgical techniques
among the male of the human species – The face-lift and
the "Sirloin Butt" – Admissions of vanity on the part of
the Author, and moral considerations thereof*

In Los Angeles, everyone is gorgeous. The women are thick-haired and
shapely and graceful; so are the men. People are so good-looking, driving
is hazardous. In Toronto or New York or even San Francisco, almost
everyone makes eye contact. Not in L.A.; most of us don't make the cut.
The average level of beauty in L.A. is so exalted it's that of a master race.

Ironically for a city where so many people are so good-looking,
everyone talks about plastic surgery. The *Los Angeles Times* and billboards
on Sunset Boulevard carry daily advertisements for eyelid surgery and
liposuction, face-lifts, eyelid tightenings, liposuction of the love handles,

silastic pectoral implants, penile lengthening and thickening, calf implants, even rear-end implants, known in the trade as a "sirloin butt." The fact that these are major surgeries and entail radical procedures, general anesthesia, and copious amounts of pain doesn't matter. The operations are pitched and bought as if they're vacations. The ads promise more and better manhood, instantly.

I'm twenty pounds heavier than I was in college, my waist and thighs are thicker. One hundred and eighty-five pounds was once a distant, hideous blur on the horizon of my future, fifteen impossibly undisciplined pounds away. Now I look back on it as if that weight were a fabulous vacation I once took.

"I'm fat," I say to my wife, standing naked in front of the bathroom mirror, twisting and turning myself into a human cruller.

"No, you're not," she says, exasperated, from the bedroom.

Sometimes I believe her, most times I think I know she's lying. I imagine she sees my deltoid muscles sliding down my back; my triceps, turning into hams; my *gluteus maximus*, newly discovered heavenly bodies. I imagine she sees all these and accepts them, and allows them into her bed, but that what she longs for in her secrets is hard, slim, taut, youthful definition, a man whose body has yet to make any compromises.

Mine is already making them. Last spring my knee collapsed. The doctor tells me I'll have arthritis by the time I'm fifty. I refuse to think about it, though I did catch myself two weeks ago contemplating a subscription to *Arthritis Today*. I already have arthritis in the little finger of my left hand; on cold mornings I can't close it. A month ago another doctor prescribed glasses for astigmatism. I hate to wear them, but movies are in focus when I do. My right elbow aches, I have a chronic pain in my neck, alarming tiny bumps on my scalp, recurrent crotch-rot, my hearing is—my hearing's another story entirely. I now need two weeks to recover from a cold. These changes have all occurred in the past three years.

Ten years ago, when my body worked, I worried what it looked like. Now that it's beginning to crumble, I'd trade function for form any day.

I want my body to work. *I want my body to work.* More than anything, I want my body not to abandon me. Sometimes I fear my strength is all I have.

I tell no one about these fears. Very occasionally my male friends and I complain about putting on a few pounds here, about our dingy lungs, our cracking joints. Sometimes, if we're feeling really racy, we'll hover momentarily over the question of how often we make love these days. The ideal is still every night, but no one's making that. Well, all right, twice a week. I try to have sex that often so I don't have to admit to anything less impressive. As we approach middle age, we're loath to admit we might be losing it.

The other day a woman I know told me she and a friend recently inspected one another's cervixes. *They inspected their cervixes.* One woman had been to the doctor and in relating the experience of seeing her own cervix discovered the other friend had not. So they held an inspection. Can you imagine men doing the same thing? "So, Al—that's your prostate!" I don't think so. A woman can't ignore the reminders her body sends out: it's her thirty-day destiny, her monthly circuit. A man's body, my body, is a ride to some other place I have yet to find on the map. I don't want it to break down before I get there.

But if I force myself to think about my body—and I don't like to, because then I worry that I'm vain—I would say I'm lucky. I'm a bit short, and I bear some resemblance to a fireplug, but I'm healthy, and quite strong. Not really handsome: not like my best friend in high school. Women dropped for him like bicycles blowing over in a stiff breeze. They said it was his eyes: "He has bedroom eyes," they'd say, or, "He has such sensitive eyes." I knew it was bullshit; I knew he just wanted to bed them the same way I did.

I do have a broken nose. It makes people keep their distance, and I need that. My nose (among other features, it's true, but let's stick to the nose) frees me from a thorough excess of vanity.

That's what I want, most of all, physically: freedom from vanity. My vanity exhausts me. I don't mind a modicum of concern: I exercise to feel better and be disciplined as much as to maintain physical decorum. It's the racking fears that kill me, the hatred of my physical being that sweeps over me from time to time. Because there are those days, too: the days when I am too broad or too small, too fat or too measly, the days when I wear a shirt at the beach—days when I look in the mirror and discover I'm not there at all.

True, I am a man, and a man can still get away with decrepitude. I've never considered having some part of my body surgically altered. There's this voice in me. I'm not sure where it comes from, and I'm not sure I want to ask. It says: you are what you are. Make peace with yourself. Your dignity requires it.

Of course, that was before I lived in California, and before I had heard about Dr. Charles David Valiant, a plastic surgeon for men.

Each time I called Dr. David Valiant's office, I ended up on hold listening to a recorded message. The message was narrated by a woman with a pleasant voice and set against the strains of baroque music. She advised callers to ask for literature about any number of plastic surgery operations; informed them that they could pay with Visa, MasterCard, Amex, or on a financing plan; boasted of the benefits of "hand rejuvenations" and "cheek, chin, and calf implants." The message was witty ("While plastic surgery is usually performed to improve the way you look, there's nothing superficial about it"), gripping ("A chemical peel is an exciting procedure"), and, in general, evidence that male vanity was becoming a public affair. Maybe it was the woman's voice, so clean and efficient and friendly; maybe it was what she was saying, so alarming and exciting; but calling Valiant's office gave me a thrill, as if I were contacting another planet.

A week later, I drove out to see Dr. Valiant. The reception area of his office resembled an organ, an inner pocket of flesh: low-lit mauves and pinks, curving sofas, huge paintings of vulval poppies, ridiculously huge bird-of-paradise flowers. The waiting room emanated a subliminal message: here you will flower. A thin blond patient was making an appointment when I arrived. "I use all three names," she said to the receptionist. "If you were to call out Lucy, I would turn around." The receptionist was wearing a studded white jean jacket, open to accentuate her breasts. They were lovely breasts. Valiant had made them for her.

Valiant was late. He was wearing a white lab coat with his name stitched on its breast in blue script, as if he were a beautician. For one of the most prominent plastic surgeons in the United States, he seemed surprisingly young—though just how old he was, it was hard to say. His gray hair put him at least in his forties, but his face was as smooth as a twenty-eight-year-old's.

"Have you had plastic surgery?" I asked, as we walked to his office.

"Yes," he said, "I've had collagen injections in my forehead and cheeks, to erase the nasal labial folds around my mouth. And I'm going to have liposuction of my flanks, and at the time of that, my tummy. I want to get down to my ideal weight, and I'm almost down to it. I've dropped about sixteen pounds, and now I want to have my flanks liposuctioned and my abdomen liposuctioned and I'm going to have my ears—well, you know, we can say pinned back. I'm going to have an otoplasty done. My right ear sticks out more than my left ear. Both ears stick out more than I would like them. So I'm going to have them both pinned back at the same time."

His voice was quick and confident, but his ears looked pretty much the same to me. But Valiant had moved on. He wanted to point out that reconstructive surgeons were real doctors, and particularly good ones; that plastic surgery was an increasingly sought-after specialty; that, despite the quacks, good cosmetic surgeons trained for anywhere from eleven to fourteen years. It was the sort of self-justification one seldom heard from cardiologists or neurosurgeons.

There was a reason for that. In 1953, the year Valiant was born in Orange County, cosmetic surgery was the white trash of medicine, barely respectable. The first principles of its more established cousin, reconstructive surgery, had been stated by Ambroise Paré in 1564. Sir Harold Delf Gillies, the British father of the field, had published *Plastic Surgery of the Face* in 1920, in the aftermath of the disfigurations of the First World War. Reconstructive surgery wasn't recognized as a specialty in the United States, however, until 1941. And it was 1982 before Eugene Courtiss, the Boston plastic surgeon and Harvard professor (and, it so happens, Valiant's hero), published *Male Aesthetic Surgery*, the first textbook to deal exclusively with male cosmetic surgery.

Even then plastic surgery had its taboos, most of which grew out of the unsteady status of male vanity. A woman's obsession with her appearance was acceptable, and even essential, many said, if she wanted to capture a man or succeed professionally. Men who worried about their looks were weird. "Three decades ago," Courtiss wrote in the 1991 edition of *Male Aesthetic Surgery*, "we were taught as residents that most men interested in cosmetic surgery were severely disturbed and most certainly neurotic, if not psychotic, and that we were at risk accepting them as patients." Courtiss still fingered men over the age of thirty seeking nose jobs as "potential problem patients. . . . Since many men having rhinoplasty, in my experience, have been homosexual or bisexual . . . the patient may not truly know emotionally whether his nose should look ultimately more masculine or feminine."

By the mid-1980s, the postwar generation had reached middle age. Demand for male plastic surgery outweighed any lingering belief in the practice's taboos. In 1986, the American Society of Plastic and Reconstructive Surgeons discovered that thirteen percent of the 600,000 aesthetic operations performed that year were performed on men: nose jobs (rhinoplasties) and baggy eyelid removals (blepharoplasties), mostly, followed by dermabrasions (skin peels), rhytidectomies (face-lifts), otoplasties (ear jobs), and liposuction. (Liposuction, the procedure in which fat cells are sucked out of the body with a vacuum-powered pipette, was developed in the early 1980s by a French surgeon.) In 1986, roughly sixty percent of David Valiant's practice was cosmetic surgery, and fewer than ten percent of his patients were men. By the time I met him, six years later, ninety percent of his practice was cosmetic, and nearly forty percent of his patients were men.

Why more men wanted plastic surgery was a question of considerable speculation. Several social scientists, not to mention dozens of journalists, claimed feminism lay at the root of the new craze. Traditionally, men brought status and income to a marriage, while women brought beauty and their procreative bodies. With more women working, and therefore financially independent, the theory ran, more women were demanding a standard of beauty in their men—a fact reflected in the growth of body building. At their weakest, men sought to look strongest. The number of divorced men had also increased fourfold between 1975 and 1985, and most of them were over forty. To catch younger women, they went under the knife.

David Valiant had thought about all this. "We have been given license as males to probe into areas that heretofore we were discouraged from probing into," he said. "Women have been encouraged since young adolescence to apply makeup, to heighten the contours of their cheeks, to enhance the image of their eyes, to manipulate their bodies to effect a given response. Men, on the other hand, have been taught historically just to be reasonably well-groomed, put on a nice pair of pants and a tie, and go off to work. Many of us never gave a second thought to, if you will, altering the contour of our eyelids.

"What I began to see as the job crunch took place, as the wild eighties came to an end, was high-powered businessmen in their early forties, through their fifties and sixties, coming in and saying, 'Can you do something with this skin? It makes me look tired. And the guys at work are saying to me, why don't you go home? You look tired.' And they felt comfortable asking about that. Although some of them would come in sheepishly, and ask about a possible skin cancer on their face, and say, 'But Doc, what I'm really here to talk about is my eyelids.' And that still happens today. I kind of chuckle with them and tell them not to feel uncomfortable. I tell them, we're all in it together."

Valiant told me about a police chief who'd been in his office a couple of days earlier. "He was in for liposuction. He'd done the usual thing, lost twenty to thirty pounds, changed his diet and eating habits, and still had recalcitrant fat up and over his belt line—love handles, call them what you will."

Love handles they were, then. "I could hardly believe I was interacting with a chief of police. Five years ago it just would not have happened. I wouldn't have talked to a chief of police, period. He came in, and he looked buffed. He looked great. And he said, 'Hey, what do you think about this fat on my hips?' And I said, 'I'll suck it off.' And then he said, 'Well, I broke my nose a couple of times.' And I said I could fix that. And then, right off the cuff in my office, he says, 'What do you think of my calves? Do you think I could use implants?' I was bowled over. And I think to deny somebody like that access to cosmetic surgery is reverse sexism."

It was nearly time for lunch; I was getting hungry. I wanted a large hamburger. I asked Valiant what he thought of the theory that feminism was responsible for the new popularity of plastic surgery for men.

"Well," he said, "if feminism has given all of us men, directly or indirectly, the ability to become more introspective and more sensitive, and more self-analytical, and maybe more free with our thoughts, then I would extrapolate we would take more interest in our appearance. If feminism gave women the ability to be more masculine, it may well have given men the ability to be more classically feminine."

"It's a form of emancipation?"

"That's a good word," Dr. Valiant said.

"Well," I said, "I'm not sure. Emancipation means freedom. Among other things, feminism was supposed to free women from having to be concerned about their appearance. But, according to your argument, men have only been freed up to be more concerned about theirs."

"It's an interesting argument," Valiant said. He was making I-have-to-go movements with the papers on his desk. "Have we really emancipated ourselves, or have we actually shared the bonds that women had already? Have we really just intensified our bondage? We are freer to seek out and pursue activities that we otherwise might have been criticized for. Can you imagine twenty years ago saying, as a man, uh, I want to open a floral shop? Or I want to change my nose? Or I want to spend ten hours a week in a gym to alter the form of my body to have a big chest—and I also want to have my nose done. A lot of people would have thought, back then, reflexively, this guy needs a psychiatrist. Or how about this? I'm starting a ballet class with my daughter. Now, I'm not certain I could have said that twenty years ago without raising a lot more eyebrows."

"But what about dignity?" I asked. I felt like an idiot, and a twelfth-century idiot at that. "Cosmetic surgery seems somehow—insincere, I suppose. There's a certain nobility in making do with what you have, in not being distracted by appearance. There's a dignity in believing that your inner self is what matters."

Valiant looked puzzled. "You mean it's more noble not to have plastic surgery?"

I nodded, noble Ivanhoe, he of the natural double chin.

"You'd have to give me time to think about that, to formulate an answer. Because it's so alien to what I do that I'd like to think it over. Because of what I do, I think people should have the right to change their bodies as easily as they change their clothes. Whereas what you're talking about is sort of a theological concept, right? Accepting the body that God gave you. You'll have to let me think about it. That's deeper than the stuff I normally consider."

I hadn't thought my question had anything to do with God. I meant the body had its own dignity, its own imperatives. But it really was time to go. "May I ask you—This is rather a personal question," I said.

"Sure."

"How much money do you make?"

"I can't answer that," Dr. Valiant said, smiling broadly, and shortly after that the interview was over. Out in the parking lot, I counted a dozen Mercedeses. Across the street, in the marina where the doctors moored their boats, a forest of masts waved back and forth.

At 8:15 one morning a couple of weeks later, David Valiant picked up a huge needle. It had to be a foot long. The needle was full of epinephrine, to quell bleeding. Boom! In went the giant needle, straight into the forehead and jaw of Ted Hackett. Valiant leaned into it with the weight of his entire body. The tip left tiny droplets of blood. Tears appeared at the corner of the patient's eyes. Hackett, himself a doctor, was an unusually ideal patient. "Most men need more attention," Valiant said. "More reassurance. Men are afraid of dying."

Hackett looked like a samurai. A pale gray samurai, but a samurai nonetheless. It was the pony tail of hair held back from his face by rubber bands that did it.

As the epinephrine took effect, Valiant took a call in the hallway. "Yes," he said into the telephone, "you may go to underwire bras." He was famous for his breasts.

At 8:25 a.m., the team was ready. "Okay," Valiant said. "Everybody set?" Hackett appeared to be smiling in his sleep.

Valiant cut deeply into the flesh over Hackett's left eye, following the heavy blue felt pen line he had drawn across Hackett's wide brow. Drips of foamy antiseptic made bright pink plops on the gray operating-room floor. "I'm purposely making it interrupted a little bit," Valiant said, "so the scar will be invisible in his hairline." A thin line of blood followed the knife, like a row of spectators, down each temple, in front and along the bottom of each ear, and then back into the hair behind the ears, the so-called flaps. They were taking Hackett's face off.

The hide of Hackett's forehead was surprisingly thick—the scalpel cut was half an inch deep. As he cut, Valiant scraped fat from beneath the skin and pulled the flap of Hackett's forehead back down over his eyes. The forehead looked like a toque that had fallen too low.

When he wasn't cutting and scraping, Valiant dabbed at Hackett's forehead with an electric cauterizer. The cauterizer was a form of soldering gun and made short fizzing sounds as it burned off the ends of Hackett's blood vessels.

By now, Hackett's forehead had been pulled back to his eyebrows. The flap reached well down his nose. The fringes were already curling up like a strip of beef jerky.

"Tell me when you want more pressure," said Ellen, Valiant's anesthetist.

"Yes, crank it up, please," Valiant answered. "We're actually on his skull right here." He tapped the bone. It made a sound like china.

The speaker phone rang. "Floydo!" Valiant said. Floydo was his brother. He was an investment banker.

"Hey!" Floydo cackled.

"How are you?"

"Do you have my sunglasses?" Floydo said.

"You're very muffled."

Floydo tried again. "Thanks for giving me back my sunglasses."

"I don't have 'em," Valiant said. The cauterizer was going wild now. The operating theater smelled like a butcher shop with a small flesh fire burning in the corner.

"You were wearing them," Floydo said.

Zzzzst. Zzzzst. "I put them down next to you."

"First thing to go, buddy. Your memory's the first thing to go."

"You called me when I was on my way to work yesterday. I was glad to note I was going to work before you did."

"Tell you what, buddy. Why don't you give me a call when you're done there?"

"Sounds good," Valiant said. The phone clicked off. "What's his systolic?"

The blood vessels in Hackett's face were squirting blood on Valiant's chemise. "You notice I double glove, even with a guy in the Mormon

Church. What is he, a bishop? A lot of people would do anything he asked them to do, but even with him, I double glove. Because I'm scared to death of blood."

Now Hackett's forehead was completely filleted. The flaps behind the jaw and ears were next. Within minutes, at 8:53 a.m., Hackett's face was attached only by the skin around his eyes, nose, and mouth. Without his face, Hackett didn't look human. He looked like a machine under repair.

For Ted Hackett's pre-operative interview in David Valiant's office, where she signed the anesthesia consent forms, Dotty Hackett had worn her orangey-pink silk top, the one with the roses, and her gray stretch polyester slacks. The slacks and the rose blouse were kind to her thickening figure, and Dotty looked good: plump, golden-pink hair, and certainly younger than her sixty-odd years. Dotty's abdominal wall had been rebuilt after her fourth child, but her real secret was her face-lift ten years ago.

Still: ten years. The effects wore off. Now she wanted a second one. Dotty and Ted had planned to have separate face-lifts a day apart, but then Dotty got to thinking about a dual recuperation, and it all began to seem a bit much. Now she planned to have hers right after Christmas.

Dotty was all for face-lifts. The first time around, she told her doctor she didn't want to look like a movie star. She was thrilled afterward when her friends asked her if she'd been on vacation. That was the thing: having a face-lift was as good as going on vacation.

"You just wanted to look a little refreshed," Hackett said. He was wearing a very snappy blue sports jacket.

"Not like a thirty-year-old," Dotty said. "Because even that's . . . women at thirty want to look twenty. That's because you guys want younger and younger women." She smiled at Hackett.

"I couldn't compete with her," Hackett said, "because she'd always win."

For his part, Hackett wasn't worried at all about the surgery. He was a doctor and familiar with the procedure. Nor was he the sort to feel afraid. He'd been a Navy pilot. He went helicopter skiing in British Columbia every year. He traveled all over the world, to Japan and Fiji and the Maldives, to scuba dive. He'd raised four kids. He'd been one of the first doctors to buy land in Santa Barbara, and today everyone wanted to work there. Now he was having a face-lift. Just another adventure, like his hair plugs ten years ago, $10,000 worth of scalp transplants. "They've been highly successful from an entertainment point of view," Hackett said. "We've had a lot of giggles."

And of course there were celebrities like Phyllis Diller talking about plastic surgery all the time, how her doctor had said her next face-lift would have to be performed by Cesarean section. "That kind of openness with a celebrity made it easier to be open about it," Hackett admitted. "I would like to look as well as I could look. It's not a central thing in my life. I think good health is as good as good appearance. But I have good health, so I guess I'd like to work on the other a little bit."

What convinced him, finally, was a patient in her sixties who came in one morning to have some varicose veins removed. Hackett thought she looked terrific and said so. She thanked him and said she'd just had a face-lift. She said it was one of three valuable things she owned. The other two were a mink coat and a Lincoln Continental. "They all cost about the same," the woman said. "But I get infinitely more satisfaction from the face-lift than I do from the mink stole or the Lincoln. Because I find that when I look better, I feel better. Though of course I realize you can't turn back the clock."

"That seemed to me to be healthy," Hackett said. "She got value for her money."

So when Hackett began to have trouble shaving, the decision to have a face-lift was an easy one. He wasn't fat, but he had his father's fleshy triple chin, and shaving his neck was like trying to shear a sheep. He was always pulling the skin out, yanking it down, and stretching it to get at the gullies of his neck. One morning he decided he'd had enough.

One thing he did know: the face-lift was going to be a great source of jokes. Hackett and Dotty didn't worry about one of them looking younger and more attractive than the other. If anything, it was just the opposite. Hackett and Dotty knew they were aging. "We say, when we get older, maybe we'll need to turn the lights down," Hackett said. "Or maybe we'll put sacks over our heads. But the face-lift took years off Dotty's appearance."

Valiant was taking Hackett's blood pressure. They coordinated well—two doctors who were also friends. "That's probably another thing, too," Hackett said. "I don't have to pay the full fee for this." Valiant was giving him a discount. Hackett would be good advertising for Valiant's skills whenever Hackett saw a patient. "If I did have to pay the whole thing, I'd probably go diving instead."

There it was again: vacation or face-lift? That was the real debate when you were sixty-four and living the good life in California, with the kids grown up and struggling to afford their own houses, and your retirement more or less taken care of: vacation or a face-lift? Hackett's appearance had become one more zesty material comfort, like some fabulous new scuba respirator or a brand-new camera he picked up on sale. You couldn't buy youth yet, but you could buy the appearance of youth, and what was wrong with that?

Valiant was telling Dotty how to care for her husband after the operation. No extra Vitamin E, no aspirin, lots of hydration, no big steaks or potato salads, nothing to eat or drink after midnight. Valiant wanted Hackett to have a week off, breakfast in bed, "plenty of TLC. We can give you a prescription for that."

"I don't know if I can get it filled at our house," Hackett said. It was a joke.

"He took care of me when I had mine," Dotty said. "Now it's my turn. Payback time."

"How'd you two meet?" I said.

Dotty said, "I think we met at a dance. A church dance."

Hackett said, "It was in England."

"And this dapper fellow came over, with a moustache, and this English suit, a very boxy, heavy suit, and I thought, 'He's different.'"

"It was my animal magnetism."

"Yeah, right. But he was very good-looking."

"I was pure and undefiled before I met her."

"On Friday was our anniversary," Dotty said. "Fourteen thousand nine hundred and sixty-five days."

"Forty-one years," Hackett said.

"It's a long time," Dotty said.

"It's like those hostages in Iran," Hackett said. "They count the days, months, hours, minutes."

"That's how you do it?" Dotty said. She was joking, but she was asking.

"The question is," Hackett said, "which one of us is the hostage?" He was joking too.

Valiant yanked Hackett's face tight and tacked it temporarily to his skull on either side of his forehead just above the ears. Nearly an inch of extraneous skin overlapped the original incision.

The tensility of Hackett's new face established, the trick now was to make it look natural by "sculpting" the fat in the once baggy zones. Sculpting meant liposuction through an eight-inch plastic straw known as a cannula. The cannula was attached to a vacuum pump that dumped the fat into a calibrated glass cylinder on the floor.

Valiant began to plunge the cannula back and forth into Hackett's neck, slipping the pipette under the skin flap behind his ears and through a tiny incision in Hackett's neck. "I'm creating tunnels like Swiss cheese in the neck," he explained. The pump made a sucking, slurping, slightly musical noise; the tube from the cannula ran intermittently red and white, as blood and fat disappeared from Hackett's neck, down the cannula, and into the waste-fat cannister. Hackett's carotid artery, jugular vein, and greater auricular nerve were in full view, yet Valiant could have been a cook carving a turkey, a taxidermist stuffing a duck. This was not so far from the truth. The margin between sucking fat and paralyzing Hackett's face was narrow, but nothing seemed to phase Valiant. The end of the cannula jumped about visibly under Hackett's neck skin, as if a mouse were inside, trying to erect a small tent.

As Valiant pushed and pulled and sucked and tunneled, he talked: about duck and goose hunting with his brother on the Snake River, about his brother's legendary duck call (Valiant performed a loud imitation, mid-suck), about the look of disdain his dog gave him when he missed a shot, about steelhead and Canadian geese. He interrupted himself only once to say "I'm gonna suck his neck a little here."

Valiant was on the home stretch now. He'd clamp the face, cut off the excess tissue, and sew what was left back together. "Nothing to it," he said. "Just a little cutting and sewing."

"He's going to look at least fifteen years younger," Ellen said.

At a quarter to ten, another doctor dropped by. Did Valiant want to go deep-sea fishing after lunch? That was the great thing about being a doctor with your own practice in Santa Monica. Valiant couldn't go. "But I'll see you tomorrow," he said. Friday, the two doctors were performing back-to-back abdominoplasty/face-lifts: Valiant knitted and purled the face, lifting years, and his associate helped him tuck the tummy, erasing stretch marks and pot bellies. The double-enders ran six hours apiece—hence one in the morning, one in the afternoon—and netted the doctors $20,000 each.

"Oh, it's going to be a good year," the other doctor said. "Good clothes." He peered over the operating table. "What's he going to look like?"

"At first he'll look like the end of a baseball bat," Valiant said.

While he joked with his associate, Valiant trimmed the excess off Hackett's new face. The mark of a real man! The ability to do two things at the same time! Pee and talk! Work and chat on the phone! Hack great chunks off a man's puss and fling them into a wastebasket like bits of fat off a newly barbecued steak, while bantering with your partner!

Meanwhile the other doctor was deep into a story about a recent fishing trip in which one of his party had suffered a heart attack and died just as the other doctors in the party were hooking onto big yellowtail tunas. As the man had already died, the doctors landed their tunas and then stowed the body below with their new fish in the boat's refrigeration tank. From the doctor's telling, it wasn't clear if he intended this as a true story, a funny story, or both.

"Can we put on a little rock and roll?" Valiant asked. He liked to close up to invigorating music. "Classical to start, then once they're asleep, Def Leppard. No, it's only a joke, Springsteen."

Hackett's face was almost finished. Valiant worked in silence. Hackett's forehead was ready to be re-attached to his scalp, and the forehead is always the trickiest part: the sutures have to be invisible and require a superfine needle and thread. A minute passed. Then: "Did you know I did my own mother here?" Valiant said. "Four times." Her eyes, her face, her clavicles . . . he refused to work on her breasts, though. "That would have been too sexual," he had explained earlier. "And did you know I did my wife here?"

"And did you know," Ellen said, marveling, "that he didn't seem any more uptight than he does today?" It was a compliment. On the table next to the telephone stood before and after photographs of the surgeon's mother. David Valiant made his mother young again. No wonder they got along.

The job was almost complete: a new face, a new man. So simple. It was 11:26—three hours since the doctor made his first cut, according to Ellen's notes. The forehead was seamless. "Okay, let's wash him off," Valiant said. "But you keep him real deep, because I'm not sure we're out of the woods." The bandages went on, rolls and rolls of white sterile gauze under the chin, up the sides, across the top, Hackett's head growing larger and larger. Wrapped, it was the size of an overinflated basketball, a huge white beet. He still seemed, unbelievably, to be smiling.

As he wrapped, Valiant was back on his favorite topic—why cosmetic surgery is a boon to mankind. He knew he'd done a good job. "Ted was a very young-feeling, young-acting person, who looks into the mirror and the face he sees looking back is not the person he feels," Valiant said. "I don't want to denigrate anything that people who feel cosmetic surgery is shallow say, but—their day will come. They'll see the light." We all get old, he seemed to be saying, and we'll all want to be young again. A few months later I saw a photograph of the new Hackett, and he looked at least twenty years younger. He made *me* want a face-lift. I wondered if David Valiant knew me better than I knew myself.

In the locker room at my health club, it's always the old men who catch my eye. Something happens to a man's body when he reaches eighty. The rest of us are more or less indistinguishable, but the old birds have frames all their own. Hair sprouts on every conceivable surface; they're squabs, all chest and no legs. Their skin is as white as feathers. It's the old guys who talk, who make all the noise. "Boiled chicken!" they shout, loud enough to be heard across the room. "You never see that any more!" They start conversations with whomever happens to be standing next to them in the shower. They never curse, and they're always talking about a "good-looking woman."

The rest of us are aware of one another: we keep our eyes to ourselves, go briskly about our business. The old men gaze openly, admiring strength and ease that is no longer theirs. But there's a calm, a possession in their cranky postures that we younger men don't yet have; in us, there is still a struggle, between the body and the mind, one debating the other. I can see it in our stiff, muscular moves, our inadvertent posturing. The old men never posture. They own their bodies outright, have paid the mortgage. Their bodies remind me of mobile homes on autopilot, old horses whose movements and creaks and habits are so economical and well-established they operate without instructions from the driver. They concentrate on the moments dead ahead and long past, apologizing for nothing. I don't think many have had plastic surgery, and if they have, it can't help them anymore.

3

Sex and the Golfing Astronaut

Secrets of the infamous "golf weekend" – Justifications
of the game, and the reasons it is played – Hair styles
and oral gratification – Sex, consensual and otherwise

Six weeks later I was heading into the desert in Jerry's leased Nissan
Maxima. I was playing with the car phone while Jerry talked about
"getting to yes." I'd known Jerry back in Boston; now he hoped to spend
the rest of his working life selling bonds in Los Angeles, until he made a
killing and retired at forty-five. Jerry and six of his buddies were making
their annual golf pilgrimage to Palm Springs. Jerry had invited me along
for the weekend.

The desert was light tan and looked like a large vacant lot. We were
doing eighty and talking about a woman someone had admired in
Playboy.

"What month?" Don said. Don was thirty-two, six-foot-four, the best golfer in the group, and extremely confident. He smiled constantly. Naturally he had the front passenger seat.

"July," Spence said. "Nineteen ninety-one."

"Wendy Kaye," Don said. "Memphis, Tennessee." He knew the name and birthplace of all the *Playboy* centerfolds, right back to the first issue.

The traffic was terrible. It was seven o'clock by the time we arrived in Palm Springs. The lush irrigated green of the city jumped out of the desert like an attack dog. The entire town appeared to be dedicated to the proposition that only the rich can die happy. We dropped our bags at the hotel and headed for a club called Pompeii.

The music at Pompeii was so loud it made your stomach dizzy. The bass alone shook my diaphragm and blurred my vision and made the room tremble, as if it might fall apart.

None of it affected Spence. Spence was Jerry's best friend. He cocked his ear closer to the woman's mouth, a wide wet oval. She was very tall and wore the standard-issue Palm Spring Desert Bloom look—tight white miniskirt and Spandex tights to the mid-calf, a white T-shirt. She looked exactly like every other woman in the place.

She tried again. "Did you play sports at college?" she screamed in Spence's ear.

"Actually, I did," he screamed back. "I played lacrosse for Princeton."

Spence had never held a lacrosse stick, and he certainly hadn't attended Princeton. But the Ivy League routine was one of Spence's staples when he played the Big Lie Game.

Spence had invented the Big Lie Game years earlier in a bar in Los Gatos, California, inspired by the basket of business cards by the door. The routine was simple. Spence's friends picked four cards; Spence drew one and assumed the identity of its owner. The first night he ended up impersonating an astronaut-in-training and a Maserati dealer. The thrill was inventing convincing details—engine sizes, lift-thrust differentials, close calls. Spence indulged his greatest fantasy—he could become someone else to get a woman into bed. I knew women who would have considered that a form of rape. But Spence said, "If a woman wants to go to bed with me just because I'm a NASA astronaut or a junior senator from Idaho, I don't have to give her an explanation for that. She doesn't deserve an explanation."

The lacrosse story was a bust. Princeton the woman probably bought—Spence had the tall parboiled whiteness of a model Princetonian—but lacrosse? What was that? Spence gave it twenty solid minutes, then left her alone. Picking up women was a lottery. He had no illusions about his appeal. "I can make 'em laugh," he said at the bar. "I make 'em feel comfortable. A lot of times, I make 'em feel pretty." He was a philanderer, but he seldom felt the need to defend his habits. He seemed to think of himself as the last defender of the male empire. Disapprove as I sometimes did of his behavior, I couldn't help liking him. Something in Spence appealed to my most basic, primal, idiot male mentality—the same part of me, I suspect, that laughed at a pair of friends who once showed up at a party wearing Depends adult diapers under their jeans. They picked up a pair of girls, stepped onto the dance floor, and in the middle of the slow number, lazily smiled at one another. They were peeing. Something in me liked them as I liked Spence, because some part of me always wanted to break the rules.

Jerry was the only one who knew everyone on the trip, but we took to one another eagerly. Later we ran out of things to say, and then the old reliables came in handy: corporate power and money and professional sports and women. When even they failed us, we drank, and then it didn't matter what we said.

And of course there was always golf. Golf was our obsession, but it was a mistake to admit it. Never mind that twenty million men and women play golf all over the earth. The truth is this: a man in his thirties who takes up golf is admitting to the arrival of middle age, to a self-imposed retreat from football and baseball and collective team effort—the work of society!—into puny individualism, where one's struggles are private and full of compromise. Jerry, for instance, had taken up golf at virtually the moment he promised his wife he wouldn't visit strip clubs any more.

Spence felt it, too: not that he had failed, but the possibilities of his life were shrinking. At thirty-three, the future was no longer a great open highway but instead a small secondary road, and an increasingly familiar one at that. The consequences of his life were coming home to roost.

A month before the golf weekend, for instance, the girl Spence was seeing had an abortion. She was twenty-four. Spence flew her to Arizona from San Francisco to have it taken care of. "I felt like shit for about a week," he said. We were sitting in the lobby of the Ritz in Palm Springs. "Which was surprising. Well, not surprising. But—well, it shouldn't have happened. An unborn child." He shook his head.

The strange thing was, Spence wasn't entirely unhappy with his more settled landscape. He wasn't as hopeful as he had been at twenty-two, but he wasn't as frantic, either. Something had happened. It wasn't the date-rape scandals, or any of the other public scoldings men were subjected to frequently on television and in the newspapers; Spence wasn't the type to be intimidated by the questionable behavior of others. But he'd been promoted at the company, and he'd found a job he thought he could be good at. (In fact he was laid off a year later.) "I won't go as far as settling down," he said. "I don't like those two words—'settle' and 'down.' But for the first time in my life I'm starting to feel guilty. I don't like to pull the wool over women's eyes so much any more. I find myself feeling a little—"

"What?" I said. This was most unlike him.

"Callous."

For years his Friday nights had been planned. Now, if he found himself at home on Friday reading a book—well, that was fine, too. He could stay at home and make his list. By his own count, he'd slept with three hundred women—not in Wilt Chamberlain's league, but at least fifty times one estimate of the national average. All those women; he felt virile when he thought of them. He never worried about AIDS. He'd had everything else: for a while, Spence had so many genital infections, so many lesions and sproutings, his friends called his penis "the lawn sprinkler." It always got a big laugh. Now Spence uses condoms a good eighty percent of the time.

That's not to say Spence was all tenderness. We were filing out of a bar called TGIF when Tito hissed. Tito was Spence's brother. "Hey! Three o'clock at the bar. Blow-job hair."

"You're right," Spence said. "Blow-job hair."

Spence had been ordering the drinks, as usual, first beer, then Long Island Teas, then a shooter called Slammers mixed from tequila and Triple Sec and three other even more medieval ingredients. It tasted like solvent. Spence was one of those extroverts who became your personal host whenever he stepped into a bar or restaurant. He called himself "the cruise director." "I do it," he once told me, "because I like the attention." I was only too happy to have someone else make the decisions.

Outside, we piled into Desmond's rented cinnamon-red Lincoln Town Car and headed to the liquor store. It was hard to believe he and Spence were friends. Spence was tall and blond and smooth and sophisticated, like the office-machine salesman he was. Desmond was short, balding, and a weight lifter. The trunk of the Lincoln was two inches deep in body-building magazines, Desmond's weekend reading. At five-foot-seven, he resembled an anvil sitting on a milking stool. But he and Spence had been friends since high school and shared the iron bond of adolescence, of becoming men and killing brain cells together.

"What did you mean," I said, "when you said 'blow-job hair'?" The tequila had been very powerful. My lips felt like two leeches on my face.

"Blow-job hair?" Tito said. "You never heard of that?"

"Actually, no."

"The girls had short hair, right?" Spence said. "Short-haired girls are better, because you can see your own blow job."

"You like to see your blow job?"

"Doesn't everyone?" Spence asked. He was shocked I had to ask. "Why?"

"It's just great," Tito said.

To watch a woman fixated on your erection, to be aroused by the sight of oneself imbedded in the center of a woman's mind—true enough, I thought, it's one of the highlights.

"Why is that? Is it the sense of having power over the woman?" I actually said this.

"Sure," Tito said, "that's part of it."

"No," Spence said, "it's not power. It's because men want to be the star of their own porn movie."

That's very true, I was thinking to myself, when the door of the Lincoln opened and Desmond flung himself into the front seat carrying a bottle of Cuervo. "She wanted ID, for fuck's sake. I said to her, 'Look at my hairline, for fuck's sake.'"

"We were just talking about how great it is to watch your own blow job," Spence said.

"Oh, yeah," Desmond said. "And watching a black girl give you a blow job is the best. It's like your cock disappears into this black hole."

Desmond's unwitting instinct for self-exposure made me wince for him. Sex with a black hole? Charming. Trying to pretend there was no one on his other end. But that was part of sex as pure pleasure, the privacy of it: the early play, then a greater hunger and vigor as she locked in, and bingo, that was it, the bobsled was now out of the gate and tearing down the track and taking the first and the second and the third and at long, long last the final turn . . . and the twin tumbles of pleasure and disappointment that inevitably followed, leaving just the faintest tincture of defeat. Thrilling defeat, but defeat.

And then nothing. Emptiness. For a long time there is nothing but this silence. And then, as slowly as if you were being born again, you come to. You feel the outline of your skin again. You open your eyes.

I kept quiet in the car on the way back to the hotel. I wasn't about to admit I liked to watch my own blow jobs. Even the words embarrassed me. As a young man, making my way for the first time through the tar pits of sex, I found being on the receiving end almost too intimate for comfort. *Better to obscure the fact that I was in pursuit of my own pleasure.*

Eventually, of course, I came around. But how had Spence and Tito and even Desmond passed through the sexual wash cycle guilt-free, so blithely unrepressed? Yes, they labeled the hairdo that worked best for them—an objectification of the female person, to be sure. But they were paragons of emotional health next to, say, my friend Andrew, who over lunch a couple of days earlier had admitted "masturbating wasn't even acknowledged in our house." Andrew was forty-two. "And so it didn't exist. Anywhere. No one else masturbated: I was the only one in the entire world. And yet I needed it—every day! I couldn't do without it!" He was still agonizing over the fact.

At least I knew it would stunt my growth. For several years as a boy, I spent five minutes every morning stretching myself on my bed to counteract the effects of the night's activity.

I envied Spence's thoughtless love of pleasure. He was alive, and he wasn't about to let anyone forget it. It was a rare thing to find in a man these days. But he needed pleasure a lot. He used women to get it. Even a woman's pleasure, about which he professed to be seriously concerned, sometimes seemed more about Spence than it was about her. He had a way of grabbing a lot of stuff for himself. He could be greedy.

Spence's sex stories were always hilarious, but later they sometimes had a quality that made me wish I hadn't heard them. I found myself wanting distraction. If I thought about my wife at home, I felt more virtuous. Sometimes I thought about golf.

The charms of golf were largely private. The game was said to present multiple opportunities to "do business," but in my experience its appeal was the very opposite, that I could spend time with my pals and not talk about work. The equalizing nature of golf—"man's battle against himself," as some golf writer called it—gave the game its glow: the companionship of men involved in their own fervent private battle with a ball that, unlike the one used in tennis or squash, waited for you to come to it, thence to drive it from its sleep. Golfers were always making decisions.

Of course, we never talked about that either: such sentiments were too introspective and inert. Better to treat the game as a science, a physical challenge to be repeated again and again. To do that—and this was the real paradox of playing golf, the mental wow that could thrill or frustrate me—to play well, I had to perform a truly creative and spiritual act: I had to repeat my swing over and over again, *without thinking at all*. In its pure physicality, its fervent concrete anti-intellectualism, golf was perfect.

When one's swing worked—when all the elements fell into place like a casual step, and the ball rocketed into its beautiful swept-up arc, first low, then rising high to its apex before falling steeply to its target—when it worked, each shot, each round, held within it, like an invisible code, what I thought all men sought: an open-ended adventure, its outcome unknown, a question of purpose demanding to be answered. And each well-hit shot, punctuated by a brisk but contemplative walk to the ball, was a reply. Playing a round of golf was like playing a round of life—and yet not like life at all, because in the end you knew just how well you'd scored. "Plus," Jerry said one afternoon, "it lets you bang a ball."

But not for me, at least not often, because my golf game "sucked the large bag," as Jerry put it. Still, I remember the moments when my game worked. I remember walking the fifteenth hole of a quiet course north of Toronto, the dew thick on the ground (it was May, still early in the Canadian season), complaining to a friend about an argument I'd had the night before with my wife. I'd forgotten the details of our first date, to her distress. She could remember what we did, where we went, what play we saw, who starred in it, what I ate, what she was wearing, what I said. I could barely remember the year, for Christ's sake, though I have total (and frequent) recall of our first night in bed together. I often feel ashamed of this fact; my faulty recollection is a sign of disgrace, of my crass physicality, of my emotional hollowness. But when I stepped up to the ball and knocked a four iron 180 yards onto the green, my whole body lengthened and a buzz of joy ran down my arms like heroin. That I remember.

Spence carried a list in his wallet wherever he went. He'd seen the list in a magazine in Singapore and copied it out on a bar napkin. The list encoded his personal philosophy.

1. Never regret not doing something.
2. Thank people who do things for you.
3. Don't let life cheat you.
4. Compliment people you care about.
5. Don't take life for granted.

Whenever he actually took the list out and read it, wherever he was, he thought of his father. His father was the reason Spence treated women the way he did. Spence's father had been a director in an aerospace firm, married at twenty-four, a father at twenty-five. He'd grown up in Philadelphia and had always been a big party man, even a brawler. But marriage and fatherhood had changed everything. Half the fight had gone out of him. That was what Spence called it: the fight. His father, his entire generation, had fallen into marriage. Spence wasn't against marriage per se; he wanted to get married, provided the girl pushed at least six "buttons." For a while he carried that list in his wallet, too:

1. Beautiful
2. Sense of humor
3. Sensual and sexual
4. A challenge
5. Spontaneous enjoyment of life
6. No preconceptions

So far he hadn't met her. He wasn't going to marry just to be married. He hated it when his friends got married and suddenly disappeared. "I'm not sure if it's the fault of the woman for wanting to make over the guy, or the fault of the guy who allows himself to be squelched," Spence said. He needed the companionship of men, valued their recklessness; maybe, in a non-sexual way, he would only ever love men, because only men would understand him.

As I say, Spence wasn't afraid to face what he was, and for that I liked him. A lot of people did. Spence made you feel you shared sexual adventures—racy truths the world didn't approve of. Yes, there were people (a number of women, for instance) who thought Spence was an asshole. Spence's old man said Spence wouldn't get married until he loved a woman more than he loved himself. Whereas I figured Spence'd get married when he found a woman who let him love himself as much as he loved her. Not so unreasonable. As to whether his father was ever going to approve of him, Spence found it impossible to say.

What amazed me was that I could pick up the newspaper any day of the year, or turn on the radio or the television, or even just kick up a conversation on a bus, anywhere at any time, and find a lot of people agreeing that men had oppressed women since time immemorial—and yet despite that, Jerry and the boys, all executives in Los Angeles or New York City, still lived in a universe where they devoted a mind-boggling amount of time to, as Jerry put it, "chasing pussy."

It was always better to chase it with your buddies. That way, there was always someone around to keep score—keeping score was important—and there was always someone around to "jump the grenade."

Jumping the grenade meant taking the ugly friend of a pretty girl off your pal's hands while he tried to get onside with the pretty one. "You know, like in war," Jerry explained. "You know how you're all in the foxhole, and a grenade rolls in, and you jump on it to save your buddy's life? That's jumping the grenade. So you know how pretty girls hang out with ugly girls. Because pretty girls are the most insecure people in the world. Because they've always been appreciated only for their looks. By having an ugly friend, the pretty girl gets to be friends with another woman who won't threaten her by getting more attention. But when someone's trying to cut one of the pretty girls away from the herd"—another common term—"someone has to jump the grenade."

The converse of jumping the grenade was "fucking a buddy over"—the sexual term in this case denoting domination, just as "blow me" was for Jerry and company the ultimate degradation. They "fucked each other over" in the course of trying to "do her"—pursuit, competition, triumph, and failure being all part of the same thrill, the thrill of domination.

An instance, one night in New York. Jerry asked a waitress for some service, and she became frazzled and started to cry. A couple of minutes later, he noticed Don commiserating with her—the Sensitive Guy routine. It worked pretty well most of the time unless you tried it out on a non–Sensitive Guy girl, in which case you crashed hard and were perceived as limp.

The problem was, Don was using Jerry's impatience as a contrast to his own Supersensitivity. Don was saying, Don't worry, Jerry can be like that, but I'm different.

Not that Jerry begrudged Don any of the women they competed for. He just didn't want Don to win the prize at his expense. The principle of competition was at stake. The competition was sacred. You had to earn it. So Jerry found a napkin and a pen and wrote a little funny note of apology to the waitress. Then he grabbed a couple of straws—and this was a stroke of genius, an inspiration he would have a right to talk about for months afterward—and what did he do? He made a plastic rose out of the straws! Red and white stripes! Amazing. He presented the note to the waitress. Just as she was about to say something, he handed her the plastic rose. As soon as she saw it, he knew he'd won. Her face collapsed into a smile. She gave Jerry a hug, thanked him, touched his arm. She turned away to deliver a tray of drinks, and Jerry turned to Don.

"You're out, pal," Jerry said.

Was Don mad? No, all is fair in love and pussy. Big, tall, movie-star-at-tractive Don knew he'd been outsmarted. And then, so they could slip away before the waitress came back and chose between them and turned the game into something it was not supposed to be—before the emotional ante was raised out of the Comfort Zone—they all took off for steaks, as they'd intended to all along. Jerry knew there wasn't enough time to really get the girl. He just played the game for the hell of it, and because it mattered at least as much as the woman's feelings did.

Of all the beauties Jerry and the boys studied, challenged, and conquered, though, the most satisfying was Jerry's driver. He called it Bertha. Bertha was the perfect antidote to depression—not only because she promised to make you more accomplished with her kind, and because she was your servant, but because she represented plans, insurance against your life sputtering out.

Bertha was a golf club, but not just any club. Bertha was a Yonex ADX-TL oversized driver, with a boron-reinforced Exsar Gold Low Torque shaft and a matte black aerodynamic graphite head the size of a grapefruit—one of the new miracle clubs, "the thing of the future," as the salesman at the Roger Dunn Golf Shop in Beverly Hills had put it. For $269.99, a golfer bought himself a lighter shaft—which meant a faster swing, with more velocity—topped off by a vast clubface with a sweet spot the size of a silver dollar. Next to the rest of Jerry's golf clubs, Bertha looked like some kid with a gland problem standing head and shoulders above the third grade. She was extremely light, and almost clownishly long, and therefore hard to control. But if through religious practice and iron mental discipline you could tame Bertha, which Jerry had, you could regularly drive a golf ball three hundred yards—as long as the strongest professionals. After Jerry started to hit Bertha consistently well, she became a subject of common awe, and all of us wanted to try her. "I can't believe the effect it's had on his game," the Professor once remarked as he watched Jerry crack one into an oncoming weather system. "He couldn't drive for shit before he bought her."

All you had to do was walk into a golf shop, and suddenly you were surrounded by the warm promise of a better performance: by Snug-Fit golf gloves, and golf videos, and club covers to protect one's magic sticks, Gore-Tex pump golf shoes, cushion-sole socks, golf bags, clip-on ball caddies, golf ball imprinters ("LOST BY ARNIE JONES"), Swing-Tech training systems, putting machines, practice mirrors, shag-n-bags, golf mugs, divot repairers, grip cream, ball cleaners, Blast-Off golf tees (accompanied by testimonial diagrams drawn by Dr. Richard Brandt, a professor of physics and president of the Sport Science Research Center, Inc.), distance finders, chipping nets . . . and, of course, the pièce de résistance, fanned out on racks around the store like species of rare birds drying their wings: golf clubs.

If I timed it right, and arrived at the golf shop by midafternoon, I could transport my new purchase to the driving range for a try-out before dinner. I loved going to the driving range in the afternoon on weekdays to watch the accomplished golfers, especially the Japanese and the black guys, whack that ball into forever, their lithe bodies, compact and easy, swinging again and again and again and again like metronomes in the gold dust of the late Los Angeles afternoon.

I even bought a pair of golf shoes. White ones. With flaps. My conversion was complete. Of course, my golf still stank up the links. Spence, who was a superb golfer, with a handicap of eight, was always polite about it when I shanked a drive or hooked a three-iron into some embarrassing spot, such as the median of a nearby highway. He'd look away, or simply concentrate on his own shot. When I did well, he never failed to compliment me.

At other times, he seemed more ruthless. When he talked about his heart, about things he felt deeply or stuff that scared him, he thought he had to have answers, and then he could seem almost cruel. For instance: "The big problem I've had when I've dated Caucasian women on the career track," he said one afternoon, "is what I call built-in hassles." We were sitting in the hotel lobby, drinking margaritas and watching rich people. "Even to say thank you, for a Caucasian woman who's an executive, twenty-eight—I mean, I'd say thank you for something she did, and she'd say, 'What do you mean?' I'd say, 'I mean thank you.' She'd say, 'You don't have to say thank you because I'm a woman.' And she'd be so intent on not behaving in any way that could be interpreted as 'womanly' that she'd forget she was also a human being. What these professional women forget is that they possess the ability to help create and nurture a human life. Now, to be a guy, to live, to work and sign million-dollar deals, to dunk a basketball, that's all great, but it's not the same. And a lot of women don't realize that."

Spence took a slug of his margarita, as if to fortify himself for the utterance of his next opinion.

"And a lot of these women are tough cunts." (Now there was a word that made me cringe. It was a hard, mean thing. Whenever I heard it, I automatically pictured the commodities market, with stacks of sacks: those were the hog bellies, that's the frozen orange juice, these are the cunts. I'm not saying I never used the word. If a woman preferred the term cunt to describe her own—I knew a couple of women like that, who used the word cunt proudly, and it could even be sexy—that was fine. But I didn't like the way Spence turned something so personal into a generalization, and not a pleasant one at that.) "Caucasian women in their late twenties and early thirties, their priorities are just wrong," Spence said. "But then they hit their early thirties, and they suddenly see that it may be more important to bring a child into the world than it is to cut a deal. And then they go 180 degrees, and the biological clock thing comes in, and there are external pressures, and they compromise their own personality traits that make them attractive, so they can trap a guy. And this is terrible. But it's the way it is. The thing that bothers me is that these women are no longer fun to be with. They're just not pleasing personalities. They'll sleep with you on the first date—and coming from

42

a guy like me this may sound like shit, but I'd like to think that the woman who's going to be my wife, she's not going to sleep with me on the first date."

Spence wanted everything his way. He wanted women to yearn for babies, but he had no desire to be trapped by women yearning for babies. He hoped they would sleep with him on the first date, but he wouldn't marry one who did because she wanted a baby. He had higher standards for women than he had for himself. He loved women, and wanted them, and wanted to dominate them, and yet he wanted them to take care of him and be better than he was. He thought love and sex could be simpler than they ever are. He reminded me of a lot of guys I knew, especially myself.

Back in the "opium den" at the Ritz, as Don referred to the suite Jerry and the Professor and I were sharing, the mood was disconsolate. Everyone was back, womanless, except Don. The boys had duffed badly at Pompeii.

More to the point, Desmond—innocent Desmond, he of the black-hole blow job, a newcomer to drugs—had ingested half a gram of cocaine at once. "I didn't realize it wasn't all for me," he said, as the entire room glared at him. "Boy, this stuff's great," he added, standing to his full five-foot-seven and tossing off half a dozen chest stretches. "I feel great."

"Your brain is as small as your dick, Desmond," Spence said. "And we all know you're hung like a bug."

"What?" Desmond said. He looked confused. His best friend was insulting his penis in front of a room of male acquaintances—a serious betrayal. He plunged his hands into the pocket of his exercise shorts, green fluorescent baggies that revealed his bulbous legs. "I am not hung like a bug," he said. Everyone ignored him.

I turned my attention back to the book I was reading between snatches of a golf tournament being replayed on television. More than watching the game, almost more than the technical challenge of playing golf, I loved to read about the game—a discernible world of knowledge to be mastered. My wife couldn't understand it. "I've become a golf widow," she told our friends. I couldn't explain the appeal. What was I going to do? Open *Golf's Golden Grind*, Al Barkow's history of the pro tour—that was the book I was reading—and quote it outright? "To play golf is to stand shorn of all possible pretense, of all the tricks we learn to invent for coping and conquering in business, or, to raise the ante, for being a parent of a child. The ball and stick are ours alone to do with only as we can. We have no place to hide." No, I think not.

But my new knowledge calmed me. I became part of a tradition, of something that had existed before me, and that would exist after. I lived for golf facts. I now knew that the first formal golf ball was a leather sack filled with feathers, and that a Frenchman had once driven a feathery 381 yards—41 yards farther than I once smacked a solid-core ball (introduced by the A. C. Spalding Company at the turn of this century) on the seventeenth hole of the Malibu Golf Club with a hurricane-like tail wind. When my father-in-law hurried my putting along, telling me it was better to "miss 'em quick," he was remembering an aphorism attributed to Gene Sarazen, the first Italian-American to win on the pro tour, and linking Sarazen to us. I was getting a big fat kick out of being part of something.

Best of all, I discovered the heroes of the game. I learned with a thrill that the overlapping grip I used had been invented by Harry Vardon, the sport's first great professional. Vardon, a working-class Scot, played the first subpar game of golf on record, a 71, in 1900, thereby putting my 127 on the Dinah Shore Classic Course that weekend in Palm Springs in historical perspective. I developed an embarrassing historical crush on Walter Hagen, first pro to make a good living playing golf in America. Hagen wore plus fours and a tie and Panama hats, drank and womanized prodigiously, and traveled between tournaments in no fewer than three limousines: one for himself, one for his clubs, and another for his wardrobe. Hagen seemed Gatsby-like, a man who made himself up as he became more famous and successful.

But it was Ben Hogan and Sam Snead, the scientist and the artist, and the forefathers of Jack Nicklaus and Arnold Palmer, who really captured my attention. My father had owned a matched set of Hogan clubs—the clubs I had carried for him, the clubs he taught me to swing.

My father never took the game that seriously. His hero was Snead— "my boy Sammy," he called him on the gray Sunday afternoons in Canada as we watched "the golf" on television, after Snead had dropped some wondrous shot within an arm of the pin. Hogan lived for golf; Snead was too humane for such intense concentration.

Golf was never my father's game, the way squash and rugby and cricket were. He never took a lesson, never became obsessed the way other men did, never even used a driver on the tee, preferring instead the unshakable consistency of his two iron. And yet he played as well as most men, because like Snead he was a gifted natural athlete. I began to suspect that my father's admiration for Snead lay in their physical similarities—especially their long-muscled, loose-limbed ease, the same ease I had copied in my father all my life with hopeless results.

As my father embodied physical grace for me, Snead embodied for my father the careless perfection of *sprezzatura*, the grace of the spirited, accomplished amateur for whom the game is not so much a task to be perfected through repetition and discipline as it is a gift, an expression of the natural. Snead and my old man made the difficult look easy. They both bent at the waist, keeping their legs straight to pluck a ball from a hole. They had both lost most of their hair. And both offered the lesson of inspiration. True, that easy-going grace had its pitfalls: Snead's putting was a disaster, his game often fell apart, and in the end he was less respected as a golfer than he was enjoyed. But his very failing made greatness, however occasional and haphazard, seem that much closer.

My father golfs less now, but he continues to play squash (and beat me) in his late seventies. His speed, his awesome quickness and physical alertness, isn't what it used to be; if I remember to play the corners, and keep him running, I can win. But more often I concentrate too hard on the technique of my shots and forget to play the game, and he triumphs, three games to two. I can see us now, two pale men battering the air in that small, cold, white windowless room; can hear his yelps bouncing off the walls as he misses a shot—yelps of frustration, but of joy as well, joy at being bested by his own progeny. If I have a son, will he and I play that game? My father and I share this physical presence; my body, his body, his body, my body, circling one another, aping one another in every flick and turn. I never thought to call it love.

Afterward, in the shower, he thanks me for the match. We have the same build: I have broader shoulders, he has longer legs, but beyond that, we are much the same man, from head to cock to toe. "You look fit," he says, tilting his head up to let water course through his sparse fringe of snow-white hair.

"You don't look bad yourself," I say.

"No," he says truthfully, "I'm shrinking. I'm all skin and bones now. Seventy-six. I look like an old man."

That was two years ago. He called before my weekend in Palm Springs, his voice floating over the long-distance telephone wire as if out of the past. "How are you?" he said. "Just called to see if you're all right."

I said I was.

"Take care then," he said, before I could elaborate. "Love you."

"Likewise," I blurted out, but he was gone.

Suddenly the door to the Opium Den burst open. "Okay, listen up," Don said with brisk military efficiency. "I've got two women in my room. My roommate can't fuck one of them because he's married. So I need a single, virile, horny, *single* man for her."

Spence had been comatose in a chair in the corner of the Opium Den, his eyes washed with fatigue; instantly, he was sober, standing, scoured, and combed. "Me, me, please sir, me," he said.

And so Spence set out on his adventure. According to him, this is what happened: By two a.m., the women were floating in the hot tub by the

46

pool. Don's—they used the possessive to distinguish their consorts—was tall and dark.

Spence's date was five foot five and weighed 140 pounds. But she carried a good heft in her breasts, and Spence loved breasts. (He told funny, appalling stories about placing classified ads in San Francisco weeklies for extra-large-breasted women interested in recreational sex. The ads were often answered.)

Spence's girl had short, artificially yellowed hair. "Do we take all our clothes off?" she said—undesirable hesitation, from Spence's point of view, in a woman in her late thirties about to plunge into a hot tub in Palm Springs with a man she had known for three minutes. She was not the greatest beauty he had ever known. But, he told himself, I *need* to get laid.

They made conversation in the hot tub. Don and the thin girl were necking. Spence's date nattered on, clearly nervous. "Linda, I gotta go," she said more than once. "This guy's freaking me out. There's too many people here." Spence figured it was the pot they'd smoked. She was a local, that was certain. A waitress in a bar here in Palm Springs, maybe. She was quite drunk.

"Hey," Spence's girl said. "Do you have liquor in your room?"

"Sure," Spence said.

"Let's go." She swilled the rest of her tequila and slithered up onto the edge of the spa. She really did have huge breasts. Spence was bright pink from the steaming water. He took her hand, and together they made their way across the soft green mat of grass toward the hotel room, stark naked.

Spence didn't know how the girl . . . Carol . . . how Carol was going to react to the fact that Desmond and Tito were asleep in his room, in the bed next to Spence's. Maybe she was used to it. She was definitely the older-horny-Palm Springs-no-questions-asked kind of woman.

"Get me a drink," Carol said when they arrived at the room.

He kept the light off. Spence could see the lumpy forms of Desmond and Tito in the next bed. He was glad they were asleep. It wasn't going to be pretty. He tried to kiss Carol, feel her. He could feel her against his chest.

"Get your fucking hands off me," she said suddenly. "Get me a drink. I won't fuck you until you get me a drink."

He stopped, pulled back, looked at her. He wondered if she was too drunk to know what she was doing.

"Is my mommy here?" she said suddenly. "But you are kind of hung," she added. Spence insisted she said this. "You do feel pretty good. Show me what you've got. Show me your big cock. But get me a drink."

Another lunatic. He could feel his spirits falling like an elevator. Sometimes it was like that: sometimes, for all the pressure of his physical urges, he'd get a girl, coax her upstairs . . . and suddenly she just wasn't that appealing any more. In the bar light the girl was ravishing. In the cool darkness of his room, he realized he'd rather go home and have a grilled cheese sandwich.

What was it with the lunatics? He was always running into them. There was that time with the weird girl who'd asked him to pretend to suffocate her while he was drilling her. What had he said to her? "Um, this is not healthy shit." All that night, Spence had a recurring vision: his name and photograph on the front page of the *Chronicle*, and the headline: Copier Salesman Suffocates Woman in Bath.

Then Carol stood in front of him, close. He looked down at her, and he could feel that place behind his solar plexus falling, as he became aroused.

"I'll get you a drink," Spence said, "after you give me a blow job."

He watched her fall to her knees, take his semi-erect cock in her hands. Her hands were small, but cool. That fine feeling. He swelled a bit, and she started in. It felt good enough. He thought of blow jobs as the "handshake of the nineties." You could squire some girl around for weeks and months, take her out to dinner, talk to her, listen to her, and she still wouldn't fuck you. But you could be hardly out the door on your first date and she'd pull your pants down and suck you off. That always blew his mind. Three-quarters of the women Spence went out with had sex with him on the first date, one way or another.

Three or four minutes went by and Carol was still at it. Nothing was happening. He couldn't get over the hump. He reached down, put his hands under her arms, pulled her up. "Let's go to bed," he said.

"Get your hands off me," she snapped. "Get me a drink."

He got her a drink.

"You're cute," she said.

Spence grabbed her by the elbows and steered her out to the balcony. As she passed the mini-bar, Carol leaned over and grabbed a tiny bottle of liquor. Outside, Spence put his arms around her, and—Christ, she smashed the little bottle on his head! He grabbed the bottle and put it down.

Carol reeled. "I should go," she kept saying. "My girlfriend."

There was a knock at the door. Spence opened it to find Don's girl.

"Is Carol there?" she said.

"Yeah," Spence said.

"Will you tell her I'm leaving? If she wants a lift home, she should meet me in ten minutes at the parking lot."

"Okay," Spence said. He closed the door. He thought fast as he walked out to the balcony where Carol was. "That was your friend Linda," he said. "She said she'll be down the hall in room 306. She's staying there." All at once, Carol seemed to relax. Her resistance disappeared. She was smiling.

Now, if you ask me, that was the critical decision on Spence's part. Did Carol independently consent to have sex with Spence or not? But Spence didn't have much time to think about it, because they were down to it. He always let the woman have the first orgasm. When he was young, he'd had a slight problem with premature ejaculation, and that was when he learned to get the girl off first, using his tongue. It made him feel like a man, potent, purposeful. He needed to feel that way. He gave them pleasure: there was nothing like it. Most of the time, he figured, they ended up having an experience unlike anything they'd ever had before. This was what he told himself.

From 4:00 to 5:55—Spence claimed he could see the red numerals of the digital clock staring at him like angry bloodshot eyes for two whole hours—he sawed away. Thank the Lord Tito couldn't hear.

Whereupon the moon, the huge glorious Palm Springs desert moon, moved out from behind a night cloud. The room lit up as if by spotlight. Spence glanced to his left, even as he worked away with Carol. And there were Tito's eyes, wide open and staring.

Jerry ordered room service. We were due at the golf course in forty-five minutes. Tito was regaling us with the story of Spence's conquest when Spence walked in.

"That woman was crazy," Spence yowled. "She was a lunatic. I wrestled with her from three to six." He looked out the window, and the sudden movement of his eyes swelled the horizon of the desert into a sea of nausea. "I can't even *think* about playing golf."

But he played anyway. There was no excuse for not fulfilling your obligations, no matter how whacked you were the morning after. This was what passed for their code of honor. Besides, that was the thrill of it all.

"I get a kick out of shit like that," Spence said, on the way to the golf course, eight o'clock in the morning, 101 degrees outside. He was still regaling us with the details of the night before. The air conditioning in the Lincoln was blasting away so efficiently it was 60 degrees in the car. Palm Springs! Golf in the desert! We were *here*, weren't we? These were the last days of the male empire! And Spence's story was going over beautifully. "I like to do shit like that," Spence said. "To create a little episode, little stories. It gives us something to talk about the next morning on the golf course."

4

Barry-Bob's Big Adventure

*Animals in the foot – Iron Bob – Revelations of the
pee-shy – Eating and Fascism – Naked drumming –
And other perilous adventures in the men's movement*

That fall, Robert Bly published *Iron John*. Suddenly men were shedding their clothes to dance naked in the woods, and everyone had an opinion about what it meant to be a man.

My hesitation to prance in the woods with fat nude men was, I realize, a bad sign. I was not open to change. Dozens of self-help books for men and thousands of therapists were willing to tell me as much. The postwar crowd was turning forty, and so forty million men were undergoing their midlife crises more or less simultaneously. It was called the men's movement.

And why was I not open? Because I was repressed. Repressed and, next to a growing flock of men who were opening their minds in ways I hadn't seen before, narrow-minded. And what was I repressing? Good question: what wasn't I repressing? Perhaps I had a fear of being touched by other men. And why was that? Well . . . it seemed unnatural. What if I liked it? I had no tendencies in that direction that I could identify, but I also had no doubt that anyone could or might get into the whole thing. Everyone, as Freud observed, had some polymorphous machinery. The question was whether you needed to dredge it out of the swamp, recondition it, and drive it around town.

I felt I did not, but in California I was in a distinct minority. The first masculinity conference I attended was a two-day extravaganza staged by the Pacifica Graduate Institute in Santa Barbara, California, at $185 a head. There were five hundred people in the room—a gross of $92,500, for a two-day conference—most of them therapists, and most of them women. "If you can't get laid here," my friend Barry whispered, "you'd have to be some kind of eunuch." The conference was a practice step; I figured if it went well, maybe I'd dance in the forest after all.

The stars of the conference were Marion Woodman, the respected Jungian analyst and author, and her equally well-known colleague Robert Johnson. For two days, Marion and Robert—they insisted we call them Marion and Robert—encouraged us, as one of the conference's organizers said, to "open ourselves to the gods and the goddesses we will meet this weekend. . . . This conference is built on the conviction that the masculinity of our time is outdated, has grown old. . . . We're not here to *define* masculinity, or say what it is. We're here to *dream it along*. To add images to the stockpile of masculinity. We need new images, new fantasies of masculinity."

Marion and Robert believed men had lost touch with their true masculine spirits and were too intent on proving themselves as boys to their mothers, which was why they were so concerned with guns and wealth and possessions and everything else we could no longer afford as a planet, spiritually and economically. That was interesting, albeit speculative, subjective, and vague. What men needed to do was to get in touch with their inner femininity, but also—and this was the confusing part, to me—with their inner masculinity. The chief stumbling block to doing this, according to Robert and Marion, was that we were all devoted to "not hurting."

"Please don't make a bad joke of it," Robert said, "but every modern man has an arrow through his testicles."

Then Marion made us stand up and pretend we were golden retrievers, "wagging your tail for your master," and whimpering. Then Marion and Robert "dialogued" about drug addicts and eating disorders and about Jung's idea of the shadow, the dark, unconscious, largely destructive—but potentially creative!—side of everyone and everything. Sometimes Marion or Robert would say something such as "Early in one's life, to name something is to own it. But later, to own it is to destroy it," and therapists in the audience would jump up out of their seats and say, "Oh, yes!" It was like a revivalist meeting in a Baptist church.

"I want to put out a plea to women," Robert said. "If you're reaching out to a man, and you touch his Fisher King wound"—the first wound a man received for trying to be himself, back when he was really still a vulnerable boy—"you're going to have 170 pounds of raging inarticulate misery on your hands."

"Look at our leaders," Marion said. "Trapped in the worship of *mater*. The little boy consciousness. It is possible that one has never seen an unwounded male in this culture."

Marion and Robert didn't feel any need to proceed by rules of logic. The faith of the audience, its willingness to believe anything they said, carried them instead from revelation to revelation.

Finally, at the end of the first day, a male "body dancer" gave a performance to the music of exotic instruments. It was like watching a man move to the sound of a fly buzzing. After the performance was over, a fat girl approached the body dancer. The body dancer wasn't wearing any shoes. "Your feet are so interesting," the fat girl said. "They're just so grounded. Me, I've been doing yoga for five years, and I'm only just beginning to get any real feeling in my right foot. My left foot is still just totally lifeless."

"Did you have an injury?" the dance man said. He looked like John Travolta.

"No, I just . . . well, you can see for yourself." She took off her shoes. Her feet were two pale New York strip steaks. "They're just lifeless."

"Well, you know, you could have an injury. You could be left-footed, your soma could be divided, it could be any number of things. You could have an animal in your left foot."

"Really!"

"Yes. What you need to do is talk to your foot. I do therapy where we talk to the body part. You really should give me a call."

When the conference finally came to a close two days later, people in the audience were weeping. Robert had to depart early—he was flying to India that day—and he left on a break without saying good-bye. This made people sad. So many people in the audience were weeping, Marion finally decided she had to say something.

"Many people are feeling what I am feeling," she said. "I have to say that I do feel the grief of Robert transitting that way." Transitting? "But this gentleman wants to call it a death. I don't feel that way."

Out in the parking lot, ecstatic to be transitting in the fresh air again, I asked Dexter, an acquaintance of Barry's, how he had liked the conference. Dexter was round and short and was wearing black tights, like a twelfth-century jester. He described himself as a "Jungian psychic."

"I got a lot of validation, and a lot of confirmation," he said. Then he turned to Barry. "How about you, Bob?"

Barry looked surprised. "I got a lot of validation, too."

"That Dexter's some psychic," I said to Barry as we walked to his Chevette. "He couldn't even remember your name."

Barry looked at me. His name was Barry Milligan. "Actually, my name is Bob. Bob Beazley. I told you about it. I think my name was Beazley before I was adopted. Plus it's my new movement name. Kind of a symbol that I'm a changed person." He was even planning to attend a reunion of the Beazley family of California later that summer. And I was going with him to a wildman weekend.

If I hadn't known Barry, the men's movement would have been easier to dismiss. He was a serious man, an ambitious intellect, and he was convinced it was real.

Barry was the first person I ever heard use the phrase "the men's movement." The year was 1983, and Barry had just returned to Washington from a winter in northern California. In those days, striding down the hallways at one of Washington's most prominent think tanks, he was a framed picture of traditional Ivy League masculinity. He wore blazers from Brooks Brothers and shirts from J. Press and brown brogues that could have served as the foundation for a twelve-story high rise. He hobnobbed with the top people in world affairs. Barry had grown up fatherless in a foster home in Chicago but still managed to win a scholarship to Princeton. He had a habit of capitalizing on his opportunities.

But a few of us knew another, secret Barry who seethed under the strictures of East Coast male life. I was one of two people, for instance, to whom Barry had confessed his growing conviction that he was bisexual. He dated women, but the affairs were short-lived, not much more than shadows, and they left him wondering what was missing. Homosexual life, Barry was convinced, was no more satisfying. The intense loneliness created by his secret life was set off only by the fantastic stories he told of unimaginably passionate sex with men. There was nothing to equal it in my heterosexual experience. His erotic adventures—the primal scene in the baths, the illicit but somehow authentic anonymity of his encounters in parks in Washington—fascinated and terrified me. I admired his daring. Next to my corybantic friend, I was an emotional gecko, content to lie in the warm sun of conventional manhood. So I wasn't surprised when one day Barry turned his back on Washington and disappeared from sight.

I received the odd letter, the infrequent phone call, but no one knew for sure where he'd gone. Vague rumors circulated: Barry was in university in Venezuela; Barry had come out of the closet; Barry had fallen afoul of the IRS and was working in a Taco Bell (albeit as an assistant manager, as befitted a Princeton graduate). He was going through "big changes."

When he called two years later, I was staring out the window at the unchanging blue of the West Coast sky.

"Hi," he said. "It's Barry."

"Where have you been?"

"Well," Barry said, "I . . ." He stopped and burst into laughter. He sounded stuffed up, as if he had a cold. "I don't know where to start. I've been getting into the most amazing stuff. Men's work."

After that Barry began to telephone regularly. Each call marked a new frontier of his explorations in the radical end of the men's movement. It was like listening to Columbus as he enthused about the new world he had discovered. He didn't want simply to retake the lost ground of men's "feelings." Barry's aim was nothing short of a complete restart of the male heart, the discovery and celebration of the divine in all male sexuality. All that men had been feared and chastised for, all their fundamental and most powerful physical urges, were, in Barry's new vision, grounds for spiritual exploration—the basis for a truer understanding of the male psyche. He was reading Jung and Freud and Joseph Campbell, and he seemed to be taking their writings personally.

His enthusiasm for his discoveries, for the new places he had found in his heart, made me envy him. *He* didn't worry about infidelity. *He* wasn't paralyzed by commitment. He looked terrific, too, better than he ever had. Next to the clear example of his rebellious cause, I felt like a guy installed permanently beside a backyard gas barbecue.

At the same time, some of his behavior shocked me, which only made me feel more bourgeois. "Erotic massage," he said one morning over the telephone. By now he had qualified as a body worker. "I've been working with men who are sexually dysfunctional—or just plain philo-sophically curious. I mean, I've discovered that half the men in America are pee-shy."

"Pee-shy?" It was all I could do sometimes to keep up.

"They can't pee in front of other men. And it's just the tip of the iceberg. Men in this country are so fucked up. I've been . . . well, I've discovered the dirty little secret of American men."

"Really," I said. "What would that be?"

"Premature ejaculation."

"This is a problem a lot of your massage clients have?"

"It's an epidemic. It's the result of a complete dissociation between what we do in sex and what it means to us. And I know the solution."

"Do go on."

"More masturbation."

"I would have thought," I said, "that there's entirely too much masturbation going on already."

"No way," Barry said. "I've been conducting workshops." He then described a long therapy session, one aspect of which (admittedly the most radical element) was "therapeutic genital massage. We erotically massage the client, building erotic energy, teaching them to breathe and relax, spreading the erotic energy away from the genitals. That can last for an hour, or about twenty times longer than the average man lasts in sex." Failing that, there was an array of different strokes to delay ejaculation and bring on "full-body orgasm," which from Barry's description was like detonating a small, personalized atom bomb.

A handy trick to know! "Doesn't sound that much like Washington," I said.

"Thank God. I look back on that time now, it seems like another universe."

Where I saw sexual adventurism, Barry spied an opportunity for self-knowledge through acts of physical and sexual daring. He found my interest in the sexual extremes of his work prurient, voyeuristic, and typical of a conformist, middle-class, old-style-male reporter. He frequently accused me of sending up the sensationalistic physical aspects of his work—which were bound to shock people—without presenting the serious thinking that lay behind it. I, on the other hand, found the Jungian/Tantric/rebirthing underpinnings of "men's work" an impenetrable and completely speculative web. Barry's goddesses and theories, his equation of his physical desires with his spiritual longings, served as an explanation of his behavior and that of all mankind, but they were still just hopeful theories—relevant *if* true.

But my skepticism and his theories both obscured the real meaning of my friend's progress, the real intent of his adventure: Barry was turning his life into a work of performance art. Masturbation class was just one high-shock example of that performance, and a small example at that: most of the time he talked about more mysterious and frightening rituals, such as men's conferences where the artist Keith Hennesey passed a ceremonial spitoon amongst the audience and then painted his body with its contents. That certainly challenged the seriousness of Karen Finley, the New York performance artist who crammed candied yams up her backside. "That's men's work, post-Bly," Barry said.

Barry began to telephone more frequently. I looked forward to his calls. Each discovery was more wonderfully implausible and challenging to my mind, more utterly logical to Barry's. One month he discovered yoga; the next, Buddha. "I have been through so much this summer," he said on another occasion, "I'm convinced there might really be something out there living in the universe."

If he wasn't grilling a new leader, he talked issues. "The Clarence Thomas hearings were the best thing ever to happen in this country as far as sexual taboos are concerned," he explained. "I mean, she said the word penis on national TV!" By then he was practicing what he called "sacred intimacies," radical Tantric sex workshops to "explore people's connections with their bodies and to reverse psychology's denial of the body."

More importantly, he'd discovered love. "I've found love with five men since June," he said. It was now September. Some of these men were dying of AIDS. He didn't mean sex; he meant love. He was probably the first man I ever knew to make that distinction sincerely. "The last time was at this men's conference. I was there to presence and learn about the Divine Goddess within. The inner feminine. You know, the Shiva stuff. And I met this amazing man, a developer. He has a wife in L.A., but he also wants to build a sexual monastery."

"Boy," I said, "that's great."

By then I knew Barry's calls were leading to something. I had always made it clear that his interest in the men's movement was his concern, but now I sensed his growing seriousness.

"Do you think you'll be down this way at all?" I said. "It'd be great to have a beer." That was good. Beer. Men being men. I must have sounded like a fat old boy from Texas.

"Well," Barry said, "I have to go to my twentieth high school reunion. Actually, I need your advice. I was thinking of going back there dressed as . . . well, I'd really like to go back in drag. I found this fabulous leopard-skin miniskirt. Do you think that's a bad idea?"

I had a slight coughing fit. *I was discussing a male friend's desire to dress up as a woman.* And the weirdest thing was . . . it seemed like some kind of progress! After all, cross-dressing was a time-honored art, the subject of several fine films, a favorite of the ancient Greeks and the contemporary British, not to mention a guaranteed hit with Norm and Betty and the rest of the package-holiday crowd in Las Vegas, happily married couples from Kansas and the like who flocked to see "Boylesque." Cross-dressing was another branch of Barry's new art, this new ongoing performance of his life as a man: his declaration that men needed to nurture what Jung had called the inner feminine. By dressing in drag at the reunion, Barry could declare his inner being on his outside, in the same way that serious tattooists and body piercers were now deliberately displaying their inner selves and conflicts, as opposed to simply acting them out unconsciously.

But as interesting as drag may be as theatre, a high school reunion seemed an unwise venue for an opening night performance. What Barry didn't seem or want to grasp was that his new life's work in the men's movement, while ground-breaking, sincere, and integral, still gave the average repressed guy the full-tilt heebie-jeebies. As for walking into a high school gym in Chicago for his twentieth high school reunion bash . . . under all the red, white, and blue crepe, with the live band winding into a cover of *Baker Street* and Miss Rennie and Mr. Loutit tapping their now arthritic feet against the wall, all the while being watched by his friends . . . Who would remember how he'd worked for the Humane Society . . . surrounded, as I say, by all that history . . . with him dressed in a jungle mini? "Well," I said—and here maybe I failed him—"actually, though it's an interesting idea, I would say that would be a bad idea."

"Yeah," he said, "I guess you're right. But there is this shadow workshop at Harbin Hotsprings. If you're going to go to one of these things, this is the one. It's the deeper end of men's work—the most serious work of its kind. It'll be frightening. I'd love to see you, of all people, in this thing. I just think this will be an historic occasion." He hooted with laughter.

"I thought we could leave early," Barry-Bob said as we climbed into the Chevette. "That way, we can get to Harbin Hotsprings early and have a massage. Harbin's famous for them; they invented this massage I think we should have, called a wazoo massage."

Stabbing pains of anxiety shot from my scrotum to my chest. I was going to have to make it clear I did not share Barry's sexual predilections. "I don't want my wazoo massaged."

"Not wazoo," Barry-Bob said. "*Wah-tzu*. They float you in the hot tub and massage you. You can have a woman or a man to do the massage."

"I'll take the woman."

"That's what I reserved for you," Barry-Bob said, without taking his eyes off the road.

As it turned out, the female *wah-tzuer* was sick. While Barry-Bob was floated in the main hot spring by a Chinese man, I retired to the Pool of Contemplation, which was a snappy 120 degrees. A dozen couples, all naked, were bobbing in the pool's mineral heat. Every time I retired to an empty nook, I was joined moments later by a naked couple, who insisted on kissing and necking in the pool beside me. The Pool of Contemplation was anything but. Later, in the dressing room, one of the women smiled and tousled my hair. I felt about six years old, but I wanted to neck with a girl of my own.

After a meal of barely cooked macrobiotic vegetables, Barry-Bob and I waited in the parking lot for the van to take us to the mountain lodge where the Shadow Workshop was to begin. Night was falling quickly. Gradually other men drove up. Sydney, a tall thin know-it-all from Marin County, was a "facilitator" in the men's movement. Alex, large and bearded, kept asking me if I was "the one from L.A." We talked about the traffic, about whether this was our first weekend. Everyone else had experience at this sort of thing. I sat still, breathed in the cool Northern Californian air, and imagined myself at home in Los Angeles, next to my wife, reading. Occasionally, I also thought about the naked woman in the hot tub. I'd been away a week, and my longing was pronounced. Do you know how bad it was? Do you know how, when you're desperate and a waitress signs the back of her check "Thanks! See ya! Doreen!" you actually wonder whether she means it? I was beyond that and into the next zone of awareness. I was examining the full-blown D itself and seeing in it the outline of her breasts and hips.

"Please remove your shoes," Troy, our co-leader, said. All twenty-two of us were standing in the wilderness lodge, a chalet designed for eight, having tea and cookies. I needed coffee, but coffee was considered counter-spiritual. After tea, we climbed upstairs, sat in a "council circle," said our names, how we came to be there, what our "issues" were, and what we hoped to get out of the workshop. I said I was trying to accept the occasional boredom of marriage. I'd managed to repress the baby dilemma so far within me, I couldn't think of anything else to say.

"The Judge," another man said. "The Judge is always looking over my shoulder."

"I'm dealing with issues of bisexuality," said another man. He was in his late fifties.

"I'm regressing to fourteen," said another.

"We want to do some exercises," said Hassan, another co-leader. Hassan was his Sufi name. His real name was Bruce. He was a building contractor. "I want you to shake your body and go zzzzzzzzzzzzzzzzzzzzz."

This we did. It felt stupid. Then we greeted one another "non-verbally." "Be aware of the Witness, the Judge, and the Participant," Hassan said, rolling his eyes like Brooke Adams in *Invasion of the Body Snatchers*. Whenever Hassan had something meaningful to say, he rolled his eyes. "Also be aware of projection, of being critical of others to distance yourself. We fear the judge in ourselves, and so we judge others. We are what we fear."

I turned around, and a large man with white hair was looking at me with a 27,000-volt stare. He was communicating the word "hello." I reached out and shook his hand. Then I pushed him in the shoulder. He measured my shoulders, made a "wide!" gesture, and touched my heart. I pushed him again. He turned around and walked away.

To my right, two men had locked heads like scrumming rugby players and were grunting. "Unnnhh," said one man. "Grrrrr," said the other. I felt faint. The temperature in the loft had to be 102 degrees. Out of the corner of my eye I watched Barry-Bob. He walked up to Hassan, grabbed him by the head, and shagged him as if he were batting a too-playful dog. "I wanted to deflate his seriousness a bit," Barry-Bob whispered afterward.

After we had communicated non-verbally, a tall, depressed-looking man with a beard and an Afro stood up. This was David, our cook. He looked like one of the acid-burnouts I saw all the time at Venice Beach, spinning plates for a living. He was wearing suede sandals. "I just wanted to speak about the food," David said. "The food is all vegetarian. And there are a couple of rules we'd like you to observe. Don't talk while you're eating, because the meals have been designed for contemplative inner work. And don't talk to the food preparers while they're preparing. And don't take carrots or whatever from the bowl while you're waiting for dinner."

Then Jim Schuenemann, another co-leader, said "We'll go to bed now." Jim was big: six foot three and a half, bearded, 220 pounds, another contractor. In fact, there were half a dozen contractors in the crowd, a fact I had ascertained illegally while on break, because job talk was a no-no, as were conversations about sports, sex, or cars. "In the morning, you'll have twenty minutes to get up and shower and get dressed. Snorers, please sleep downstairs."

That meant me. I was climbing into my sleeping bag when I noticed Wayne, a fellow participant, sitting behind a wall in the kitchen, sticking a syringe into his arm.

Back in Los Angeles before the workshop, while I waited for my wife to jump me unexpectedly and force an impregnation, I had tried to read "men's books." I kept getting distracted. There was always a movie to go to, or TV to watch, or the crossword puzzle in the *Times* every morning. There were other books, too. I read novels and stories about men as soon as I picked them up: stories about mountaineers, men who rode cutting horses, Indian chiefs, fly fishermen, alcoholic philanderers, ornithologists who took drugs, men who fell in love in Paris, men who fell in love and built boats, boxers, sailors, booksellers, and even, for two perverted weeks, de Sade's *The 120 Days of Sodom*. Learned tomes of theory about manhood, on the other hand, left me cold. I worried that I lacked the discipline necessary to become a new man.

Robert Bly's *Iron John* at least had the virtue of being the original. A moderately well-known Minnesota poet, Bly had been "gathering" with men for nearly ten years, during which time he had written *Iron John: A Book About Men*. The book dominated best-seller lists for more than a year. In Bly's view, men had lost their sense of masculine purpose sometime around the late 1700s, thanks to the Industrial Revolution.

For the first time in history, Bly speculated—and speculation disguised as objective analysis was what he and other New Male Evangelists were best at—instead of raising sons at their sides as they cut trees and grew crops and sharpened axes, fathers in the late 1700s were suddenly cloistered away in factories. Older and more primitive cultures had taken time to initiate boys into manhood through rituals. But such rites were considered dangerous by well-behaved capitalist society, as well as by the Christian Church. Thereafter deprived of any fatherly lessons in what being a man required physically and spiritually, and further confused by the fact that they were now raised almost exclusively by women, men began to compensate for their missing sense of purpose by "acting out" whichever version of manhood society needed to sell, however inauthentic it felt. This was how men gradually became unfeeling, warmongering, ultra-competitive automatons, and probably alcoholics and drug addicts to boot—John Wayne He-Men, as Bly characterized them—determined to prove their manhood to their absent fathers and their overpowering mothers by ignoring any unmanly grief and sadness of their own.

This model of manhood prevailed until the late 1960s, when feminism—an otherwise worthy cause, Bly maintained—mutated He-Man into Soft-Man, the Sensitive New Age Wimp who, in Bly's withering view, was nothing more than an already soulless and susceptible man determined to turn himself into a woman. She-Man was more sensitive than his forebears, but no less frustrated in his search to discover a sense of purpose as a male being. Hence the need for a new way of teaching men about themselves, and hence Bly's book-length exegesis of the story of Iron John—the hairy wild man of a Grimm Brothers fairy tale who instructs a golden-haired boy in the arts of curiosity, sacrifice, discipline, courage, and adventure, thereby allowing him to pursue his own personal grail and once again respect his own "masculine integrity."

By going off into the woods with other men, Bly believed—though of course there were other ways to accomplish the same thing—men could create a "safe ritual space" in which they could once again talk about how it felt to be a whole man, warts and anger and sadness and all. "Through the Wild Man's initiation," he wrote, "men learn to worship the animal soul, and that ancient worship to this day calls up from the busy adult man the sorrow of animal life, the grief of all nature, 'the tears of things,' the consciousness that is betwixt and between."

Bly was reluctant to say what, exactly, a genuine sense of male purpose is, but he was very clear on what happened if you didn't at least try to discover one. Violent husbands, missile-wielding politicians, and even cynical journalists who made fun of the men's movement were all misguided men rebelling against their elders, trying to pull the structure down, trying to exercise their thwarted warrior selves in misdirected ways.

By Saturday morning, the Ridge Trail Institute's Harbin Hotsprings Shadow Workshop was swinging. Watches were banned (to remove us from the outer world and encourage our exploration of the inner one); we had to occupy "present time," which is to say, live in the moment with our feelings, which, since most of us didn't know what feelings were, meant we had to live in our bodies, and obey our physical sensations.

Hence the spectacle of twenty-two men sitting in a circle on the floor like kindergarten children, listing their weaknesses. The collective unhappiness was startling. Half the group claimed to be paralytically susceptible to relentless self-criticism. Another quarter was suffering the aftermath of divorce. Two men were struggling with bisexuality, another handful were "incest survivors." Several admitted to being overwhelmed by inexpressible anger, especially toward their children—the result of being forced into "husbanding" roles they couldn't live sincerely. The fathers of the men in the workshop had been either absent or ultra-critical; their mothers had been repressive and repressed. New Age (i.e., repetitive) flute music bleated away in the background. Masks of ancient gods and goddesses—notably Rangda, the demonic Indonesian Earth Mother, so beloved of the New Male writers—hung from the walls. People were crying.

For two hours, we formed into pairs—dyads, in therapy-speak. The gig here was to ask your partner a question, whereupon he answered nonstop for five minutes. Then he asked you the same question. Troy had imported this technique from a "self-realization intensive" workshop where he met his wife. "I was working on the question, What is Another," Troy told me. "And she was working on, Who am I. And we're still working on them."

Our question in the Shadow Workshop was "What are you suppressing, and how is it affecting your life?" I imagined this was a big topic at Scientologist dinner parties. Jim, my partner, a fierce-looking fellow with a red beard, couldn't argue with his wife without getting angry. "I can't even answer her," he said. "I get cornered, because she doesn't hear me. And then I get mad." My next partner was an incest survivor. A third was addicted to drugs and alcohol. Most of the guys were contractors, teachers, marketing executives, lawyers.

Afterward, we felt like we knew one another. This was good. On the other hand, after each session, my partners wanted to hug. Hugging was key, but it was competitive! Hugs started mutually, as a gentle embrace, and then Jim or Troy or Hassan would hug back—just a little harder. They didn't want to seem—less into it! Less brave! Less capable of intimacy than another man! And so I returned the squeeze. I admit I upped the ante. Jim and Troy and Hassan grabbed back. Pretty soon we were locked in neo-mortal combat, gasping for breath. Then Troy said, "Change partners."

I told myself hugging wasn't such a big deal—there was no reason men couldn't express their connection by embracing, the way women often do. But hugging, I realized as a 280-pound self-proclaimed "incest survivor" crushed me in a bear hug, a genuine existential clasp, is an intimate act. I was no more intimate with Derek, despite his confessions, than I might have been with a lunatic in a pinwheel hat who had revealed his life story between stops on a bus. Our confessions weren't brought on by intimacy. They were possible because of our mutual anonymity.

Bly began meeting with groups of men in Minnesota in the early 1980s, but men's work didn't have a serious following until the mid 1980s, the same year Troy Rampy, Jim Schuenemann, and Bruce Hammond, the founders of the Shadow Workshop, caught wind of his work in California.

Troy, a dropout from the University of California at Berkeley's architecture school who makes his living writing and producing educational videos about family life (e.g., "Birthing: Making the Right Choices"), and a self-confessed "therapy junkie," was himself a classic candidate for the men's movement. "I came out of a very middle-class family"—his parents owned a hardware store—"with very middle-class values," he explained one afternoon. He had a dark moustache and an historic case of adenoids. "My group at high school were more of a fringe group. The surfers. We were athletic, but not the jocks. The outsiders. So it was really sort of a subgroup. And I have always felt that most of my life." Several hundred spliffs and six-packs and a couple of VW vans later, Rampy was introduced to Arthur Janov's primal scream therapy, which at the time was taking California by storm as an antidote to the cerebral isolation of Freudianism. (Even John Lennon was doing it; he called it "a slow acid trip.") The average primal scream workshop took place in an isolated motel and demanded three weeks of uninterrupted attention. "By then," Troy remembered, "I was living with this woman—who I guess I didn't really love. And I was drinking too much alcohol and smoking too much pot."

Always on the lookout for The Answer, Troy had moved through a galaxy of therapies—EST, rediffusion, isolation tanks, rolfing, guided visualizations, akido, human sexuality mediation sessions, and a vast number of relationships—when he met Jim Schuenemann in a therapy group. Jim, the son of charismatic Lutherans, was another university dropout and a sometime contractor and house painter. He had no more formal training as a psychologist than Troy did. But he knew the therapy game from personal experience, had an intense interest in spirituality and alternative religions, and wanted to start a "men's group" to help others move "toward their own divinity, inside and outside." One night in 1979 Jim said to Troy, "I'm really feeling this wanting. I want to start a men's group."

So they did. They sat down twice a month. The group seemed to touch a chord—"a need for truth telling and personal authenticity," as Troy and Jim liked to call it. "Now, I don't think you need a men's group to do that. There are plenty of men who can do that on their own. But that's what it took for me. I grew up in a family where that just wasn't done. There was no incentive to enlightenment, and there was a lot of posturing, learning to be a certain way. I think the family I grew up in was really about being effective in the world. There wasn't a whole lot about who you were and what your purpose is."

They were about to ride a huge wave. By the late 1980s, "workshops" on maleness and masculinity were more common than real estate seminars. One didn't want to be narrow-minded, or make fun of the well-intentioned, but . . . there were a lot of nutballs wandering around. There were literally thousands of healing sessions, practicums centering on the "dolphin-human connection," new moon study groups, dialogues with the land, and neuro-cellular repatternings, all brought on by the confluence of the New Age and the men's movement. "Sex, Gender and Polarity in Ritual" was "a panel discussion by pagans from a variety of traditions." You could study "pregnant dreams—the secret life of the expectant father." The Rite of Passage for the Powerful Male was a weekend devoted to understanding male transition through alchemical hypnotherapy, radiance breathwork, shamanic journeying, drumming, ritual, movement—movement!—sweatlodge, spontaneous celebration, and play. Play—otherwise known as goofing around—was a very big draw. You could even mourn the loss of your foreskin (explore "circumcision-violence issues" and "release and explore feelings about circumcision"); failing that, you could have it sewn back on.

In response to a generation of men teething on need, Jim and Troy and Bruce had soon formed the Ridge Trail Institute and were staging the Shadow Workshop for public consumption. In 1991, they were invited to Robert Bly's Mendocino Men's Conference, exclusively for "leaders" in the men's movement. They had it made. It was a long way from screaming primally in a motel room and being an itinerant therapy junkie, but as Robert Bly once said, "You either eat your shadow, or you marry it."

The secret to the Acting Out exercise was your "Trigger Phrase." Your trigger phrase was what your Trigger Phrase partners taunted you with when they turned on you. It was actually an old EST trick. Every man's trigger phrase turned out to be the same: I am worthless. No sooner had the exercise begun than men were screaming and crying and pounding the carpet and yelling. "Let me out!" screamed one. "Leave me alone!" sobbed another. "You left me!" cried a third. One man, a former drinker, became so violent he had to be wrestled to the ground; finally he burst into tears, a great sadness for his girlfriend finally overwhelming him. He was breaking up with her but felt nothing.

Then a man named Fred assumed the ready position in the center of our circle, and we all attacked him. He seemed to be holding up pretty well; he said he worried about being a good father, but nothing seemed to hurt him.

"If you're so worried about being a good father, Fred," I said, "what are you doing up here on a weekend, engaging in this sort of ridiculous prank with a bunch of guys you don't know?"

Fred widened his eyes. I had him.

"What are you going to feel like if you go home and discover your kids have been run over by a truck?"

It wasn't subtle, but it worked. Fred started to cry. Then he started to howl his eyes out. He slumped to the floor, moaning and sobbing. At first

I felt pretty good: powerful. Then I felt pretty bad. "I didn't mean it," I said to Fred, lying only slightly.

When my turn came, the other fellows made all sorts of cracks about my wife cheating on me. They didn't know about the baby. I didn't break down at all. Later I regretted I hadn't. I wanted to know what it was like to scream and moan on the floor in front of a group of men I didn't know. Afterward, we all hugged anyway.

By the time I took the Shadow Workshop, the gender therapy establishment had taken after Robert Bly as a dog does a raccoon. Formally trained psychologists—who had cottoned on to "men's work" in the competitive San Francisco Bay Area like hungry rodents, setting up thousands of workshops and talk-ins—dismissed Bly as a mere poet. Then there were the feminists. Tammy Bruce, the president of the Los Angeles chapter of the National Organization for Women, called Bly's boys "a degrading movement geared to spiral men even further down into an extreme that advocates primal behavior and a separatist philosophy."

Bly was anti-establishment, but he was no misogynist. He had said over and over again that the enemy was not women, but men themselves, for complicitly living conventional, unfeeling lives. Troy agreed. "Anti-feminism is not what the men's movement is about that I can see," he said. "It's about men saying, I'm doing everything I'm supposed to, and it feels awful. There are three options for women. They can be full-time mothers, full-time careerists, or half-time each.

"And men have three options, too: make money to support the family, make money to support the family, and make money to support the family. The women's movement is political: they want equal rights and pay. Those are very focused, concrete demands, so they're hard not to take seriously. Whereas the men's movement is not focused at all, beyond men saying, 'Our lives suck. We're white middle-class men, supposedly the envy of the world—so why doesn't it feel good?'"

But Tammy Bruce was a piker next to the radical homosexual caucus.

Like the women's movement, gay liberation had concrete goals: sexual freedom for all, social and economic equality for gays. The more amorphous men's movement was once again an easy target. Colin Brown, a self-confessed sexual healer and spiritual ecstatic who was director of Body Electric, "a school of massage and healing arts" in Oakland, accused Bly of homophobia and the men's movement of having a "genital hole" at its center, one that denied the male sex drive and the specific problems of gay men. This was true; Iron Bob Bly nodded hello to gay men, but never specifically addressed their own complicated need for mentors or fathers, because to do so would have brought him perilously close to opining about why gay men are gay—a politically incorrect move guaranteed to dump all sorts of heavy lumber on his head.

Body Electric had come up with a solution to Bly's reticence. Body Electric staged weekends for gay men, dedicated, Colin Brown told me, to "reconnecting their sexual selves and their spiritual intentions"—or, to put it another way, to teaching them unconventional sexual practices. The weekends featured time-honored teachings of everyone from Wilhelm Reich to Dionysus, but the highlight was the instructional sessions in Tantric spirituality, rebirthing, and mutual erotic massage (twenty-five different patented strokes), including butt-to-body massages performed by the participants on one another.

This was not the sort of event my wife and I were likely to read about in the *New York Times Sunday Magazine* over coddled eggs, which was exactly Colin Brown's point. "I think every man has his take on being out of it genitally," he said one afternoon. "And it's because we are raised by women who are afraid of sex. And it's not just our generation. It goes all the way back to the Christian Church and St. Augustine. So we're looking at generations of disembodied men."

Brown planned to open up his Tantric masturbation sessions to heterosexual couples. I couldn't imagine how Tammy Bruce and the rest of the morality police were going to react to that one.

By Saturday night at the Shadow Workshop, Jimmy was beginning to feel more relaxed. He'd endured the Acting Out sessions that afternoon, had eaten his lentils in silence, and had built himself a "shadow mask" out of plastic. Now he was standing in the loft of the wilderness lodge, wearing his mask, beating a drum.

Suddenly . . . Jimmy did a double take. What the hell was that? Over there . . . Hassan . . . Hassan was naked! Hassan had taken off his clothes and was calmly wandering around the attic of the wilderness lodge as if he were trying to find a coffee shop in an airport, bare ass gleaming like a pair of Crenshaw melons. And . . . he wasn't the only one! Now everyone was getting naked!

Within minutes, all twenty-two of us were buff naked, except for our masks, and drumming. I thought of my wife, who would find this hilarious. But that was the point. Jim and Troy had defined the dance as a "safe space" free of wives. The beat of the drums was loud and amateur, the air again thick with the revolting odor of burning sage. Suddenly Troy ordered us to crowd together, flank to shank, cheek to jowl.

"I want to hear your pain. Your growls. Your moans."

Jimmy was petrified: was this some strange sexual ritual? Jimmy was ashamed of his body, had been all his life. He was fat, 270 pounds, there was no doubt about it. He was nervous, too; he'd been abused by an uncle as a child, and being naked among other men gave him the willies. And speaking of willies . . . well, there was that, too.

Gradually, herded by naked Hassan and naked Jim and naked Troy, we formed a circle. "Sit," Troy commanded. We sat. "Drum," Troy commanded. We drummed. And then, suddenly, as we drummed, Troy jumped up and . . . began to dance! In the buff! Like some lunatic in Columbus Circle, no less! He danced round and round, crouching, moaning, rising slowly to his feet again. Troy's asthma was audible even above the drumming: he sounded like a subway train letting off steam. And what was that in his hand? He was carrying a two-foot-long forked stick—the truth stick. When he placed it in front of a man in the circle, that man had to perform his shadow dance. Naked. In front of the others.

Jimmy desperately wanted to leave. Maybe . . . maybe if he slipped out now. . . .

No. It was his turn. He looked around the circle. Everyone was waiting. Slowly, using his right hand to support himself, he hefted all 270 pounds of himself to his feet. He wanted to disappear. All he could think of was . . . his dick! Judging it, measuring it against their own! Jimmy felt strangely calm. So they were looking at his penis. So what? So fuck them! He picked up the stick. His heart was racing, but some instinct was taking over. It was like an order from his guts.

Suddenly he wanted to lie down, to crouch low on the ground in a ball over the stick, crouch low in shame. So he did. He hunkered down over the stick like a dog, his gigantic ass perched up in the air like . . . like what? He could imagine his ass up there, beaming away in the candlelight, like some raging, hairy planet. He stayed there for a full minute. The drumming was so loud, he could feel it in his testicles.

He had to get up and dance. He couldn't just sit there in a mound on the beige indoor-outdoor carpet in the attic of the wilderness lodge. After all, he paid $275, he had to find out what happened when you went through with it. Besides . . . what could happen? They could laugh at him? So what? He was never going to see these clowns again in his life. He lumbered to his feet again. He was terrified. He was ashamed; if ever that word meant anything, it meant something now. But . . . fuck them!

That, of course, was the secret, unstated power of a men's retreat: above all else, it let a bunch of guys scream "Fuck you!" at the world. Jimmy could feel it. The longer he stood there, in the dark liquid room, the calmer he felt. Weird! He'd been forced into this ritual baring—one that symbolized the emotional baring of the weekend, Troy had said—but the consequences were . . . actually less formidable than he expected. He wouldn't know it until later, but he was beginning to enjoy himself. To hell with these assholes, these judges of his life! Who the hell were they to judge him? Fuck them all!

Jimmy began to dance. He moved slowly at first, tentatively . . . three steps out . . . three steps back . . . a little jog-step . . . then he discovered the truth stick in his right hand. He stabbed himself, using it as a weapon. That was good. He stabbed himself again. A creative metaphor! He was moving faster now: the faster he moved, the faster the drums beat. He could feel his belly swaying. His belly was so big, it acted as a counterweight. If he moved right, his belly swung left, left, right, right, left . . . *boom-chacka-lacka* . . .

Suddenly Jimmy knew. He understood. He was dancing the Dance of His Confusion and His Shame. On and on, for five minutes, he swayed and jimmied around the attic, evoking with his body the shame of his life, his shadow.

At last he began to slow down. He wanted to keep dancing, but there were others waiting. He moved slower, then slower still, scanning the seated crowd of naked men for someone who hadn't danced . . . there. That guy with the blond hair, the one who never said anything, who was always writing things down, who seemed to be holding back . . . him. Let him give it a try. Fuck *him*!

Jimmy stopped dead, stuck his belly way, way, way out . . . bent over . . . placed the truth stick in front of the blond guy. . . . He felt extraordinarily calm. He'd done it. God knew what they'd think back at the office, where he had been an executive for twenty years, but he didn't care. Fuck them too!

The blond man was dancing now, a strange, scurrying dance, pretending to put the truth stick in front of different people. . . . Jimmy watched with interest. His breathing was almost back to normal. Tomorrow, when they repeated the "truth-telling" exercises of the day, everyone would be calmer. There would be less crying, less pain. Somehow, having been through this ritual together, they would have learned to trust each other more, perhaps because they had trusted themselves, if only for a moment.

What had they created? A bunch of men in a group who refrained from attacking one another. That wasn't unoriginal.

The question was, how long would it last? "I learned to trust other men," men would say the next day when the Council Circle met. "I learned that my anger toward others is anger toward myself." And then they would get in their cars, and drive back to the city and resume their lives as fathers and construction contractors and advertising executives and lawyers.

But Jimmy would eventually quit his job, go back to school, and become a therapist—at the age of fifty-one. His partner—Jimmy didn't use the politically incorrect word "wife"—would find him to be a new, more confident man, a better, less defensive lover. Jimmy was one of the few men for whom the weekend would have a lasting effect. Most of the others would relegate it to the basement of their therapeutic memories. True, a year later, one guy would still be performing "creative visualizations," sitting stock-still on the carpet of his living room and descending into an imagined cave, and seeing reflecting pools, and taking note of the reflections he saw in them, all of which required considerable discipline, not to mention a high threshold for boredom.

I admit I sometimes wanted to laugh at all of them. They confused self-consciousness with self-knowledge, and they believed in answers. They didn't seem to realize that knowing you were lost was not much different than being found. They thought it ought to be easy, being human. For months afterward, I wanted to dismiss the weekend.

But then I remembered Jimmy, fat sad Jimmy who had stewed in the juice of his own unhappiness for fifty years, and who was now suddenly able to get up in the morning, lighter by the weight of some of his shame. I thought of Jimmy, and I thought: what the hell. Let them dance.

As for Barry-Bob, he disappeared again. Nearly a year later, a letter arrived. The letter was handwritten in the looping script he'd always hated. I will say this for him: just when I thought he'd gone as far as a spiritual explorer could go, he went further. Now he was thinking about starting a family, possibly with a lesbian. "Did you survive the siege," he wrote, referring to the Los Angeles riots, "with any shreds of what one would like about L.A. still intact? I say let the exodus begin. I'm heading to Peru (another quiet spot on the globe) for three weeks of shamanic explorations with *ayahuasca.*" (I recognized the word, a serious and potentially deadly hallucinogen.) "Will I ever be the same?"

The same as what? I thought. The same as you never were? Wasn't that modern man's problem in the first place—trying to be the same?

5

Wacker's Quest

Origins of the New Man and why he smells the way he does — Throwbacks to the old ways — The red-eye special — Apotheosis in Connecticut

The first "new man" I ever saw was not a man at all, but an advertisement for after-shave. It was some morning late in 1989, as I recall, when advertising agencies were tearing their hair out trying to sell things to men who were rumored to be undergoing an identity crisis brought on by women and their rise to power in the world.

The ad consisted of four black-and-white photographs of a man, each slightly askew on an otherwise blank white page. The man was handsome, graced with rugged urbanity. His hair was just long enough that he could have been an executive in an advertising agency. He was wearing an elegant European suit and a subdued floral tie and was striking contemplative poses: fingers to his lips, hand stroking his chin, and so on.

Underneath each portrait was a handwritten caption. They tracked the man's thoughts, his reactions to a woman he could see across a room.

"I see this woman. She's perfect," read the caption under the first portrait. Then: "She's smiling." By now the man was looking directly at her.

In the third photograph, he seemed slightly frantic, and ran his hand through his hair. "Is she smiling at me? Or laughing at me?"

To which he replied in the last photograph by leaning back and laughing behind his hand at his own vanity: "Or at someone else. . . ."

At the bottom of the page was a headline—MAN IS NOT SO SIMPLE AFTER ALL. Beneath that was a bottle that looked like after-shave, but which was in fact "Claiborne: THE FRAGRANCE FOR MEN."

I looked at the advertisement again. Instead of standard after-shave fare—a giant bottle ejaculating across the page, or a clipper ship leaning into bracing trade winds—this advertisement was subtler. It sold "fragrance" by displaying a man's ambivalence toward his own desire to get to know the "perfect" woman. That was a complicated idea. He wanted to meet her, but he didn't want to be rejected. He liked her, but he wasn't sure she liked him. He thought she was a knockout, but in the end he told himself he was having as much fun watching her and observing his own reactions as he would meeting her. Maybe he was the kind of guy who read a lot of Foucault. Maybe he was a wimp. Whoever he was, he was the New Man. I went to meet his maker.

Altschiller Reitzfeld Tracy-Locke, the advertising agency that created the Claiborne Man, was on the twenty-first floor of a building on Broadway near 20th Street in New York. The offices were decorated entirely in black and white and brushed steel. I felt like I was standing in a Plexiglas pepper grinder. The receptionist was reading *Tender Texas Touch* by April Ashmore, one of many books I have not read. Then a woman in tan riding britches and a black turtleneck appeared and said, "Brian?"

I pointed to myself, raising my eyebrows.

"Are you Brian?" she said.

"Ian," I said.

"We're just going to be about five minutes," she said, and disappeared.

Five minutes later she was back. "Craig?" she said. "Craig!"

"Ian!" I said.

She nodded and led me into the offices of David Altschiller, the main man at the agency.

Altschiller was a short, bearded guy in a blue chambray shirt and tan pants. His office was black and silver too. He had a TV and a VCR on his desk and awards stacked in front of the windows. He was forty-nine years old, had been married twice, and had two grown children. He said that gave him some claim to know how men felt.

Altschiller told me the Claiborne ads were the result of an edict from Liz Claiborne herself forbidding the use of sex to sell Claiborne products. The ads had been developed out of conversations with young men who already wore after-shave. His copywriter, a woman named Roz Green, said the point of the ads was to go beyond stereotypes of men as either John Waynes or corporate bigwigs to the (one hoped) appealing contention "that men can have second thoughts, and third thoughts and doubts and be afraid and still have a lot of guts." Thus was born the Ambivalent Hero.

The Claiborne Man wasn't a real man, of course. He was an idealized guy Altschiller believed would appeal especially to women—because more than three-quarters of the after-shave sold in North America was bought by women. Altschiller hoped the ads would convince a few guys to buy their own after-shave, too, but advertisers have been frustrated for years because men tend to resist any single image of themselves.

"We found that men resented people—particularly women—who put them in either one category or another," Altschiller told me. "You know, the 'men are brutes, they're insensitive louts, they pick their noses and drink beer and they watch television, and they want their dinner on time' point of view. Or, conversely, that 'men are Kris Kristofferson or Alan Alda.' We were saying, we're neither one of those things. The cut is to the line 'Man is not so simple after all.' Because the issue for men was, please accept the fact that we are complex beings."

"What's interesting about this guy," I said, "is that, by the end of the ad, he's free of his own desire for women." This is what happens when you hit New York. You start talking about advertising as if it were real.

"Oh yeah," Altschiller agreed. "That's true. Well—does he become independent? It's an interesting notion. He does become independent. He also recognizes that he's not the master of his own universe, that he can't have all he surveys. That the woman has a vote in this. And he kind of comforts himself with that. He accepts that. He doesn't say, Holy shit, now I'm gonna find out, I'm gonna get her, I'm gonna, man, I can't lose this one, I've gotta reel her in. He says, Just as well. It was a nice encounter for about twelve seconds. That's all there is. But he's also fearful to make an advance. To make a fool of himself." Altschiller shrugged his shoulders and turned his palms out, as if he'd just given me his final offer on a carpet. "This has always been a problem men have had. The most successful men with women have always been those who had the confidence, I guess, not to be afraid of rejection, but just to go right at women. They could be the most bizarre people, but merely by asking for the order, they got it." I thought of Spence, pretending to be a lacrosse player in that club in Palm Springs. "Most men don't ask for the order. They're just conscious of the possibility of rejection. And that probably plays into the whole issue of men at this time. Because it's probably harder to ask for the order right now. It's harder for men to go out on a limb than it once was because women are no longer as retiring or as charitable or as forgiving about those kinds of advances."

Just then Altschiller's assistant interrupted to ask if he wanted another cup of coffee. "I know how you get if you don't have your ten cups a day," she said. He didn't want one. She offered me a refill, and I said yes.

I wondered if she wanted to smack me in the head because she had to fetch my coffee. "You say men want to be seen as complex," I said. "But what about beer ads?"

"It's a very confusing time for men," Altschiller said. "If you look at Budweiser's commercials, they still continue to be sexual fantasies, and fantasies of adventure. They're very much—you know, big boobs. That's because it's very, very hard to sell to all men. Men in Nebraska without education are very different from men in New York with education who are very different from someone else. The hardest thing is to sell all men. And to do that, you have to generalize more. When you have to sell to all of them, you have to deal with the largest and lowest common denominator, which very often is those clichés you see in Budweiser advertising."

In other words, if you want to talk to all heterosexual men at once, talk about a woman's breasts.

All this time I was staying at the New York Athletic Club, on Central Park South in Manhattan. It is a lush neighborhood: Carnegie Hall, the Russian Tea Room, women in furs. Central Park is across the street, a wet, soft bruise.

The Athletic Club had been my brother's idea. He was a member. The Athletic Club didn't twinkle in the high firmament of New York clubs, say as brightly as the Union Club, the Century Association, the Leash, and the twelve clubs still listed in the Social Register. The Athletic Club was famous because it was the last private club in New York to refuse women as members. Only an order from the Supreme Court in 1989 had forced the members to change their ways.

"It's cheap," my brother said over the phone, "but you have to wear a tie and jacket all the time in the club. It's a real pain in the ass."

"No," I said, "that's okay."

"No," he said, "it's a real pain. But I'll set it up."

The day I arrived I forgot my tie. "Will you be checking in, sir?" the man at the front desk said. He gave me a look that suggested I would not be.

But once inside I felt at home. My room was narrow but neat, and furnished in shiny, ugly furniture that seemed to have been there a long time. The bathroom was white enamel, with fat taps that didn't disappear in my hands. There was a reek of cigars on the halls.

The only place like it I'd ever been was its cousin, the Harvard Club, on West 44th Street, where I was once a guest. The Harvard Club admitted women, but it reeked of cigars, too—also of luxury, comfort, privacy, adventure, privilege, and accomplishment. Of men, in other words. Members and guests had to wear ties and jackets. There was a beautiful, ripe library on the second floor and a lounge full of well-stuffed red leather sofas. The walls of the lounge were scarlet and nearly forty feet high. They were dotted with the heads of dead animals mounted on plaques. The *tête de résistance* was a teenage elephant whose trunk had been mounted to stand out at full erection, trumpeting across the room.

The New York Athletic Club was slightly less imperial, but the effect was much the same. In place of animal heads, there were athletic trophies everywhere, standing in glass cases like tiny mummies. One of them was engraved "The New York Herald Power Boat Trophy for the Long Island Sound Power Boat Race Open to Cruisers rating 38 Won By Henry A Jackson's Victory II Long Island Sound July 28th 1917," the only time the race appeared to have run. A very specific trophy, the kind you find only in places that worship individualism above everything else. I was living in the very scrotum of East Coast manhood.

The clerk at the front door was wearing a brown Armani suit. He had felt it necessary to give me a copy of the dress code. "The City House of the New York Athletic Club is a formal building in the grande tradition of New York City," it said. "Members and guests are expected to dress appropriately when visiting the City House. Appropriate dress can be described as New York City Dress"—i.e., dress like a building. "For men this means a business suit and tie or sports jacket and tie. For both men and women the safe rule is, when in doubt be conservative."

Precisely. Never mind that it was 102 degrees outside; William Astor and William K. Vanderbilt, the rich white jocks who organized the club in 1868, believed privilege came at a price, and that the price was comfort. We don't permit ourselves to enjoy our privacies, the dress code said, so don't say we're privileged.

My welcome package also included a charge number—cash, proof that members engaged in anything so venal as commerce to make a living, was not permitted in the club—and a tiny directory, printed in red. One side of the directory listed all the reciprocal clubs around the world where members of the NYAC could stay. There were sixty-four reciprocal clubs in all, in places such as Akron (the Akron City Club), Winnipeg (the Carlton Club), Thailand (the Royal Bangkok Sports Club), Melbourne (the Kelvin), Honolulu (the Pacific Club), London, England (the Royal Automobile Club), Glasgow (the Royal Scottish Automobile Club), and Dublin (Stephen's Green Club).

The other side of the directory listed all the club's services. I put on my suit and a tie and set out to explore.

It was like wandering through a small, dark city that I personally owned. The city was sealed and domed, designed to accommodate my every need without ever requiring an actual exit into the harsh world outside, where the atmosphere was unbreathable, where things might go wrong, where I might sense change. Especially where I might sense change. A lot of the rooms I poked into hadn't been used in a long time. Once in a while someone in a white shirt and tie would appear and ask me if I was a member. The billiard room, a huge organ of green felt, was on the tenth floor. The card, chess, and domino rooms (one each) were on nine. Fencing studios and wrestling pits were in the basement. The golf practice net and the judo room were in the solarium. I didn't think anyone still practiced judo. Handball, twenty-first; squash courts, seventh. The gymnasium on six ran the length of an entire city block. The barber shop was on the third; letter boxes were in the lobby. One had one's own mailbox, naturally. The Tap Room, a bar and restaurant on the second floor, strictly prohibited hats and overcoats for no clear reason except to prove that this was a place where men could make their own rules. The ninth floor was completely abandoned, save for a bald man in his seventies. He was sitting in a wing chair in the far corner of a ballroom half the size of a football field, and he was smoking a cigar. This I figured was a big advantage of a private men's club: you could sit in a big room all by yourself and smoke a stogie the size of a tree and produce enough smoke to kill your mother and no one was going to spank your conscience. At first I thought it was a waste of space, until I realized that protection, and especially self-protection, is a specialty of the privileged male. You can imagine how terrified men are if they need a whole floor in a private club to avoid being criticized for smoking a cigar.

I figured the boxing room would be an abandoned closet, boxing having given way to less violent forms of communal exercise since the 1920s, when it was the aerobics of its day and the backbone of most athletic clubs. I was wrong. The boxing room was the best appointed boxing gym I've ever seen, with two full-sized rings and ropes uphol-stered in red velour, something you never see except at professional bouts. One member was wrapping his hands; another was practicing his kick-boxing. The walls were covered with black-and-white photographs of rich white businessmen boxing one another in oversized gloves. The streets of New York featured kids firing Uzis at random into the crowd, but the New York Athletic Club still honored the idea that a man ought to be able to defend himself with his bare hands, especially if he was wearing a tie.

The third floor was the Baths Department, right next to the chiropodist's office. (The club had its own chiropodist, in case someone developed a foot problem in, say, the Tap Room.) The Baths Department was fantastic. Five-foot-high towers of white towels stood in every corner, waiting to be used and discarded. There was a dry steam room, and a wet steam room that was actually three separate rooms, each one hotter than the last, that gave into a maze of shower rooms and sitz baths and hot tubs and knee- and elbow-soakers. Four young guys in the steam room were making plans for the evening and stopped talking only briefly to look at an older man whose penis hung down to his knee.

But the centerpiece was the pool—a huge, pale blue, Olympic-sized tank famous throughout New York as one of the few pools where men could still swim naked. None of the five men in the plunge, each with his own lane, was wearing trunks. I wanted to dive in, but there was no free lane, and my brother had warned me against sharing. "It can get gross," he had said. "The kick-turns. The red-eye special."

Around the pool were wooden racks marked "SPECTACLES"—specially made signs for the specially made racks to hold members' eyeglasses. Under the racks were dozens of dark oak Mission-style lounge chairs, each with a red leather cushion, on which men reclined naked, armed with a drink or a book propped on the wide flat arms of the chairs. They were all chatting, resting, and being themselves. This was the New York upper-class version of a Robert Bly Vision Quest.

I took a sauna. I always neglected to tip the porter in high-toned bathrooms in New York. I came from a class that did not understand porters in bathrooms. The porter in any bathroom was a man who wanted money for handing you a towel, something you could do perfectly well on your own, and therefore a man to be avoided. He worked in a men's toilet, too. He was the man who offered you a peppermint from a basket that had been standing on the washstand next to the communal combs, peppermints that had been fingered by hundreds of men, all of whom had been holding their penises seconds earlier. These concerns did not assail the blithe upper-class male, who had nothing to fear from his own kind. This is the ultimate privilege of being that kind of male: to have no fear, no enemies, not even any troublesome germs.

Afterward, as I changed in my personal changing booth, I heard a man in the next booth say, "I'm going to Tuscany next week." He had long, lank gray-white hair curled behind his ears and a marbled, upper-east-side accent. "Livorrrrno," he added.

"Oh, yeah?" said his companion, who looked more like Willy Loman. "You know it?"

"Yeah, it's down by the Cape, isn't it?"

"Heh heh heh heh heh."

"Me, I'm keeping it simple," Loman said. "Nantucket." They were wearing identical gray and white seersucker jackets from Brooks Brothers. Loman wasn't wearing any socks. Clearly they planned to use the club's Athletic Entrance, a back door that emptied into a loading zone.

"Oh, yeah," Livorno said, like he couldn't care less. It sounded like a put-down.

In the three days I spent in the New York Athletic Club, I saw exactly two women. At first it was a relief to be free from that distraction: according to Ancient Male Theory, self-denial breeds self-knowledge. Not that the New York Athletic Club was the Parthenon or anything. But it was definitely male. Male, because it was a lair that felt like it could be defended. I knew this from the stationery I found in the drawer of the desk in my room.

The letter paper was white and small, five inches by seven inches—just enough space to arrange a meeting or thank someone for dinner. A man never writes more than is necessary. *New York Athletic Club*, it read at the top, in small red understated capitals: *180 Central Park South, New York, N.Y. 10019-1562.* I immediately wrote four quick notes to friends in New York and Toronto.

This made the club my home. Not just a temporary spiritual sanctuary, but an actual physical location, with a dependable address. The paper was so small because the letterhead said everything that needed to be said: any other message was irrelevant by comparison. Here I am in wild-assed New York City, the letterhead implied, and yet even in this wilderness I have a place I can call my own. This illusion, that I could set up a comfortable camp no matter how hostile my surroundings, flattered me. It said: I am self-sufficient. I am a man. I have the letterhead to prove it.

Two days went by like that. Then I started to feel stale. All I could smell was meat. One evening I stepped into the elevator and stared into the face of a member. He was refolding his lapels and shooting his cuffs. The look on his face said *vestio ergo sum*, I dress up, therefore I am. He is still frozen that way in my memory, paralyzed by his privilege.

I hurried out of the club then and ate a bad overpriced meal in a diner. Then I walked back to my room at the club and watched television. First I watched a program about the riots at Berkeley in 1964. "Now that we have won freedom of speech," some student leader said, "we must use it responsibly." I did not believe he would. Then I found the J Channel, New York's pornographic cable service, which the New York Athletic Club kindly provides to all members. I turned it off after an attractive blond woman appeared on the screen saying, "Call me . . . nine-three-nine P-E-E-E, the extra E is for extra pee." Love and Berkeley seemed very far away. I decided I had had enough of the practically all-male New York Athletic Club and telephoned the front desk to say I would be checking out the next morning. Then I went to sleep.

That night I had three dreams. In the first dream, my mother came to visit me with a radio that I couldn't turn off, even after I took out the batteries. "The longer you fiddle with that," she said, "the more insulted your father is." Then I dreamed about an older, richer, very superior couple who gave a show of slides, all of which were out of focus. Finally I dreamed about David Barer, an old high-school friend of mine who was a Jew, who needed to be my friend more than I had time to be his. He eventually felt betrayed by this arrangement. In my dream Barer took out a gun and shot me, to my immense surprise, in the back of my skull. I was surprised he thought I deserved it. As I fell to the ground, my legs paralyzed, I could hear him saying, "He'd have shot me, the bastard." I always dream in sets of three, and the meanings are always the same: a living son kills his father, money destroys clarity, betrayal is a form of murder. Or maybe that isn't what the dreams meant. Maybe the dreams were simply about that sort of club, clubs that don't admit anyone but their own kind. Women, Jews, what have you.

I woke up suddenly, and for a while as I lay in the loud black New York night I thought that once you had been disappointed enough, being a man didn't amount to much more than choosing a prison. The prisons were family, lust, class, money, independence, power, and, because I seldom admitted such things could be a prison for a man, loneliness. I got myself pretty worked up for a while, but I managed to fall back to sleep. I always do.

One day Jerry told me I should call someone named Watts Wacker about the changing male thing. Watts Wacker worked for Yankelovich Partners, Inc., the trend-research and polling company, and was the company's main prognosticator. His title was Futurist. John Naisbitt, the best-selling author of *Mega Trends*, had the job before Watts. The Yankelovich boys, Jerry said, took their futurology very seriously. They'd been sending private studies, about the ways men were changing, to their clients.

I called Watts Wacker, and we arranged to meet in the Oyster Bar at Grand Central Station the next day. I asked how I'd know him. "If Santa Claus were thirty-eight years old and worked out on Nautilus, he'd be me," he said. He also confided that he'd recently returned from a three-day Vision Quest, "an incredibly sacred Indian ritual. We went through the ceremony of purification as if it were fifteen hundred years ago."

I said I'd see him the next day.

The next day turned up as usual. I was waiting for Watts to show in the Oyster Bar in Grand Central when I noticed everyone, but everyone, was reading the *New York Times*. Everyone read the *Post*, the *Daily News*, and *Newsday*. But today? The *Times*, everywhere. It's a plague of seriousness, I told myself. I had my eye out for a *Times* of my own when I saw a man who had to be Watts Wacker.

In person, Watts did not look like a pantheist or Santa Claus. He looked like a Viking, with a Brooks Brothers suit strapped to parts of his body. He ordered an Amstel. On the telephone, when I'd asked if he thought North America was changing its definition of what it meant to be a man—a pretty goddamned stupid question, now that I think about it—Watts launched an answer right at my head.

"The definition of masculinity in this century has been built around this notion of the breadwinner," he had said. "Whereas the primary concern of a majority of women when she got out of college was, who am I going to marry? Is he going to provide? And what women have learned in the past twenty years is, it may be unpleasant, but if I have to, I could live without this schlepp. And men are panicking as they try to redefine their role."

Now, in the bar, Watts elaborated. It was impressionistic, but it sounded like evidence. He talked about the four successive "upticks" that had occurred in the width of ties within the past year. This, Watts said, meant men were "insecure." Watts said the resurgence of muscle cars represented an inevitable regression before the general progression men were about to make. All these changes were very confusing for men and made them defensive. The more defensive men got, the more disdainful women would become. "Women could potentially lose their affect for men," he said. "Men could become pets." I was afraid he was right.

Watts looked at his watch, to make sure he hadn't missed the 6:03 to Westport. Westport is a highball-type suburb in Connecticut, and Watts dwelled there with his seven-year-old daughter, one-year-old son, and his wife, who was heavily involved in the women's movement for abortion rights.

"It's that loss of affect," Watts said finally, "that silence on the part of women, that's different and that's causing men to go, 'Whoa, what's going on?' I think men are scared. And men are not going to work with great enthusiasm to find the solution, either, the way women did."

He didn't think the men's movement was as universal and organized as the media suggested, but he did think men were getting together more to talk about meaningful subjects. I thought about my friend Barry-Bob, and Hassan rolling his eyeballs and crying. Watts thought the tone of these conversations might go backward before it moved forward. "My feeling is it's going to be less crying and talking about your father and more drinking beer and talking about big tits." I thought about Spence, advertising for mammaries. Between those two poles, it was a hell of a choice.

It was time to catch his train, and I decided to ride to Westport with him. A friend of Watts's was on the train, and on the ride out of the city Watts told the two of us about his Vision Quest.

I had gathered from my weekend with Barry-Bob in the wilderness hut at Harbin Hotsprings that Vision Quests were essentially long hikes with some steep hills. But for Watts it had been much more ceremonial. Watts planned to do it every year. He said it was cathartic. Very cathartic, in fact. "It wasn't all emotional. We drink, we fart, we tell crude jokes. But you can also reach a level of intimacy immediately. You can go from telling the crudest jokes to talking about the greatest pain of life within two minutes. But it's not an EST session."

Outside, Connecticut sped by, well-dressed and respectful. In the sweatlodge he and his friends built during their Vision Quest, Watts experienced a revelation. "It was the first time I'd taken my wedding ring off in twelve years of marriage," Watts said. Their guide, an outfitter and rancher in Montana, gave Watts a special Vision Quest name: Thor. "He grew, I would say, to love us," Watts said. That was a funny thing to hear on a commuter train in Connecticut. They had religious experiences. One day they met a man walking by himself in such an isolated part of the mountains that Watts believed the man had been sent by a higher power to meet them, to serve an unknown spiritual purpose. Watts believed that. He was not a fool.

One night they made a circle and told stories, and then it was Thor Wacker's turn. "And when I got into the circle I said things I had never said to anyone, even to my wife. I would suggest that everyone did the same." He "called guys on their shit"; he talked about life at home. He had never talked about life at home, at home with his wife. That was not the sort of thing transitional men did. The transitional man took it and ate it and suffered in silence.

"Part of what has happened to men as a result of the women's movement is that men have had a lot of demands placed on them," Watts said. "And part of what made the week so great was that I could reflect on that. I think the biggest demand placed on men is the whole question of who is going to be the primary care giver for the kids." His own wife had owned that role, but that was changing, as she became more involved in her causes. (Of all the complaints I heard from men about what was wrong in their lives, the most common was that they shouldered an unfair burden of child care, especially given their other responsibilities.) Watts wore a look that suggested he felt put upon. "One of the things you end up trying to do is fake it. You hear your wife's car pull up and you turn off the television and throw your kid up in the air."

We were almost into Westport. I asked Watts if that was all he had talked about on the Vision Quest weekend—if that was what he meant by "stuff he'd never even mentioned to his wife."

"What I said that weekend was that two people have tried to kill me."

Watts's friend looked at me. I looked at Watts. He had our attention.

"Someone very close to me was a psychotic manic-depressive who took a knife to my throat. Someone else was a drug addict and alcoholic who tried to kill me with a gun. He was drunk enough that he missed, but . . . I've heard that when you grow up in a psychotic family, you either make it or you don't. I like to think I made it. But I really agree with what Joseph Campbell said: it's a journey. Forget about where you've been. It's where you're going that's more important."

Watts was going to Westport, and there we were. He said good-bye and got off the train. I thought it was brave of him to admit to all this.

As the train rattled back to New York, I had one of those thoughts that seem very grand at the time but puny the following morning. The thought I had on the train was that the questions of identity men ask themselves in nearly everything they do—who am I? Why do I live this way? what happens if I change my habits, or do what I fear?—don't have answers. If they have answers, something is terribly wrong, pal. When our perennial philosophical queries became only a pretext for psychological therapies, then it was time to be really worried. And that was exactly what had happened. Too many men of my generation had abandoned those questions, and the spirited, fuck-you posing of them, because we were told they were childish and privileged—queries that had no definite answers and therefore weren't worth asking. We believed what we were told. I thought perhaps we might have let ourselves down for lack of nerve. I thought about promising myself, right there on the train, that I would always ask myself those questions. I thought about getting up every morning and saying, out loud, in front of the bathroom mirror like some character in a Truffault movie, "Life is not perfectible, even through the repeated use of modern kitchen appliances." Then I felt like a fool for having such thoughts. And I remembered the notes my father wrote to me when I was a boy. Stay clean, my father wrote, every time. To which I thought he might have added, Don't be afraid.

Someone had left the morning paper on the next seat. I picked it up, and there on the front page was the reason everyone had been reading the *Times* that day. Two scientists claimed to have discovered a genetic cure for impotence.

6

Howard's End

*A courageous foray into depravity – The heartbreak
of impotence – Portrait of a sensitive porno girl –
Jane Pauley's revenge – And other ups and downs of life
on the set of a pornographic movie*

Peter Major's member was twelve inches long and nine inches in circumference. It was a respected and somewhat alarming sight. I knew the math because Major's thing was two feet from my head. I was sitting in a warehouse in the dry rut called the San Fernando Valley, on the set of *Dream Lover: A Tale of Sexual Awakening*, a pornographic film, watching Peter Major, the biggest man in the business, fail dismally.

It was the first time it had ever happened. The mood on the set was somber, as if the president had just died. Major's pals called his penis Beer Can—and that was soft. He was thirty-four years old, and a Canadian, and no matter which girl he was working with, no matter what the circumstance, he could raise his monster to life. But today, in roughly the eight-hundredth porno film of Peter Major's twelve-year career, he was jelly.

He'd taken sleeping pills the night before. That was what he told himself was wrong. What else could it be? He'd been working out, taking his vitamins, as he had for ten years. He was actually a small-framed man pumped up to larger proportions: you could tell from his wrists.

But this . . . this was awful. Being crippled had to be like this: he could feel the desire, he wanted to have sex with the girl, but he couldn't plug his wish in.

All he had to do was give Lauren, the new girl, the bada-*bing*, as J.D., the cameraman, called it, and then move on to Jennifer, and that was it. Half an hour, max. He had to climax but once. If it were twice, or three times, the sort of performance directors normally entrusted only to twenty-year-olds, well, okay, a little anxiety would have been understandable. But once? Unimaginable. Besides, the girls loved him. *Loved* him. Some were willing to work with him for no pay. They liked just to look at him. Hadn't his next-door neighbor stopped him on the street, told him how she and her husband liked to lie in bed and watch him walking naked around his apartment, how just looking at him had improved their sex life? He was high on that for months.

It was just a matter of focus. Focus was how all porn stars had sex on command. You blocked out your surroundings and your secondary thoughts and zoomed in on a body part—Lauren was flat-chested, for instance, but she had a pretty face, and a nice backside—and then you did the job.

But this afternoon his zoom was kaput. He couldn't seem to lock in on his confidence, on the image of his own perfectly executed performance.

Major touched his hair, to make sure it was in place. He was obsessed with his hair. The others made fun of him, but Major's credo was that if he looked good, he felt good, and if he felt good, he performed well. He shut his eyes. Maybe Plan B, a fantasy, would work. Fantasizing your way to an erection was standard operating procedure in the event of faulty focus.

You floated a whole derangement of past women, other women, forgotten women, women who had been thrilled to have it in them, across the heads-up display of your imagination. . . .

Still nothing.

Fall-back position number three was to get off on your own power. Major looked down at his own body. He looked good. Sometimes the sight of your own muscles working, the subcutaneous pulse and sheen of your pecs and your forearms, did the trick. You ignored the girl and watched yourself stuffing the girl.

But he didn't know Lauren, and she didn't know that she had to be turned on for him to be turned on. "It's like she's there," he muttered to Paul Thomas (P.T.), the director, "but she isn't there for me."

Or maybe it was the fact that her boyfriend Jordan was lurking to one side, watching the scene. He was watching Lauren, and Lauren was glancing back. He was a young kid, just breaking into the business. Unbeknown to Major, the kid was frantic. Major was so huge, the kid was afraid Lauren would never want sex with him again. Jordan was trying to maintain what the porn boys called "mental discipline" by reminding himself that she was just doing it for money, but he was getting depressed. Meanwhile Lauren was thinking of her boyfriend! That would never do.

Wait . . . what was this? A light swell. Major grasped the advantage, pushed it quickly into Lauren. . . . She breathed out audibly. . . . He began to pump. He could feel her pulling back, trying to keep it from hurting. He swelled some more, pumped some more. Ten seconds . . . twenty . . . thirty . . . she was breathing more easily now . . . but there were no whimpers.

No whimpers! He could feel his excitement dropping off the face of a sheer cliff. He was soft again.

Major pulled out and stood alone in a corner on the set, a dejected Greek statue with a drooping phallus. He just couldn't get wood. "Sorry," he said to Lauren.

"Oh, that's okay," she said, smiling as she looked back from her position on her hands and knees.

"J.D., back off," P.T. said to his cameraman. "Back off and give him some space. Don't rush in. Let him get into it."

"He's starting to burn out," Alan, the makeup man, said. Sucking on his pipe, Alan looked like a leftist professor at a small state college settling in for a discussion of the causes of the Civil War. "He's having problems."

"Killer bod, man," Howard, the production assistant, said admiringly, shaking his head. "Killer face. Killer dick. And the longest cum shot in the business. He can put it in the corner."

"He hit the dolly guy, once, offset."

"He hit the camera."

But this afternoon, Major couldn't hit his own pocket. J.D., the cameraman, had seen it right away.

"Major," he said, "get some rest."

"Yeah." He hadn't had sex at home in a week in preparation for today, and he certainly wasn't going to now.

But J.D. knew that home was part of Major's problem. He was settling down, had a house and a girlfriend. J.D. was married himself, and he believed the transition to domesticity could sap a man's sexual energy. Sex, and the chase and anticipation that preceded it, suddenly seemed pointless and unexciting. He thought of his own wife, "taking root on the couch in front of the TV with her hundredth Diet Coke," and he understood Major's problems.

"That's the way it is with women and sex and marriage," J. D. said. "Women get into the house and into making it businesslike. Gradually the man loses his sense of maleness, his sense of adventure. I can feel it happening to me. You get the money and the home, and insurance, and even health insurance, but you can become too caught up in that. After marriage, women become materialists. They say, 'Sex, what is that? That was the whore in me, before.' And men miss that. So they lose their maleness. Women use their feminine wiles to attract us, and then use social conventions to keep us there." I wondered what plans he had had for himself before his own fall.

The script for *Dream Lover* was forty-four pages long—half the length of a Hollywood script, though the final product would run ninety minutes and contain a full ten minutes of dialogue. Stage directions let the sex handle itself: *Amy finishes jerking off Doug and watches in awe.* By the standards of porn, the script was positively Kierkegaardian:

AMY: Laura? Do you like sucking penises?

LAURA: Cocks. Mmmmm.

AMY: Why?

LAURA: It's the only time I feel like I really know what I'm doing.

This was high-class smut—the so-called "yuppie porn" that Paul Thomas, *Dream Lover*'s forty-six-year-old director, had made his specialty. He was the Bergman of porn: in its categories and genres, the world of porn films resembled legitimate Hollywood, just compressed and exaggerated. P.T. had impatiently abandoned his promising career as a legitimate actor (he was Jesus in *Jesus Christ Superstar* on Broadway, and St. Peter in the film) to be a big star in porn back when the industry was almost glamorous. Marilyn Chambers and Linda Lovelace were international celebrities. Jim and Artie Mitchell, who gave the world the infamous O'Farrell Theater sex club in San Francisco, spent millions to make 35-millimeter films that were shown in "art" cinemas and reviewed by full-time porn critics who gave out their own awards. Then came 1984 and the video cassette recorder. The $3,000, shot-in-one-day-in-the-producer's-living-room ultra-cheeseball video pornographic wonder was born.

Now P.T. was trying to reverse the trend. *The Masseuse*, his masterpiece, was famous for depicting only two sex acts in ninety minutes, when at least five were *de rigueur*. In *Rockin' the Boat*, another pornographic watershed, he eliminated dialogue completely: instead the flick humped along to a rhyming rap narrative. *Adult Video News* called Thomas "the guy willing to take chances," but many critics found his films pretentious. "Sex or Story?" a think-piece in a recent *Hustler* had asked. "For the author, porn's best plot is one he can't remember. . . . Should Kassi Nova concentrate on delivering dialogue or devouring dick? Can she talk and ride rod at the same time?" P.T. knew he was making porn; he just didn't want to be completely bored, which was why he was arguing about lighting with J.D., alias John Dirlam, his cinematographer.

"This is based on *Carnal Knowledge*," P.T. said.

In *Dream Lover's* opening scene, Christy Canyon and Jennifer Stewart, two college girls, practice fellatio using Christy's finger as a prop, only to find themselves roused to lesbian passion. P.T. wanted to film in total darkness. "That's how *Carnal Knowledge* began. I want the flashlight to be the only light source."

"I saw *Carnal Knowledge*," J.D. said. "And there wasn't a black scene in the whole movie."

"The movie opens in total darkness."

"But that was the opening scene, and it was art, and it was 35 millimeter, and it was 1972."

Aside from P.T. and J.D., the crew included an assistant cameraman, two lighting gaffers, a sound man, a makeup man, Howard, P.T.'s wife Judy, who served as office manager and script girl, two stills photographers (for publicity shots and video box photos), and two visiting journalists from *Hot Video Magazine* in France. The floor was littered with box after box of Sweet 'n' Fresh disposable douche, douche bags, Today sponges, doughnut boxes, film cans. None of the actors used condoms. "We're safer than we would be going to bars," one of the boys said, "because we're working with people we know."

The finger-sucking scene finished, P.T. raced on to the next sequence. He had three days to shoot the entire movie. While Marc Wallice and T.T. Boyd, two of his actors, stroked their penises through their pants to gain a headstart on their erections, P.T. coached Christy on her lines. Her character was supposed to be reluctant to have sex with two men at once. P.T. was trying to coax more reluctance out of Christy.

"On one condition," Christy said, rehearsing. "I don't want either of you in my behind." When she wasn't acting in porno films, Christy studied to be a fashion designer.

"Christy," P.T. interrupted. "Not like that. It's more, 'I don't want anyone in my . . . behind.' Don't say it so forthrightly."

Christy tried the less forthright version. "'I don't want anyone in my . . . behind.' This dialogue's really good," she said. "Sensitive."

"That," the script assistant said, "is because a girl wrote it."

Action. The scene moved from kissing to hand jobs to cunnilingus to fellatio to intercourse to a modified DP (double penetration) in less than five minutes. The actors didn't stop between takes, for fear they'd lose their erections and delay filming. They hardly ever kissed, save for occasional "porn kisses," weird lizard-tongue flickings. The lads pumped away in six-eight time as if attached to a machine, displaying the amazing stamina they were hired for a hundred times a year. The other day a cameraman had missed Boyd's ejaculation, and Boyd had simply served up another one thirty seconds later.

"Kiss down to his balls," P.T. shouted. "I want more hard-core ball licking." When Christy flipped her hair in front of Wallice's long, thinnish penis, it was soft-core for the Playboy Channel. When she swung her hair out of the way, it was for the hard-core version of the film, which was to be sold independently.

Watching live human beings have sex ten feet away, erections flying and breasts flopping—watching people do in public, without a shade of embarrassment, what for me had always been private and fraught with secrecy—was like a hallucination. Time seemed to pass quickly and slowly at once. But I was a newcomer. The crew were bored blind. They could have been watching a long uphill stretch of the Tour de France. Christy was mounting Boyd and fellating Wallice and moaning loudly when J.D. suddenly spoke up.

"Look at that," he said. "She's hot."

"I know," Howard said. He was a former stick boy for the Philadelphia Flyers. "Every time I look at her, I get a hard-on."

They weren't looking at Christy Canyon. They were looking at a photograph of Jane Pauley in *People Magazine*.

I was looking at Christy Canyon, however, and at everything else. So that's what another guy's erection looks like! And that's how you do a threesome! It was like a 3-D anatomy lesson, a hyperintensified version of a stripper taking off her clothes. At first it was riveting. Some days I couldn't wait to get on the set. I didn't know what I would find titillating; I felt like a puppet, controlled from above by some invisible wire of desire. If I'd been arguing with my wife, or my work was going badly, if I felt overwhelmed and even more than usually inept, I could run, not walk, to the porn set, where I'd be freed, however momentarily, from all expectations, all criticism, and all self-knowledge, through the obliterating consolations of voyeurism and the narcotic wash of desire.

What was even more surprising, though, was how quickly I always wanted to leave the set. After half an hour I was ready to run. I wanted to feel something. I turned to porn to be freed from the momentary unfeelingness of my life, but the scenes I saw only trapped me more. I needed pornography for its momentary freedom, but despised it for making me less than I was.

I never talked about it much with my wife. She didn't approve. She thought I was over-researching.

Jennifer Stewart was especially disappointed by Peter Major's collapse. She'd waited all day for her big scene with Peter, and then it hadn't happened. But it was just as well. She had to get home for her dad's birthday.

All in all, Jennifer had had a terrible day. She'd been late for her call on set that morning. Her boyfriend of ten months, who had no idea she was a pornographic actress, had discovered the *Dream Lover* script in her handbag. There'd been a scene. Jennifer told him it belonged to a friend. Jennifer had already starred in ten porn flicks that year, but with 300 million erotic videos rented out annually, the odds were good he hadn't seen her work. Still, at twenty-two, Jennifer was porn's favorite debutante. She'd been named starlet of the year by *Adult Video News*, which praised her as "an absolutely beautiful woman, an excellent actress, and one hell of a hot fuck." In the parallel universe of pornography, which created *Total Reball*, *The Wonder Rears*, and *Edward Penishands (I and II)*, Jennifer had just won the Oscar.

But how could her boyfriend have guessed? Jennifer didn't look like a porn star. Blond and blue-eyed, she was a born-again straight-A product of a private Christian school. She brought her stuffed animals onto the set and admired George Burns and Gracie Allen "because they were so obviously in love." Her parents were accountants and called her Jennifer-Poo. In fact, her willowy, corn-fed prettiness was why men liked to see her moaning her lungs out in bed with the likes of Peter Major: Jennifer Stewart was the porn industry's contention that nice girls wanted it, too.

Jennifer hated lying to her boyfriend, but she couldn't bring herself to tell him the truth. "I don't know if I'd want a guy who said it was okay," she told Alan, the makeup man, as he painted her lips. "Because if he knows I'm with other guys, it's okay for him to be with other girls. And—well, I do this, but it's my job. It's not like I'm in bars or anything."

Not all porn had been tainted by P.T.'s high standards. In Pacoima, the Los Angeles suburb where Rodney King was beaten by Los Angeles police officers, I met Loretta Sterling. Loretta Sterling is his *nom de porn*; his real name is Eddie. Eddie/Sterling was the auteur of "the low-low end of porn." His specialty was "shock porn"—films that featured six-hundred-pound women (*Fatliners I and II*), weird special effects such as the milk-spurting nipples he had invented for a recent masterpiece, and, always, "boobies." A Sterling flick without huge breasts was like a day without oxygen. "Don't you think," he explained, "that the ultimate sexual experience is something that horrifies you? I don't think a lot of men have had sex with a fat woman. And they get to see what it would be like. Fat is taboo, but the sexual appeal is still there." More to the point, breasts were an obsession that netted Sterling a fine living. He also ran the industry's biggest video duplicating service and rented his studio out to advertising firms and the occasional Disney production.

The economics were impressive: with overhead, Sterling's films cost $20,000. He would easily sell six thousand of them for $12.50 each, or about $75,000. (His distributor retailed them for $24.95.) He made two films a month. All in, he netted half a million a year. He had three cars, three homes, a membership at the Baja Country Club, a wife who was his partner and business manager, a twenty-one-year-old son who knew what his father did for a living, and a thirteen-year-old daughter who to Sterling's knowledge had not yet figured it out.

Sterling looked like a life insurance salesman, running to portliness with most of his dark hair still nailed in place. Instead, he was one of the great explorers in the ancient land of repression. He made shock porn and fetish porn because he couldn't forget his first sexual adventures, which is another way of saying nothing had come along since to compete with that excitement. "Those early experiences stand out in my mind. When I think back on the good old days, I think of the first, second time I had sex."

This day was an especially busy one. All morning he'd filmed *Tit Tales III*, which not only had no script—it had no dialogue. Highlights included a bouncefest on a trampoline with three vast-breasted women, and a sex scene between Leanna Foxxx (*Foxxx Hunt*) and Joey Silvera (at least fifteen hundred films in his fifteen years in the business) in which Silvera lowered his genitals through a gap in a string hammock, whereupon Foxxx administered to them as if she were a mechanic under a car unscrewing its oil pan. It was Sterling's idea.

Conceptually, this was standard fare for porno—"sex for the terminally bored," the sound man called it—but technically it was a stunt on par with Mel Gibson's multi-story jump in *Lethal Weapon II*. "Whoa, this is good, man," Silvera said, hanging on to the hammock for dear life, "but it's a son-of-a-bitch." Whenever Silvera stood up, the rope marks made him look like a waffle.

Sterling set up the shot and peered through the viewfinder. "It's art, Eddie," the cameraman said.

"Oh, yeah," Sterling agreed, "it is." But he wanted the light down. "Because it's not very pleasing on her buttocks. It's giving her celluleet." That's how he pronounced it: cell-u-leet. "And I want to get more boobies if you can."

"You gonna shoot from underneath?"

"Yeah. Make sure you get her boobs right through the holes."

"This is one of the best things you've shot in a long time, Eddie," the cameraman said again. "It's very erotic."

"It's interesting. It's a mixture of the fetish and the bondage."

"So, she sucks him off through the hammock?"

And they were off. The scene wandered on for ten, fifteen minutes. It was hard to pay attention. Even this grotesquerie became boring. The sex was irrelevant. It was slapstick, dirty Laurel and Hardy. I kept thinking about basketball.

"Now he comes on her tits?" the cameraman asked, never leaving the eyepiece.

"On her boobies." Boobies, a word Sterling uttered fifty times an hour. "And after he comes on your boobies, give him a little more head. Because I like to shoot the come shots long and loving. Cock-worship, in a way."

"Aaaagh," muttered the sound man. "Nobody wants to see people fucking in bed any more."

Howard, *Dream Lover's* production assistant, worked like a dog and earned $40,000 a year. "It's a great job, dude," he said. "Where else can you look at beautiful babes fucking all the time, man?" He was always hoisting lights, grabbing smoke makers, hauling cable, fetching Albolene vaginal lubricant and smokes for the girls, or burgers from the Carl's Jr. down the road. He endured constant abuse in return for the promise that one day he would direct his own porno feature. From there he planned to move on to his screenplay, about a hippy seduced into being a used-car salesman against his principles. "It's my life, man," he told me one afternoon. He had hoped to be a professional hockey player, but "I drank too much beer and smoked too much pot, man. But I had ten good years of partying." You could always count on Howard to see the bright side.

Sometimes he got to date one of the "porno girls," as he called them. Like Heather, the new eighteen-year-old with double D breasts. She had a sultry, lazy look about her, as if she might have enjoyed having sex while slowly turning on a spit. She was bisexual, but Howard planned to take her to a movie.

"Don't do that," P.T. said, overhearing him. "It'll fuck up your job."

Howard was going to take her anyway. He'd been working on Heather for two weeks. When she walked downstairs to the set, Howard sprang to her side like a cocker spaniel. She was at least eight inches taller than he was. "I really like to have my nipples squeezed," Heather said to him.

"I'll squeeze your nipples all you want," Howard replied.

Exchanges like this made me think I had missed something when I was growing up. They also made me want to wash my hands.

Howard couldn't take his eyes off her. He was so engrossed, he kept forgetting to move the smoke maker, whereupon P.T. would call him an asshole in front of everyone. Howard didn't mind. "She's hot for me, dude," he said. He had a thick, beery voice, his stubby Pennsylvania accent rounded out by ten years on the beach in California. "I'll fuck her."

"Really?" I said. He reminded me of an onion pulled straight out of the garden, fresh and raw and still clumped with dirt.

"No, dude, really. I fucked a couple of them. Me and Cal, we get them, because we work here. And when there's nothing in production we call up all the porno girls. Yeah. But I don't have any feelings for 'em. I just fuck 'em. Because you fall in love with a porno girl, you break the first rule. It's stupid. How could you fall in love with a girl who fucks guys for a living? But I date regular girls, too. I'm trying to date this veterinarian. Thirty years old. She's great. She gives me breaks on my bill for my dog. And I hit on girls on the beach. They laugh at me. But once in a while, you get a hit."

A couple of days later, I saw him moping around the back of the set. "What's the matter?" I said. "How's Heather?"

"She turned me down," he said. He was off porno girls. We sat in a back alley and smoked. "I tried it once, you know," he said, leaning on his broom. "Having sex for the camera. It wouldn't stay hard. Got it right in, and it went soft. Every time. Because there was nothing in it. No emotion. It's not even like a quick fuck. It was way worse." He paused. "So cold." He shook his head, and looked at the floor. "It's in the mind, man."

Halfway down another set constructed to resemble an alley behind a college town pub, Jennifer Stewart was performing orally on Marc Wallice. The scene was supposed to depict Jennifer's first experience with oral sex. It was eight o'clock in the morning.

"It's good," J.D. said, one eye squinted against the camera.

"Okay, Jenny," P.T. said, "start to come."

"Oh, oh, oh," Jenny moaned. Then, to Marc: "Are you ready?"

"Yes," he said to her, "but don't look at me." Marc had a habit of falling for new girls. He was finishing when the camera ran out of film.

"We shouldn't let this happen," P.T. snapped. "They shouldn't have to stand there while we reload." He cared for the dignity of his actors.

"It's new stock. Sorry about it, guys."

"I don't mind," Jennifer said. "But he's . . . " She looked at Marc, stroked his shoulder. "I know the last thing I want to do after I come is stand around."

"You see, that's where we differ," the sound man said. "After I come, I *like* to stand around."

J.D. shot some fills, some angle shots, and it was over. Jenny kissed Marc, but his face wore no expression. He could have run into her in the mall.

Marc knew, just as Major knew, that most men envied his talent for unemotional sex. Most men settled down; we traded the sexual freedom of our twenties for the intimacy we hoped lay on the other side of familiarity. But the porn boys held out, resisted the pressure to conform. To a lot of guys, they were heroes.

But having a conversation with Marc Wallice or Peter Major was like talking to a man made of mirrors. Wallice was a poor kid from Flushing who lived from paycheck to paycheck, who never spoke unless he was spoken to, and then only sparsely, as if he begrudged you each painful, dangerous word. If you asked Wallice about his father, he never said his parents had divorced; he just said, "I don't have one."

But there was something inside Wallice, something he didn't know what to do with. All the sex, the sex that couldn't have any emotional consequences if he was to stay in focus, had forced him way, way back into his maleness, into the most heavily fortified sector of himself. It was like talking to the audioanimatronic Lincoln at Disneyland, except that sometimes the computer loop went wild.

"I enjoy myself at home," he told me one afternoon. He was sitting alone, as usual, smoking, as usual. The scene of ten minutes earlier had already evaporated in the indiscriminate orgy that made up his sexual memory. "I enjoy my spare time. I love to watch TV. I smoke a little pot. I love cooking. I cook amazing shit. Sushi, even. And I have my musical instruments, and I have my little doggy."

A thirty-two-year-old man who has sex for a living using the word doggy. "Yeah," he said, "we wanted to get a little funny lookin' dog, somethin' we could laugh at when we got stoned." The dog was a Bassett hound. "He's really funny. He's really clumsy."

"Have you ever thought of doing anything else?" I said.

"I'd rather be doing this," he said. Rather than what, he had no idea. "It's a nice way to come and see people every day. The crews are cool. It's nice to be driving and come to see who's going to be here today. It's like"—and he paused then, for a long time—"it's like conversation."

All afternoon, a kid named Nick had been hanging around the set. He wanted a part in one of P.T.'s movies. All his life, growing up in Ohio, he had wanted to be a porn star. "I'm basically the product of two nymphomaniac parents," he said, and right away you knew he was far removed from common feelings of shame. At twenty-one, divorced twice and separated again, he wanted to get "paid to get laid," and he wanted a girlfriend, because "two or three times a day on set, that won't be enough." He had a girlfriend, but then he went to visit her one weekend and ended up in bed with her roommate. The roommate had no complaint with his aspirations, and he felt so liberated he wrote her a song. He planned to make it as a musician as well as in porn. He said, "I'll eventually probably be the most controversial person in the world." The song was called "Laying the Cards on the Table":

I'm going to tell you exactly how I feel
And see what happens
If I lose at least I tried
And I won't cry.

In four days, P.T. shot sixteen blow jobs, twelve courses of cunnilingus, countless hand jobs, and twelve acts of sexual intercourse. The scenes gradually began to blend together—"into one big dick," as one of the girls put it. But the "cum" or "pop" shots—the scenes in which the man ejaculated—were never routine. They were the center of gravity in a hard-core picture, not only proof that the sex was real, but that it could be reality: the squalid, leaky banality of ejaculation was the one thing the predominantly male audience was certain to have in common with the movie, the link by which the audience could associate and believe. When men who watched porn films learned I'd been hanging around porn sets, it wasn't the women they wanted to know about; the names they recognized were those of the male stars. P.T. didn't call ejaculation "the money shot" for nothing.

Good thing, then, that by the third day of shooting, Peter Major was back in form. He felt terrific; he arrived early, stripped off his shirt, and wandered around the performer's lounge in his underwear, chatting. "I always wondered whether girls like hairy butts or smooth butts," he said to the girls in the makeup room. He was possessed of the smooth variety.

"Hairless!" they squealed.

"Really?" Major said, thrilled.

"You see how much more on he is today?" J.D. said. "He's got an audience, he's the complete center of attention. He's in his element. This is Valhalla for this guy."

Down on the set, after the girls had douched, after the lights had been set and the camera was ready to roll, Major dropped to one knee, crossed himself, said a mantra, and waggled his fingers like an Olympic gymnast. P.T. was going straight to sex with Jennifer Stewart, just in case.

Action. Major took Jennifer *à la chien*. He held her hips and pushed home hard. Jennifer's pale body crumpled against him, her back arching, her eyes closed, her hands gripping the sheet. Seconds later she was screaming and moaning and biting the bed covers, as the script suggested.

"It's so big," Jennifer moaned. This was in the script.

"Too big?"

"No . . . it's perfect. Where am I?" This wasn't in the script. Later she said she had three orgasms. They certainly sounded real.

"Ready for re-insertion!"

"Shoot two more minutes of hard stuff, then a pop shot."

"I get the furthest squirt when I do it myself," Major said. Jennifer was lying on her back now, her head buried under his scrotum. She looked dazed. Her temples were damp with perspiration.

As Major worked on his hand-held climax, people began to take cover. J.D. held the camera at arm's length, his head arched back out of the way. The gaffer wielding the "hoona-hanna light"—a small lamp taped to the end of a pole, for those hard-to-light organs—was crouched behind a screen. The assistant cameraman had retreated behind the spotlight used to backlight the semen as it shot across the set. Even Christy Canyon, who was completely out of the way on the lower bunk, hunkered down, her arms over her head, as if expecting a bomb to go off.

When the big moment arrived, the volume was there, but it landed where it started, on Jennifer's chest. Still, everyone was enthusiastic.

"Gobs!" Howard shouted. "Gobs of the stuff, man!"

"That 2K light makes it look so incredible," the lighting man sighed. "Makes it glisten!"

"I had the volume," Major said. "But I didn't have the distance. It'll take me a couple of days to get that back." Still, Peter Major was a man again, and everyone was hugely relieved.

There were days when I never wanted to see another depiction of the sexual act again in my life. The scenes from the movie were devoid of individuals and therefore of tenderness and humor, and the real-life set wasn't much different. So driving home at night, dropping down out of the Santa Monica Mountains that separate the San Fernando gulch from Los Angeles and its sea of lights, I could feel the temperature dropping, and the dew settling on the car, and it was as if I were being washed clean.

I could breathe again, having returned from a distant, airless planet. I could feel the welcoming, normal presence of my wife and my own bed drawing me home. My life, my desires, all of them, the full range, were mine again.

My wife still wanted to have a baby, but my enthusiasm for sex with her (or anyone else) disappeared, and weeks went by before it returned. But the images of those days have never left my brain. Jennifer, mouth working furiously. Heather, moaning in the steam room. They are scalded into my memory, and nothing I can do makes them disappear. I don't know why: whether I lodged those craven images because they meant heat and freedom, or because they tethered me, like a miner on a chain, to the specter of my own inadequacy. Pornography may or may not make men violent—the scientific evidence is widely admitted to be inconclusive. But no matter what else it does, pornography enters your mind, and sits there, a radioactive lump.

Watching porn made me feel like the guy in the Hertz ad—the one who is dropped by unseen forces from the sky, into the driver's seat. Pornography put me, the voyeur, in charge—gave me control. The drawback was, it told me what to feel. Porn let me feel one thing only, and one thing is as close as you can get to nothing at all.

7

Beemyn

An unwelcome stranger in the land of many wives —
Double-digit grandchildren — The Author's paucity of
soul — Four lawn mowers in Iowa

I was halfway through a Utah town called St. George when I spotted a temple of the Church of Jesus Christ of Latter-day Saints shining in the twilight like a department store dressed for Christmas. I don't know why, but before I knew it I was in the parking lot.

This was the first Mormon temple in Utah. Brigham Young, the second Mormon prophet, commissioned it in 1871 after settling St. George with a colony of 309 families, Mormons in exodus from persecution in Ohio. Like the founder of the Mormon Church, Joseph Smith, Young had been a polygamist. But the Mormons outlawed polygamy in 1890. A middle-aged woman in a brown dress and a lively perm met me at the door of the temple, introduced herself as Sister Park, and told me, "People are not just married till death do you part. They're married forever." She meant this to be reassuring. Then she sat me down and showed me a movie called *Temples Are for Families*.

In the movie, a clean-cut dad was explaining family life to his clean-cut children. The children were very blond. "Families are eternal," the dad said. "If we're always good, our marriages will last forever." Then a narrator quoted the prophet Matthew ("Whosoever thou shalt bind on earth shall be bound in heaven"), and then the dad said, "Isn't it wonderful to know that we'll be together forever?"

"Yes," said his son.

"Me too," said his baby daughter.

Then Sister Park handed me some pamphlets and told me to come back anytime. The likelihood of my doing so seemed small. Dozens of Mormon families were driving up to see the temple's Christmas lights. The parents seemed young to have borne so many children, but they were all smiling. I couldn't imagine why, which only made me feel lonely and cynical and about as out of place as I ever have. I got in my truck again and headed northeast to Colorado City, up in the red mesa country of Utah and Arizona, land the Navajo still consider sacred. Colorado City was a town of five thousand, and home (I had read in the *New York Times*, which claimed that plural marriage was now out of the closet) to a large population of polygamists. I didn't know what to expect. I mean, I actually fantasized about getting involved in some kind of group sex thing. I was afraid of infidelity and fidelity alike.

The town didn't even have a motel. The whole place looked like a new suburb under construction. Finally I spotted a gas station under an electric light at a corner. Three young men were leaning back in their chairs. It was a scene out of *Village of the Damned*. The men were blond and in their late teens and wore long-sleeved shirts with the collars buttoned, and they looked as if their collective IQ might crack three digits.

"Hi," I said.

One boy nodded. I explained I was a reporter looking for polygamists.

"You'll have to come back in the morning and talk to the mayor," the boy said.

"Great," I said. "Anybody else you'd recommend?"

"The mayor's the only one who can talk about that," he said.

After that I wanted to get out of town fairly quickly. The nearest motel was the Best Western in Hurricane, Utah, thirty miles away.

By daylight, I could see Colorado City for what it was: not a suburb, but a fort of resistance, a shuffle of semi-finished frame and adobe buildings perched under rusty cliffs. The polygamists kept their houses in a state of constant extension and their wives registered as unmarried mothers, all in the name of tax write-off. The color of the land made me frankly nervous: blood-red ground that soaked up the intolerance of the outside world toward the polygamists who lived there and oozed the frustration of the polygamists toward the outside world that refused to understand them.

There were children everywhere. Half the population was in infancy: the average age was five. Vehicles ran to trucks and old Cadillacs. The Colorado City Dramatic Society was mounting a production of *Little Women*. Girls and boys stared openly at me, surprised to see a stranger. Their isolation was a wall of separation from anything that threatened them. The principal of the school told me, "We've had about enough nonsense from reporters," and Clyde Barlow, the mayor, refused to talk to me. (There were a hundred Barlows in the phone book, which was as thin as the owner's manual in my truck.) Ditto the chief of police and the local superintendent.

I bought a coffee at the Early Bird, the only cafeteria in town—I was surprised Mormons served coffee—but everyone avoided me. Their lives looked hard and dry and private and poor, maybe even mean. I felt like some form of ambulatory plague, so I left and headed back to Hurricane.

Eventually I found a polygamist in Colorado City who'd talk to me. Then again, he'd talked to a lot of people: his whole family, three wives and twenty-three children, had been on "Donahue." The man's name was Tom Williams. He was forty-three. He put the sex part of his three marriages "on the rotation"; he made love to his wives on a regular, unalterable timetable, except on birthdays and anniversaries, and then he took the wife in question away on a weekend holiday. That way they found some time alone together.

Time alone was important. Sex wasn't so much a recreational thing as it was a way of being tender. He said he didn't have that much sex anyway because he was so tired, except when one of his wives wanted a baby, and then it was automatic. That was one of the benefits for Mormon women if they wanted children: they wanted one, they got one. That made me nervous.

Tom had grown up in Colorado City. The town was on the Arizona-Utah border for good reason. The Mormon Church had renounced polygamy in 1890 under severe pressure from the federal government, and the dissenting polygamists who moved to what became Colorado City needed to be able to jump jurisdictions quickly if the authorities came after them. In 1952, when Tom was four, the National Guard did just that and raided the town, taking Tom's father and other men to jail. Tom had carried a picture of that night in his mental wallet all his life. Tom's father wasn't a polygamist at the time, but he became one after the raid, marrying three more women. His fourth bride was a girl of nineteen. He was in his sixties and had another ten children.

Coming from that background, Tom didn't think polygamy was anything odd at all. "The Catholics believe marriage is so important they require their priests not to marry. So we just sort of overmarry to balance things out. So what's the difference? I mean, I have to smile at the Catholics a little. Their nuns, they all take vows to become the wife of Christ! It's a Puritan American custom to stand aghast at a life style that differs from their own, and consider it some kind of crime."

As Tom described polygamy, its benefits were that you were never lonely and there was never any jealousy. Plural life was what saved you from jealousy. "By admitting that these things"—he meant sleeping with more than one woman—"are natural, and that men have the ability to live that way, we free ourselves up to deal with other more important things. A woman who grows up expecting monogamy lives in a society where men pretend to be one way. Whereas a woman who grows up in the environment where a man can be what he is is more realistic. They realize they can't make as many demands of a man. In a monogamous relationship, there's always a little, what if? What if a man meets another woman? But it's not an issue with us. Because if a man meets another woman, she'll just be included."

He spoke these words and they made sense, but they were so far outside the morality I knew as to seem like the language of tongues.

Tom had served in Vietnam and as a Mormon missionary. His first marriage, to a seventeen-year-old named Charla, was arranged by a town elder, one of the Barlows who controlled Colorado City. Charla's father had three wives and thirty-three children, so she was used to plural marriage. She and Tom courted for a week—he was twenty-three—and then married. Over the next twenty years, she bore him twelve children. Twelve children in twenty years: she'd been pregnant more than half her married life.

After seven years, Tom and Charla decided to take in another sister-wife. But the girl they liked was snatched away by one of the ruling Barlows, and Tom was forced to marry an awkward girl named Jill. Tom and Charla were devastated. "But when a man of God sits in front of you and tells you it's your duty," Charla told me, "and you will be cursed if you don't accept this woman into your family, it really means something. At that time we had to accept her or be damned."

Part of the problem was physical; there was no chemistry between Tom and Jill. Still, they eventually had four children together. Tom found it hard, but Jill wanted to marry him, and that was that. Sometimes outsiders thought plural marriage was for men, but Tom didn't see it that way. The women made the choices.

What saved him was his faith. Without his certainty that he was doing God's will, he couldn't have done it. But he had faith, and so he didn't have to control every corner of his life any more. He could trust in a bigger scheme, the way he believed he had a guardian angel watching over him on the road, when he was driving his truck thousands of miles across the country, hauling pigs or stone. There were too many inexplicably close calls otherwise, times he snapped to at the last possible second. In the presence of that sort of faith, its very weight pressing down into you, suppressing your doubts, enforcing a calm into everything that transpired, it was possible simply to tolerate life. I envied him that. He didn't have to find a sense of purpose as a man because God had given him one.

God's purpose included his third wife, Maria, in 1988. By then Tom was thirty-nine; Charla was thirty-three; Jill was twenty-nine. Maria was sixteen. Sixteen! She lived down the street from Tom's sprawling bungalow, and she was the one who initiated the contact. She kept dropping over, and they got to philosophizing about life—polygamists apparently did a lot of that—and finally she said, "Well, I'd really like to be part of your family."

The problem was Charla. Normally it's the second wife who causes problems, what with jealousy and old wives wanting to measure up to the new ones, and vice versa. But Jill's difficult nature had only brought Charla and Tom closer. Maria was a different story.

"When Maria came along," Charla said, "that was a trial." Charla at thirty-three had the body of a mother of eleven children. Maria was the aforementioned sixteen. "That really took a lot of struggle for me, to overcome the jealousies I felt, and the pain I felt. You can't imagine the feelings a woman feels when you've been married seventeen years, and you're really close, and you get ready to go to bed with your husband, and he takes the hand of another woman, and goes to bed with her."

But Maria was the new wife. She needed attention; she needed to believe that she belonged in the family. So Tom paid a little more attention to her. Charla still had her moments of jealousy, but Maria had gradually become her closest friend. Maria was in college, training to be a nurse, just as Jill had gone to college for nursing while Charla looked after her kids. Plural wives said polygamy was the perfect arrangement for working women; there was always someone to look after the kids. "My kids call her mother," Charla told me, "and hers call me mother. They probably will as long as they're treated right."

Not that domestic life was a snap. Everyone had her own agenda, and sometimes the agendas didn't mesh. Still, the life wasn't bad at all. Luxuries were limited to a microwave and necessary appliances, but nobody seemed to miss the others. Each woman had a room of her own, with a cradle in it. Each wife was free to do as she wished: she could work outside the house or not, learn Spanish, go to college. They all had their own money, and everything they owned was part of a trust.

There were three bedrooms upstairs, and three bedrooms down, and more bedrooms and a big bathroom in the addition. As well, there was a nursery upstairs, for the one- and two-year-olds. The older boys and girls had rooms of their own, and the fours, fives, and sixes were in bunk beds. Jill and her four kids lived in a trailer at the end of the property, as she preferred. But everyone ate in the house. Tom kept an office out of the house and went there every day to have time to himself. The office struck me as a necessity.

Together, they had nineteen kids living at home. I watched them make and eat their lunch together. They were extremely well-behaved. The girls served the people, the boys fed the dogs. Charla knew everyone's name—Heber and Ray, Alma, Timothy, Paul, Victoria, Charla Jane, Leslie (she was one of Maria's), Rose (one of Jill's), Lorian, Tom, Sarah. . . . There were more, but you get the point. Charla kept track of everyone's chores. Some of the kids intended to live in a plural arrangement when they grew up, some—the oldest boys, for instance—didn't. Tom didn't push it on anyone.

The summer before they'd driven up to British Columbia to see Charla's parents. Four cars, three wives, Tom, twenty kids, and fifteen hundred miles. Why not? "That's what memories are," Tom said. "If you don't live and give your kids memories, what are they gonna think about when they get old and die? I don't want them to think, 'Gee, we sure had a dull dad. He never did anything.'" The next day, on the other hand, was the anniversary of his marriage to Charla. Tom and Charla were going to spend the weekend in a motel in Salt Lake City. It wasn't London, England, or Hawaii, or even New York, or any of the places Charla dreamed of, but at least it was some time together.

What impressed me most about Tom was how calm he was. He was like a small manmade lake on a windless day. With the eternal family life the Mormons believed in, Tom figured he had two million years to get things right. He liked to experiment. "I just believe in having the freedom to get into as much trouble as you can stand," he told me, and that didn't sound too different from anything I believed.

Over the next few days I met other polygamists, and I concluded they were brave people. One man, Alex Joseph of Bigwater, Arizona, had nine wives and more than twenty children; his wives were lawyers and designers and real estate agents. Three of them had been roommates at college and liked one another so much that when one of them married Alex, she convinced the other two to try it as well. They were all still together. In the twelve hours I spent with him—the whole clan was most hospitable—I never saw Alex lift a finger around the house. I also never saw him do a stitch of his own work. There were too many interruptions. He was like the chief executive officer of a large corporation—delegating, delegating. He excused occasional lapses of fidelity on everyone's part, so long as it was "an accident." But if there was an argument, a big question of direction in the family, Alex's word was final. "It's my vision," he said.

But when I tried to imagine living Tom's or Alex's life, I couldn't feel it.

It wasn't just the weight of their responsibility. It wasn't just dozens of children or twelve wives or the absence of privacy that bothered me; or the constant togetherness; or the steady subjugation and annihilation of my own will to the will of God; or the inevitable subjugation of one's women, no matter what the polygamist party line said; or the impossibility of ever simply taking off and marrying one's secretary; or even the terrifying possibility of becoming tied to so much and then losing it. None of those things put me off. I *wanted* to be inspired, to find the source of the calm and modesty and devotion these family men seemed to feel in abundance. I *wanted* to find the grace they found by submitting.

But to find that grace, I'd have to submit: to give in to domestic life. I was back in my room at the Best Western, watching cute Katie Couric, when it struck me (no great revelation) that to start a family you have to believe in something bigger than yourself. Out there in the red desert, sharp and tiny and strangled by the TV in a cheap motel room, I still hadn't found it, and it was all I could do not to blame someone else for that fact.

One day in Iowa not long after that I met four men who represented the official range of possible male reactions to the rise of women's rights in the late innings of the twentieth century. The University of Iowa in Iowa City, where it happened, attracts feminists of all description, and Iowa City is often called "a hotbed of feminism." Sexual politics are daily fare. I was introduced to all four men by an artist I know. It was as if I'd been looking for a new lawn mower, and he showed up with a catalog describing all the latest models, all of which were in stock.

The first man was still married to his first wife and had three sons. He was what I would call a reconditioned lawn mower. He was in his fifties, and he'd recently started to do the household laundry "because it's the right thing to do." He was still an old model in some ways; he still defined himself (much as he wished he could stop) by his work, by what he did. But he liked the way his sons had women as friends, the way they weren't so competitive, the way they accepted homosexuals. "The dog and I are the only two in the house who don't wear earrings," he said. He claimed his boys were proof that socialization mattered. "We're all bitching and moaning, men and women alike," he said, "because we've all lost someone to take care of us." Men had lost women and women had lost men. What needed to be found or at least redefined was a sense of family. He was grateful for his own. "I'm fairly convinced if I had not gotten married at twenty-seven, I would have seriously gone off the deep end by the time I was thirty." I didn't mention my own prospective family to him; like most men, he brought the subject up on his own. They all wanted to talk about it.

The second man managed a bookstore. He'd started out as a new-model man, but found he couldn't cut certain varieties of grass; now he just stayed away from those parts of the lawn. He'd been a feminist—"it was manna for me," he said, "because it meant the wimp/nerd style of guy would get some sex once in a while." But gradually he became disillusioned, as "women in groups"—it was the group that was the problem, he said—"became as obnoxious, narrow-minded, and censoring as the macho men who had caused me to support feminists in the first place." He hated being called a "white male" by women—it was a common put-down in Iowa City—and he didn't think he was part of the male power structure.

Instead, he now belonged to a men's group. This being Iowa City and the midwest, it was the talking kind, rather than the drum-beating, whacking-off Barry-Bob species I encountered in California. "Some things are easier to talk to guys about," he said, "even guys that I hardly know. I can't talk about performance anxiety with a woman. They don't get it. And believe me, I have it. Women don't have to get erections, damn it. Like when your wife really wants to come big, and you can't do it." (I couldn't believe he said that, especially right there in the bookstore.) "Plus, when you live in a feminist town like Iowa City, you have to watch what you say. But in the men's group we say anything we want. Sometimes I feel like we're little boys without their moms. We're being naughty and sexist."

The third man was an unreconstructed male chauvinist—a classic El Toro lawn machine, if you will, with the extra-large grass bag. He was a banker who'd been divorced twice, had a town-wide reputation as a philanderer, never dated women older than himself (he was fifty-seven; his most recent date had been thirty-eight), insisted that good sex was the basis of any lasting marriage, thought suckling a child at one's breast had to be the most transcendent feeling in the world (and wished he could—I thought he was insane), and now couldn't stop thinking about death.

His conversation always came back to sex. "There's nothing like the effort," he said. "The conquest bit. And the scalps, we come back and nail them on the wall. I would rather hurt a lot than not feel anything." The night his first child was born, he heard crying and thought it was a girl. His world collapsed. He was as disappointed as he had ever been. And then the doctor walked up and told him his son was "very well endowed. I couldn't have felt prouder at that moment. I'm not sure I wouldn't feel the same today." He reminded me of a character in a novel, a frightened libertine, and by the end of dinner with him I wanted to be free of his company. He made me nervous. He made me ashamed of myself.

The fourth man was the most "politicized" man I met. His name was Brett Beemyn. It had been Beeman, "but I didn't want to have a name that was perpetuating a gender language," he told me. "So I changed it to a Y in solidarity with those women who have changed their names to womyn." It was the sort of decision that wouldn't have gone over in Buffalo, his home town, but it was quite correct while engaged in African-American and women's studies at the University of Iowa, where he was a twenty-five-year-old Ph.D. candidate and teacher. He was thin, long-haired, white, and bisexual. There were signs on the walls of his office: Don't Know Any Bisexuals, Lesbians or Gay Men? Think Again! and Support Lesbian, Gay and Bi Rights. Fight Against Right Wing Bigotry!

It was unusual to meet a man who had chosen to become expert in so much that was the exact opposite of what he was. He was the latest model, the revolutionary new lawn mower: it still cuts grass, but it triples as a public-address system and pool vacuum. His livelihood depended on creating and maintaining distinctions between men and women, blacks and whites, on saying who was and who wasn't onside.

"I have a very strong desire to see people get a fair shake," he said. "To see that the country lives up to the standards that it so frequently touts about liberty and justice. Being marginalized myself, I have much more sensitivity, I would say, to people who have been marginalized." He saw himself as the enemy of stereotypical masculinity and what he considered to be its consequences: of streets where women couldn't walk at night without the protection of a man; of the John Wayne type who always wants to be in control; of the idea that you can have power only if you don't have emotions; of homophobia; and of what he saw as the tradition of white male rationalism that he claimed had suppressed minority thought. He believed the system was the culprit, and so anyone who was part of the system was to blame. If a man in Montreal killed fourteen female engineering students because he thought they were feminists, men were not to "see this as the act of a deranged man who had something against some feminists. They have to see it as an extreme form of the misogyny men are culpable for. Because they have been born men." He certainly did not see the killings in any way as the responsibility of women, as the result of orthodox feminists alienating a "marginalized" man. Brett didn't think the point was to feel guilty, but to do something about this state of affairs. What he did was walk into his first class every semester and announce: "I'm a racist. I'm socialized to have certain biased or biological opinions. It's almost like you're born with it. In a culture like ours, you can't avoid it. And it's also true of gender."

Just then someone stuck his head in the door of Brett's office. A pro-choice rally was about to take place at a local abortion clinic.

"Are you going?" the intruder asked.

"My drum is going," Brett said.

I asked him why he'd chosen to study African-American studies rather than women's issues.

"My goal," he said, "my ambition, as somebody who is white, is to teach white people about racism and race. And that's not very hard to do since most of the colleges are white. But if I was in women's studies, I would like to teach men about sexism. And in the women's studies classes I've been in, the vast majority of the students are women.

"And plus," Brett said, "there's the whole question of a job, to be quite honest. Because it's easier to be white and get a job in African studies than it is to be male in women's studies. I'm very sensitive to breaking into where I'm not wanted. I'm very sensitive to the need for women's space."

I left shortly afterward, got in my truck to head home, and mulled over my feelings about Brett. They were not altogether positive.

For instance, I liked him more six months after I met him, when he wasn't around, when I didn't have to listen to him reduce all human endeavor, ultimately, to one intellectual dogma, that white men are evil. I admired his courage and his enthusiasm, but I didn't think I could ever be his friend. Not because of what he was or because I take issue with a great deal of what he said; rather, because I'll never trust anyone who reduces the world to one problem and one solution. I loathe intellectual certainty. Not only because it limits and even denies the human imagination, because any thought outside the prescribed chain of thinking is considered offside. No, I object to forcing people to see only one cause of injustice and one solution because it's boring. Brett had no doubts, no uncertainty in his chosen cause. I could drive his mind with my eyes closed. Behind his causes and his idealized politics I saw little tolerance for real human beings, not to mention for "locker rooms and deal-making spas," which he especially disdained, but where one can find as much peace and intelligence and stupidity and narrowness as one can find anywhere else, if only you have the patience to let them appear. I like

Brett on paper, as a point of view, but in person he reminded me of what George Orwell so famously called the "smelly little orthodoxies now contending for our souls." Orwell wrote those words in 1938.

After I left Iowa City, whenever I thought about Brett Beemyn, I thought of something a good friend of mine once said to explain why he stayed friends with some men, while others fell away despite years of acquaintance. That can happen with men: you go through the rituals, the jokes and the drinking and the drugs and the sports and the sex talk, but if you don't break through once in a while to something true and sincere and daring—something that approaches what others might call an act of trust or love, which is what all communal daring entails—the friendships dry up and blow away. "I stay friends with people who still surprise me," my friend observed. I thought Brett Beemyn was a clever young man, but surprising he was not. The flaw in the idea that every problem in the world boils down to the sad fact that men are men, to patriarchy and its eradication, is that, for the answer to work, everyone not only has to be equal, which is probably desirable, but to think the same way and to feel the same things. I don't want to live in such a world, for love of human grace and fear of boredom; furthermore, I don't think it would have me. Or most anyone else.

8

The Talking Car

How to steal a van — Trials and tribulations of the
criminal justice system — Semiotics of shag interiors —
Thrills of the assembly line — Comeuppance and liberation

When the salesmen at the car shows in Detroit's convention center said, "The van is holding this town together"—and they said it often—Danny had to laugh, because it was true in more ways than one. Vans and trucks and mini-vans were the best-selling vehicles in the country, but they were also the easiest cars to steal.

He and his brother Dwight had specialized in them all, but vans were their favorite. They started piking them in high school. Danny was eighteen. There weren't many appealing jobs to be had, so they stole cars. It was easy. "And once you got your first taste of it, it was different."

They worked a five-man crew—two women and three guys. The

women were the lookouts. They carried walky-talkies. Their gang preferred sport-utility and "recreational" machines because they were popular with chop shops, the garages that broke the stolen cars down and resold the parts. GMC Jimmys were their all-time favorite. The tires alone on a Jimmy fetched $400. The stereo was worth another $70, at least if the hot stereo market wasn't flooded. Danny could sell the seats for $100 if he needed fast money. They sold nearly all their purloinings to collision shops—"at least, that's the cover they were." The collision shops did some legitimate body work, but mainly they were chop shops. They'd buy whole cars for $1,000, or the chopped parts for between $2,000 and $3,000. Danny and his brother preferred to unload whole cars—everything was easier and faster that way. Rarer models were naturally worth more. "You could make $10,000 on a Corvette, stripped," Danny said. The tires on a Vette were worth $1,000. The aluminum wheel rims alone were worth $200.

He never worked more than two full days a week. He'd leave in the afternoon, hire a U-Haul, and once it was dark they'd steal at least three cars. They always stole at least three. They'd park them somewhere out of the way, chop them, load the parts into the U-Haul, and then sell the parts to the shops.

Danny and his gang stole only new cars. New cars were less likely to be equipped with anti-theft alarms. But there was also a principle involved. "I wouldn't steal a used car, like from an individual," Danny told me one morning. "'Cause you, say, you're like me. But a new car, that's like stealing from a corporation." True: anyone who has had a car stolen knows the intensity of the fury that ensues, the helplessness you feel. Someone leans into your life and takes your car, and you lose days of time and money just because some little asshole kid takes your car? Danny knew the feeling. He didn't want ordinary people to go through that.

Other outfits—there were black car-theft rings, and white gangs, it was all very competitive in Detroit—were more organized than Danny's group. Other gangs sent spotters out with a notebook to find cars for which there was regular demand—Blazers, Chrysler mini-vans, Toyota Celicas (especially model years in the early eighties, which were a goldmine of parts). The spotter would wander neighborhoods, list locations, and then, when the shop called asking for a Bronco, check his notes and head out to the predetermined location to steal the damn car. That way, you didn't have any warehouse overhead: the owner of the car to be stolen did your warehousing for you. This was an especially popular technique in L.A., where the winter never interfered with your stealing and driving plans. Most nights in L.A. in any neighborhood you could sit by your upstairs bedroom window and watch the inventory-control specialists, sixteen- and seventeen-year-old white kids, mostly, in baseball jackets and long shorts, wandering the neighborhoods taking notes on every decent car on your street.

Danny and Dwight didn't get into it that way. That sort of vertical operation was too top-heavy, too structured. They specialized in quick in-and-out, low-overhead car theft. The best part of it, besides the easy money and the excitement, was that they were good at it. They were running a business. They got to make their own rules. Dwight did the alarms—his specialty. "He could take an alarm out and leave it on the ground," Danny said. He was full of admiration for his brother.

Danny was nimbler. He could start a van or a Trans Am in thirty-eight to forty seconds—that was his record. They often had races, two guys next to one another in a GMC dealer lot, say, with security guards on the lot, racing to see who could get the engine started first. It was great. You went in through the window; then you "tilted" the wheel, which meant busting the steering column housing at the tilt-wheel lever. There was a spring and a horseshoe-shaped piece of metal that you had to pop out. Once the insides were exposed, you jammed a screwdriver into the steering column and ratcheted up a serrated rod. One notch turned on the auxiliary power; another notch sparked the engine.

Two grand a week in spending money had a big effect on Danny's popularity at school—and he was already popular because he was a clown. "Nobody likes a guy who's gonna sit in a corner and cry," he told me. "They like the guy who's gonna go and bust that guy's head. And of course I had the money. So if you're gonna go and buy your way through the mall, of course you're gonna be popular." Some days he had $1,000 in cash in his pocket. When that disappeared, he just went out and picked up more cars. He figured that in twenty years he could save $100,000.

But the best part of it, the part he always remembered, came down to one night. It was a weekday—they usually headed out to work early in the week, when the streets were quieter. He'd stolen a van, and he was making his way up Mound Road in Warren, a suburb of Detroit, when two black guys cut him off and shot him the finger. They were driving a light beige Nova.

It wasn't that they cut him off that made him angry. It was the gratuitous finger. They just gave him some jive, some black-to-white shake-off. They were saying, in their own way, You can't do anything about this.

That was when Danny realized he wasn't driving his own car. He was driving a stolen car. Then he thought, *I really do not have to take this shit.*

So Danny gunned it and pulled alongside the black guys, who were surprised to see him and who were now giving him serious business out the windows of the Duster. He looked down at them—he liked the high seats in the vans, the way you commanded a full view of your windshield world—and suddenly he swung the wheel, ramming the Duster. Then he did it again, and pushed the Duster onto the shoulder of the road.

The black guys were out of their minds. They couldn't believe he was doing this. They were screaming, and freaking out, and worrying for their lives, and for what was probably their mother's car, and they just couldn't believe this white motherfucker in the van had rammed them. They hit the brake and stopped on the side of the road. Danny kept going. He could see them screaming and shouting and jumping up and down in his rear view. It was as funny as hell. But even more than that, it was thrilling.

"See," he said, "that was another big thrill: getting the chance to pay back. Because I was outside the law, you know? And not just outside the regular law, but outside the law of the outlaws. I made my own rules. It was like the most freedom I've ever had. And that state of mind, when I was able to do that—that was the greatest feeling I ever had."

Danny was twenty-four. His wife was twenty-two. Naturally, her name was Kim. They'd known each other six years, been married four. I asked if he liked being married.

He grinned. He was a decent guy and had a sense of humor. I think he permed his hair. He was scrappy; you could see that in his arms and shoulders, in the way he walked, chest first. "Honestly," he said, "no. A lot of my friends, they said they never pictured me married."

"Nobody sees themselves married," I said.

"Yeah, but I don't like it because I have responsibilities. You make your cake, you gotta clean it up too. However that saying goes. It forced me to grow up. Because, you know, I was wild."

That was what I liked about him. Danny didn't care that any single day of the week you could turn on the TV and find someone saying that a man had to grow up; that adulthood meant responsibility, duty, weightiness, and if you didn't like that you were some retarded, shameful, backward, immature, adolescent species of human being. I think Danny knew some people never make it to full-blown sanctified responsible weight-bearing maturity, and I think he knew there can be more than one reason why. He did know that "growing up," so-called, felt like an anvil on his head a lot of the time.

Of course, a lot of guys say they were wild. I often pretended I was myself. I told people I once burned down the neighbor's porch. I wanted to break free of something and the fantasy of being criminal did the job. But Danny, with that ugly streak of moustache that he thought was so cool—he *was* wild.

"I mean," he said, "you have to give a wife notice. Maybe she wants to surprise you, and make your favorite dinner tonight. And you say, hey, babe, I'm going to the ball game tonight. And she gets all bent. So you have to say to your friends, I can't. Next time you gotta give me more notice. Like the other night, my friend had tickets to the truck pull? I really wanted to go. I been thinking a lot about pickups. They're easier to go through snow, easier to carry stuff, and the prices ain't too high.

"Anyway, we were gonna go drink some beer, have a manly night. Except I can't, because I gotta go home and kiss up to her because I been spending the last two days shoveling snow, to make some money. I've been away, so I have to go home. And for that I get to make my dinner and go to bed."

On the other hand, a guy like Danny would never divorce. It was the Catholic in him. He saw it simply: he'd made the vow. Kim was his wife. You had to stay with it. He never even said, "Honey, you're putting on a little weight." Never. His whole family was like that, they worshipped the mother and the women. Danny still looked at his wife and said, "You still look good to me, honey," even if she didn't. He could be tempted, but he wasn't going to order. One night, for instance, he was driving down the street in the middle of a blizzard and some woman smiled at him. True, she was walking in the middle of the road, probably a hooker. Forty dollars for a blow job. And Danny thought, If she weren't wearing any clothes, I don't think I'd be able to help it.

But she was wearing clothes. Plus she probably had some disease. Marriage kept you healthy. He liked Kim's parents, too, because they liked him, despite all the garbage he'd been through. He and Kim had even lived with them after they were married because he didn't get along with his own father and mother. He never had. He didn't think this living arrangement was strange, as people whose lives have been dominated by circumstance often don't.

Still, had things been different—a big wide old question—he wouldn't have married. "When you first get married, and you have all that lovin', it's great. But then it gets old."

He flapped his jacket a couple of times. He was wearing a navy blue bomber number with orange lining. "Like, once in a while I'll make her breakfast in bed on Sunday morning."

I knew it was once in a great while, because I knew he did nothing around the house. He never did dishes; he just pushed his chair away from the table and stood up and walked away to watch the TV. He said he never learned how to wash up; his mother told him to keep his mitts off her new dishwasher. Sometimes his sheer idiot nerve took my breath away. "My wife loves it when I make her breakfast," he said. "Especially if I clean my dishes afterward." Talking to him was sometimes like coming upon a creature that had wandered out of a swamp where it had been living for four or five billion years, thereby shocking experts that it was still alive.

"Does she go for that?" I said.

"Then it's the best," he said. "I get good lovin' then. Good Sunday mornin' lovin'. Ain't nothing like it, you know."

I laughed a bit, so he wouldn't get upset with himself for being so personal. Guys like Danny were like that sometimes: they'd realize what they'd said and clam up. As if they were always waiting for that crack over the head for being who they were.

Danny saw his marriage as a domestic version of natural selection, as pure power and domination. If a woman's standards were low enough, you could get away with murder; and if you could get away with it, you were supposed to.

"But that's not the reason I married her," he said.

"Why did you, then?"

"The reason I married her"—he stopped for a long moment—"I married her because she was true and faithful to me for nineteen months. Because I went to prison, and she came to see me every week."

So he went to prison, for stealing cars, and served his time. When he was released, he got a job, and now, two and a half years later, he'd been laid off. The Michigan Employment Security Commission office up near the car plants was a wide yellow box, fifty yards square. Numbers, black on white plastic, hung from the ceiling on chains. A sign read, "!!Everyone!! This Means You Report To Line 12 Information."

Line 12 ran down one wall and halfway across the room. The floor was tan, the walls were yellow-brown wood-grain veneer. After you waited in line, you walked to a table at the back of the room and filled in a form and then you stood in line again. The table was littered with pencils, like discarded frustrations. The asbestos tiles of the ceiling were sucked and blown to a coffee brown by the air vents in the ceiling. Despite the lineup, only three of the twelve booths were occupied by clerks.

Danny was waiting in line. He'd been there an hour already. An hour was nothing; he'd been out of work six weeks, having worked overtime up until the last day. That was what he couldn't figure, how he could be working overtime one day and redundant the next.

Danny had liked his job, too, but his boss said the car industry wasn't coming back quickly enough. For a year and a half he'd been working a plastic injection molding machine. His weekly pay dropped from $416 a week at the factory to $226 a week on unemployment. He'd been looking for jobs, but there was nothing. Sure, he could have gone to work at McDonald's, but he had a trade—"plastic injection molding, that's my trade. I don't want to make $3.25 an hour flinging fries."

Kim was on his ass at home, too. She paid the bills, and she was used to having money every week. Then suddenly not having any, and having to tell him it was okay . . . he knew money was what lay behind her nasty tempers these days. She spoke to him as if he were a dog that had done something bad on the rug. That was why she was so bent about him staying home from the truck pull, for example. She wanted him to make an obvious sacrifice. Especially around the beginning of the month, when the big bills came in. He'd even quit smoking. That was $700 a year, which was a lot of money now.

But the worst part was losing the dream of it all. "I always bought something new," Danny said, looking down Line 12. He wore his jacket open, his boots unlaced. "Always bought stuff to better ourselves. I bought my wife a new car, furniture and stuff."

Kim made a big fuss of Christmas and liked to start shopping before Thanksgiving. He'd known it was coming, so he'd paid all his bills. A good thing, as it turned out, because he was laid off the day before Thanksgiving. "So I had all my Christmas presents, and all my bills paid up to Thanksgiving. I just didn't have any money."

A couple were arguing in front of us in line. It was a small argument, about their baby. Kim wanted a baby. So did my wife, but listening to Danny's money problems gave me chest pains when I thought about it, so I tried not to. We watched the couple for a while. Hardly anyone ever spoke in the unemployment office.

Danny's problem wasn't just having no job, either: the problem was that even with a job, the future was so dark. A secure future was a thing of the past in Detroit. His own father-in-law had walked into Ford's—that was the way they said it, emphasis on the possessive, as in the Ford family, the great benefactors of Detroit who Danny and his ilk still liked to think were part of their lives, watching over them like guardian angels; it was such a naive notion I wanted to shout at him—his father-in-law had walked into Ford's twenty years earlier and was handed a job. Thanks to the United Auto Workers, he still had the job. The company even paid him to go to school.

You couldn't get that job now, even if you wanted it. Nor could the union help you. The union had done its job so well, protected its members so well, they'd priced themselves out of the market. Cars are now made in Mexico. Union membership had dropped from 1.6 million to 800,000. In 1950, when Danny's father-in-law had come out of high school, thirty-five percent of all the workers in the United States were unionized. Now fewer than seventeen percent were. In the early eighties, before the Japanese invaded and everything started to fall apart, a tradesman working overtime could earn $80,000 a year.

Those days were gone, just like Danny's job. He had stood by a plastic injection molder and watched the machine as it inserted a template, lowered a frame, lifted the frame up, removed the plastic piece, replaced it with another template, lowered the frame, lifted the frame, removed the piece, replaced it with another template, lowered the frame, lifted the frame, removed the finished piece . . . over and over, day after day. The floor shook when the frame was lifted and dropped. The generator made you deaf. He had done that for two and a half years. Sometimes he counted it up: two frames a minute, a hundred and twenty-odd frames an hour, nine hundred something frames a day, forty-five hundred plastic frames a week, two hundred twenty-five thousand frames a year. . . . Working out the numbers gave him something to do standing there. Some people had done the same thing for thirty years.

Eventually the repetition got to people. The union had studied it. Doing the same thing again and again without cease or change for thirty years made people incapable of doing nothing. They became terrified of inactivity or stillness. They were afraid to retire; if they retired, they'd die. They didn't have any skills or hobbies, because you weren't exactly in the mood for stamps or woodwork when you came home from a day of pressing a button and shifting plastic frames. The boredom was exhausting. The thought of having no purpose to repeat obsessively, of doing nothing for eight hours a day, day after day, was terrifying for paradoxical reasons: it was so unlike what they'd been doing, and so like it. The union said monotony made people alcoholics.

Before he was laid off, Danny had been looking to buy a new pickup. He liked pickups, and so did Detroit. They weren't sold as haulers any more, but as the latest embodiment of masculinity. According to the auto industry, gays bought Hondas, while men bought pickups. Everything about pickups said Manly Man, even though most of them were smaller than Suburbans, the giant rolling back yards you saw out West, where trucks were still trucks. The new urban pickups were sporty. By way of compensation they wore huge tires and higher seats, which meant a more "aggressive" and therefore more "male" vehicle. What a Triumph TR 3 or a Spitfire said to men when I was a boy in the early 1960s, apparently, pickups said in the nineties.

According to some estimates, fewer than five percent of the trucks were bought by women. Sixty percent of the men who bought them never carried anything in the back. There was a huge aftermarket in plastic anti-scratch truckbed liners in the unlikely event your pickup had to pick something up.

If a man didn't buy a truck, which represented the high point on Detroit's masculinity scale, he bought himself a sport-utility vehicle—half truck, half station wagon. They had names such as Pathfinder, Four Runner, Trooper, Cherokee . . . cavalry and Indians, in case anyone missed the connection to a 1950s childhood. Sport-utility vehicles were station wagons jacked up on bigger tires with four-wheel drive added. No postwar man worth his salt wanted a mere station wagon. His parents had owned station wagons! He wasn't like his parents, domesticated the way the old man was! True, the wife liked the Blazer because she could tootle the kids around town and buy groceries . . . but what about that four-wheel drive? One car company had done a survey and learned that ninety-five out of a hundred owners never used their four-wheel drive. But North American masculinity was so fragile men coveted four-wheel drive anyway.

But the strangest zone of Manliness in the car business was occupied by van conversion enthusiasts. Van conversion was a mid-Western eccentricity. The men who bought converted vans claimed they needed one for "vacations"—that is, for two weeks of the year. A converted van was an ordinary child-, pet-, wife-, and grocery-friendly van with a fancy door jacked into one side, four to eight swiveling "captain's chairs" installed next to coffee tables and multiple drink holders, and every surface upholstered within an inch of sanity, often in shag carpet. A couple of bunks . . . all manner of floodlights and pot lights and spotlights and map lights . . . a toilet . . . gimbaled stoves . . . converted vans were yachts on wheels. "They just turn them into these wretched statements,"

Bill Chapin, a car-marketing consultant in Detroit, told me. "The excuse is they're family vehicles, but they're really for Mr. Macho."

Curtains were a must, though only a fraction of van owners ever slept in their movable mansions. Hardware and a devotion to comfort at all times were the keys, to maintain the appearance of being ready for anything, of being so well-equipped that no eventuality could throw Our Mighty Driver off his highway stride. God forbid that we should have to stop at a motel! Or drink our coffee in a restaurant! We have foldaway bunks and non-spill drink holders! And below-eyeline side mirrors, and side window defoggers, and a self-aligning steering wheel, and deep tinted glass, and Silverado trim, and a six-way power driver's seat . . . I had a secret theory that converted vans were the car of choice for former acidheads, after they had kids. Acidheads were total systems guys.

Detroit was convinced men were becoming more emotional about cars. They'd never been paragons of rationality where automobiles were concerned, but as recently as ten years ago car manufacturers believed men bought performance and women bought style. Now women were being sold on mileage and engine dependability while Daddy was off buying Shag Hell on Wheels to compensate for the sudden realization that he was married, a father, trapped in a dull job, twenty pounds overweight, and not about to attract a sidelong glance from an unknown woman ever again. It was true that Latinos in East L.A. still worked on their cars, lo-jacking the tail up into the air while chopping the entire car within inches of the ground, clamping on drag wheels—but they were virtually the only ones who did. Technical mastery of a car's engine was no longer necessary (or even possible, given computerized electronic systems) to display one's mastery of manhood.

Hence pickups, van conversions, and sport-utility vehicles. They had "life-style associations"—people who drove them were "outdoor peo-ple" or "road vacationers" or "house-at-the-beach types." (I hadn't realized house-at-the-beach was a life-style association; I thought you either had one, or didn't.) Image mattered more to men, and especially to postwar men approaching middle age, than ever before. They wanted to make a statement. The statement was I HAVEN'T LOST IT YET.

Not that there weren't old style muscle cars too. The Dodge Viper filled that anxious little niche. The Dodge Viper RT/10 cost $50,000 and was red. Period. The concept was Corvettean, but the entire car was actually—and this is key—retro technology. Yes, this is what a real man needs in the strange and changing nineties, boys: a retrofit! Back to the future! More of the same! Fond memories of things to come! The Viper was modeled on the ultimate muscle car, the Shelby Cobra, last popular immediately before the ascendance of feminism. The Viper was the Old Way, The Way Things Were and The Way Things Ought To Be. A Viper paced the seventy-fifth Indy 500 in 1991 and hung an 8-liter, V-10 engine. This mass of pre-civilized excess generated 400 horsepower at 4800 RPMs . . . awwwwwooooo . . . had brazed aluminum intake manifolds (whatever brazed aluminum was) . . . dual-throttle bodies . . . it was the Mustang and the Corvette and the Cobra and the Trans Am and the Triumph and the MG of the New Age.

And there was no doubt who was going to drive it. As Bill Chapin explained, "It's pretty much the same as the Corvette market. Huge, huge numbers of Corvettes are bought by men who've just been divorced. They've got their penises free again. They're for a man who wants to go and get laid again." Freedom, speed, and danger were most desired by infantile and regressive men—that was Detroit's opinion on the subject.

All this had been apparent at the car show. In addition to the lights and the colors and the yam-shaped concept cars powered by mulch and the car babes in shimmering fishy sequinned dresses answering questions about manifolds, there was something in the air. You could hear it, and feel it, and see it in the way people touched fenders. It was the hysterical urgency of people in search of something that told them who they were.

The irony was, men had become the cars they were buying. The snakes and dinosaurs, the re-emerging, newly divorced adolescents, bought Vipers. But what were the rest of us buying, and what did those cars make us? Hybrids. Pickups that were puny (but zippy!) and didn't need to be pickups. Sport-utility vehicles—how perfect was that name for New Age Man?—that were exercises in schizophrenia. Vans that were the mechanical embodiment of your weirdest teenage Sergeant Pepper magic mushroom shag carpet fantasies, crossed with convenience, the idol of domesticity. Men had become mobile mutants.

Personally, however, my favorite display was the talking car. The car, a purple Plymouth Laser, sat on a turntable that swiveled, like a Lazy Susan. I walked up to admire it and a woman's voice purred, "Hi. I'm Laser. What's your name?"

It was the car.

I looked around. No one was looking. "Ian," I said.

"Cute guy," the car said. "Do you have kids?"

I couldn't see where the woman doing the talking was hiding. "No," I said. I was flirting with a car.

"Do you have a garage?"

"Yes," I said. "I do."

"Are you married?"

"Yes." My heart sank. The car would leave me now.

"Who's the better driver?"

"My wife."

"It figures," the car said. "I love driving with women. They stop and ask for directions."

I smiled. It really was time to leave. I waved good-bye. As I walked away, I heard the car say, "Oh, you don't want to be the only one talking to a car?"

After his brother got nabbed, Danny ran the auto-theft operation alone. Then a guy in their gang turned state's evidence and snitched on him. "They had us under surveillance," Danny said, and you could tell the thought made him sick. He felt stupid for succumbing to the inevitable. The entire gang was arrested one night as they were asleep in a motel. It was humiliating. The DA wouldn't even plea-bargain. And Danny was the only one they wanted. He was the ringleader. At least he could take some pride in that fact. He was the smart one. The rate of car thefts in Detroit dropped so steeply after they took him, the local paper ran an article about him and Dwight.

His pride in his cleverness evaporated instantly at his arraignment hearing in downtown Detroit. There was a sign, "NO TALKING NO EATING NO READING," in the courtroom, which was always packed, mostly by mothers and spectators. It was terrible, standing in the anteroom with animals, guys who were being charged with felonious assault of four-year-old girls; being hauled in front of the judges; having your misdeeds rattled off so they could set bail, of which you had to produce ten percent if you wanted to be released until your court date.

Compared to the goons in the anteroom, Danny was just a step beyond innocent. Listening to the charges brought against real criminals was like having nails driven into your skull. Assault and battery, aggravated assault, assault with intent to murder. No, the arraignment court was not the sort of place that made you feel terrific about your gender, not if you were a man. I had read domestic violence statistics that suggested there are as many women who attack their husbands as husbands who attack their wives, but I see one thug in a $600 raincoat and a fur-and-leather porkpie charged with criminal sexual assault of a twelve-year-old girl, and the statistics mean nothing. All you could smell in court was muscle and power and criminal imbeciles wearing too much cologne. Cologne, worn by men who ought to have been ashamed. It was here, among other places, that someone could convince himself he could kill. Danny said straight out that he'd kill any moron who messed with Kim or their kid. He had no doubt about that.

The detention house at the county jail held only 1,485 men, so bail levels were constantly being lowered to make room for more serious offenders. Non-assaultive drug charge? You'd be out the same day if you had $500. A man who assaulted his own mother with a telephone—that appeared to be her in the audience, dressed up like a dog's dinner in a leopard pillbox hat—was bailed at $65,000. That much money would tell the judge on the circuit court that the accused ought to await trial in jail. But they'd still have to call the chief judge and ask him not to lower bail. Nearly all of the accused were men; the few women were charged with assault, stolen property, possession of firearms. Receiving stolen property and operating a chop shop was five years and $5,000 bail. Danny should've smuggled drugs; a lot of the arraignment judges supported decriminalization and were lenient. Some guys actually thanked the judge when they got off lightly. "Thank you, boss," they'd mumble. A guy named Antoine was called—assault with intent to kill, felony possession of firearms, bam, an automatic ten years.

"Have you ever been convicted?" the judge asked.

"I don't think so," Antoine said.

"You would know," the judge said.

It turned out Antoine hadn't shown up for his last arraignment. The judge set bail at $150,000. Antoine wasn't going home tonight.

Charges continued to ring out: fugitive from justice . . . receiving and concealing stolen property. . . . There was something vaguely grand about it all, the way the clerk's voice reverberated, the bustle of the audience, the mothers and girlfriends in their Sunday finest, the spectating crackers in three-piece suits, the lawyers moving in and out without emotion like so many carpet salesmen, the judges ramming the cases through, the kids of seventeen with a forty-year-old look in their eyes.

Eventually Danny's turn came. The charges against him sounded so strange—unlawfully driving away an automobile, four felonies. Sounded barely illegal—the kind of thing you do by mistake in an amusement park, which was actually not so far from the truth.

Danny pled guilty; his reward was two to five years in prison for each felony. The sentences were to run concurrently. The cops said his sentence would be reduced to two months of actual time, but on his first day in prison he found a fight, and he ended up serving nineteen months. The fight was necessary because without it he would never have earned any respect in the house. "I got my ass kicked a lot," Danny told me the only time he ever talked about jail. "But I stood up for myself." That was the important thing, in jail or out. Danny's first day inside, he had an argument about using the phone, fought, and lost. He fought every day for six weeks about the phone, his jacket, and just about everything else. Finally he was stabbed in the backside with a knife. But by then the other inmates had stopped harassing him. "Why am I gonna come and take your coat if you're gonna fight me for it," Danny explained, "when that guy over there is just gonna give his to me?"

That was when Kim wrote him every other day and visited him every week for nineteen months. "That saved me. Oh, yeah, that helped me cope with all that shit. That's why I married her."

Finally he was released from jail. He had to tell everyone about his parole, and at first nobody wanted to hire him. But the parole officer impressed the boss at the plastic injection factory. Danny had to hand over his urine once a week for drug tests. He turned out to be a model employee, capable of hard work and worthy of overtime, until they canned him. He'd been collecting unemployment ever since.

Now Dwight was getting out of jail in a month. Dwight was his brother, and Danny loved him. But he didn't know if he wanted to see him. It was confusing.

"No," he told me one afternoon. We were walking through a mall parking lot. The Michigan snow was cold and wet. "No. I won't do that no more. I already had a rough time in prison. My wife would leave me if I went in again. So I wouldn't get no nookie."

"Plus," he said, and waved his arm out in front of him, "now, I can go and run two hundred yards out there in that parking lot. I can't do that in there."

Two hundred yards in a parking lot. It was no farther than that to my car. But it was all the freedom he needed now, and with one exception he was never going to forget, a night he stole a van and took the wheel of the world in his own hands, it was really all the freedom he ever had. And do you know, for a moment it seemed almost enough for me.

9

Toad's Last Wail

Instances of extreme male stupidity – An appalling
confession – Why men are the way they are – The story
of a stag – Lament for emptiness

One morning in Montreal I decided to call all my old girlfriends. I sat in a hotel room on the seventeenth floor and telephoned out. I could see a long way from that height, and it was like orbiting the city, orbiting a place I had once been.

Calling my old girlfriends was something I did occasionally, generally at crisis points. I wanted to know how they remembered me, to see if I was different. I probably wanted to see if they were still interested, at least in a theoretical way.

I called Elizabeth. She was my third girlfriend. She was a brilliant, multilingual young woman who was also, in my skittish view at the time, an emotional wide-load. Once, she wanted to smoke some grass. I tried to dissuade her, because I knew it wouldn't agree with her, but she insisted. She took two puffs, got on a bus, and burst into tears and started to scream—a quiet scream, but still a scream, especially on a bus. "My arms have fallen off," she sobbed.

Years after we broke up, I took her for a drink and she said she remembered me as an eel. An eel. After the drink she said, "That wasn't fun, was it? What did you expect?"

This time, the first thing she said on the phone was, "Which Ian Brown is this?" I said I'd call her back, but I never got around to it.

The house I grew up in is thirty miles west of the hotel, in Montreal's western suburbs.

The house reminds me that for years my emotional life was all departures—my own, fast-footed, ruthless, gasping for air, women left behind. Let me tell you about the first one.

I am eleven at the time. It's 1965—the very year *The Feminine Mystique* was published. I would guess my ma didn't read it, though she could have used it, and would have appreciated same. I am leaving for school, traversing the golf course that ebbed to our front lawn. My mother is at our front door.

Good-bye, Mum, I shout.

Good-bye, she says.

Ten feet further on, I wave again. Good-bye, Mum!

Good-bye!

This goes on five or six times until I am out of sight in a grove of cedar trees in the middle of the fairway—a grove of trees I pass through because it provides an easy end to the game; I don't have to be seen to be ending it, therefore disappointing my mother. I don't have to say good-bye any more. I always begin the game, so my mother doesn't feel left out, but my mother keeps it going. I leave, she stays.

For a few hours this morning I visit with my mother. I arrived late last night, after she'd gone to bed, but the front light was on. For me. I'd barely fallen asleep when it seems I heard the first stirrings, the preliminary unbandagings of my parents' day, beginning, as it has for as long as I can remember, before the sun is up.

By the time I make it downstairs, my father's dressed for work and my mother is sitting up in bed in her room—he snores too much for them to sleep together—drinking her morning tea. They've been holding these morning conferences, too, for as long as I can recall. This morning's exchange of intelligence is concerned with my father's head. Last night, coiling the hose, he stabbed himself in the skull with a nail some clown left sticking down through the roof of the garden shed. He has been to the hospital, had a tetanus shot, and now wears a flesh-colored bandage over the glabrous dome of his head. "You'll take some ribbing at work for that," my mother says.

"Will I!" my father replies, clearly relieved that she's in a good mood.

After my father leaves, I embark with my mother on a tour of her garden. This is her daily waking task. My mother's garden is her soul. When I remember my mother, she is standing in the kitchen, cooking, exasperated, steam pouring out her ears, pleading with us to please, please come to the table before the meal is stone cold. But in her heart she has always lived in the garden, her great and most lasting work of art.

For twenty minutes she makes her rounds, checking the garden's various wards: the herb garden by the kitchen, the lettuce patch next to it (are those spider's eggs on the rusty lettuce? No; fine, then); the rock gardens by the side of the house, the vegetables near the river, and, finally, her pride, the flowers surrounding the patio.

"You see this Irish moss?" she says, pointing to the cracks between the stones. "You see all those tiny little flowers, like stars? Beautiful, isn't it? The well man told me I ought to pull it up. He thought they were weeds." Such ignorance astonishes her.

"What are those?" I ask, pointing to a batch of tiny yellow purses.

"*Calceolaria*," she says, barely looking. For years she couldn't keep the names of her children straight, but she can haul the Latin phylum for every flower in her garden out of her head like a handkerchief. "They were my mother's favorite flower."

"I can never remember the Latin names for flowers."

"No, your brother seems to have more talent there than you."

I let this minor calibration of her offspring pass. "What's yours?" I say.

"Sweet peas."

"Has it always been?"

"Always."

I realize with a start how little I know about her. I don't know my own mother's favorite flower. How much effort would it have required to learn and remember that detail? But my attention to her passion opens her up. I fix the sprinkler, she tells me secrets of the garden. It's not her passion I want to grasp, but my own. I want to say something— but what? I want to reach her, show her I care, take her thickened stout body in my arms and tell her, I love you, I think of you all the time, I wish I could show you how grateful I am for your having borne me, raised me, tended my fears. I want to tell her what she has meant to me; that I know her life as a mother has been one long sacrifice, of her body, her life, her attention, her private concerns, and even of us, the beings she cared about most, as we sailed off, as children inevitably do, to leave her behind.

Now she's showing me her knitting. It's a recent passion. She's making me a pair of green socks. A great honor. The patterns are taken from a booklet called "Socks by Beehive," an English pamphlet, her knitting bible. She leafs through the black-and-white pictures, pointing out the work she admires, pulling out her handiwork. She plumps them up and folds them on the table for me to see, to admire. The realization hits me like a shock: she's proud of her work, wants me to admire her, to see some significance, some importance in her latest years. Such a small thing, so full of care. Household art. It touches me more than I expected it to, and I praise her extravagantly.

But it's getting on. I have work to do, but I have a lunch appointment too. I know I should stay. Every time I see her, I know the number of our meetings grows smaller by one. But my temper was forged in hers: conversation can go ballistic instantaneously. I cannot imagine the world without her, but . . . but this is painful. The more time I spend with her, the more I have to face the pain of my love, the aching depth of it.

The sun is already high and hot by ten o'clock. She walks me to my father's car. I lean to kiss her, she turns her cheek; I grasp her face, turn the other cheek, and kiss it too. I reach down, hold her in my arms. She stands limp, unyielding, but yielding inside, wanting me to show her how much I love her. I wish I had the courage to show her, but it breaks my heart, and I can never show all that there is.

On the highway, people are driving quickly. I feel tired and hung over. A car cuts me off, and I think, I could die. I could die here on the highway if I'm not careful. And then I know: it's not me who will die. It's her. My mother is going to die. My mother, who bore me, held me, tried to keep holding me, who fought my every step away from her, as every mother does, who resented my inevitable departure until she felt pride for my courage. I am flying down the highway, doing eighty, Ma, flying away from her, tears streaming down my face. I must be hung over, I say to myself. That's why I'm so fragile. It's the hangover. It happens all the time these days.

Back at the hotel, I called Georgina. I'd dated her fifteen years earlier. When I think of Georgina, I think of her apartment, a loft above an old fabric store that was never open. I see her eyes, which were huge, and her body, which was very youthful and sexy. I met her on a bus. Her stop was in front of her door, and I saw her try her key. The next time I was in her neighborhood, I left a note. She remembered me from the bus, called me back, and we went out. I asked if she wanted to spend the night together, and she said no. I didn't call her for a couple of weeks after that.

She sewed her own clothes, and often made me dinner—she worked as a dentist's secretary, but there was a wide stripe of homebody in her. I liked going to her flat: you mounted some steep and very dingy stairs, but when you stepped into her apartment, it seemed hers, somehow, warm. She was good with money, thrifty, but adventuresome: on our second date, she asked me to go to Africa with her. I said I would, and she slept with me, but then I couldn't afford it, and she thought I lied on purpose. She went to Africa anyway, and I looked after her cat, a seriously disturbed animal. It would eat only in the dark, for instance. By the time she got back, the cat was completely normal, which somehow made her trust me more. She said she'd seen God in Kenya. That scared me a bit, but we started going out seriously. She was willing and responsive in bed, and she thought I was some kind of genius, and that was a pretty formidable combination, from my point of view. But she didn't trust me completely, which in turn made me defensive, and distant; she believed in astrology, seriously believed in it (she said she was good in bed, for instance, because she was a Gemini), which made me nervous (my mother is a Gemini); and she had an odd habit of never talking about her family. She hated her father, who was mean and violent and somehow deranged; I used to tag along when she visited her parents, and when I walked into the kitchen, he always stood up, swore, and went up to bed. For this and other reasons, Georgina had a therapist, but the therapist seemed to need Georgina as much as Georgina relied on her. The therapist died while we were dating: something very dramatic, as I remember, something along the lines of spontaneous combustion while she was sitting in an airport. All in all, much as I liked her, I thought Georgina was a bit dizzy, but later I figured out she just didn't care to tell stories in an organized manner. She had a baby after we parted, not mine.

Anyway, she sounded pleased to hear from me after all those years. I launched right in. "How do you remember the time we were together?" I said.

"Very fondly," she said, and I almost fell out of my chair. I thought she hated me. I was so unpredictable in those days.

"You talked to me," she said. "I always appreciated that. And you were a good listener. That excused a lot of stuff. Even though you were sleeping around. You couldn't seem to tell me about that."

"How did you know?"

"Oh, there were clues. You'd say you'd been to a movie alone, and then there'd be two tickets in your pocket."

I didn't think to ask how she knew what was in my pocket. Instead, I said, "How long do you remember us going out?"

"Well," she said, "how long do you think we went out?"

"Six months."

"I thought you'd say that."

"What do you mean?"

"Well, you went out with me formally for six months. But then you met Cathy"—my next girlfriend—"but you kept sleeping with me for another six months."

I'd forgotten about that. I mean, I knew I'd hopped in the sack with her a couple of times, but I'd forgotten it was another six months.

"I'm sorry," I said.

"Oh, I didn't mind," she said. "I always appreciated you did that. I'd quit my job, and gone back to school, and it was very traumatic. It kind of let me down slowly, for one thing, and I needed the company then."

The whole conversation was like that: good news that made me feel great, followed by bad news that made me feel like a rat. "What did your friends think?"

"Oh, they told me I had low self-esteem," she said, and laughed.

As I say, I'd forgotten all this stuff. I must have been ashamed of myself. But I couldn't stop going to bed with her. Georgina claimed it was because of our astrological arrangement. She always wanted to, and that was rare in my experience. Everywhere, too—the kitchen, on the stairs up to her bedroom, outside. Once in bed in her friend's cottage with her friend in the next bed. Once under her mother's dining room table while her mother was upstairs reading. But it was more than just the sex. It was our enthusiasm for one another.

I asked her how she remembered the sex.

"Very athletic," she said. "Great sex. It was the best sex I've ever had."

Man whose wife wants to have baby phones ancient girlfriend to ask if he was good in bed. I was pathetic. Of course, I wouldn't deny that I was impressed with myself. "How's your sex life been since?" I asked.

"I haven't had sex since," she said. Fifteen years, and no sex.

"But you had a baby," I said.

"Apart from that." The compliment of a few moments before shriveled and clattered to the floor.

"Well," I said, "during sex . . . when we had sex, did you . . . were you satisfied? Did you have . . . satisfaction?"

"Well, yes," she said. "Of course I did."

"What do you mean, you did? I did, too."

"Well, you did at first."

"What do you mean?" I didn't remember any of this. I was flabbergasted. I was worried.

"After you met Cathy, you were guilty about sleeping with me, so you stopped."

"I don't remember being impotent."

"You weren't. You were capable of having sex as often as always. But after you started seeing Cathy, you'd make love to me, and I'd carry on through, but you always stopped short. You said that to do otherwise would be unfaithful to Cathy."

I was embarrassed. I would have been more embarrassed, but I was so astonished by the lengths to which I went to find peace, so bowled over by the desperate optimism—hey! This isn't such a bad thing to be doing!—of the spirit that could behave that way, that my embarrassment just fell off the truck. All I could think of as I hung on the telephone was Shakespeare's line: "an expense of spirit in a waste of shame."

But the truth is this: part of me was even rather impressed—not just by the sexual performance it must have entailed, which was not inconsiderable, but by my own oceanic fallibility. I was imperfect, there was no doubt. Finally, the truth was known. What a pig. What a cad. And what a relief. Over the years, to ward off the sniping of my guilty conscience, I had set myself up as a fine, upstanding man, and the effort was killing me. Now I could breathe out. Yeah, yeah, officer, it was me, I can't keep it inside any longer, I did it all.

"I'm sorry," I said.

"Oh, it's okay," Georgina said. "I thought it was quite sweet. It showed you had a conscience."

I said good-bye shortly thereafter. I got up out of my chair, and I went outside. It was spring in Montreal, and spring in that city is unlike any other season anywhere: a reprieve, a sudden jump in the air, days of breeziness, as if a certain new sadness, a sense of how much everyone has waited for the warmth, blows around. I listened to French being spoken. I felt lighter than I had in years.

When I was dating Georgina, the same plates on a table from one meal to the next scared me. Nicknames, terms of tenderness, drew me closer, but they scared me. I was like a new animal, one that had only recently escaped to the back yard. I didn't want to go back in any time soon.

The physical thrill of infidelity was its own best argument: sheer sexual pleasure, not to mention freedom from physical and moral constraint. A different woman's skin, tracing the outlines of my own body. Different breasts, pushed against my chest; unknown hands, new breath, coming and going in its own new way. Newness. That's what I remember, what I'm nostalgic for. I know women miss it, too; my wife does. Newness is a hot iron in my memory. Still, I remember that time as a remote tropical swamp: exotic, sure, but desirable mainly in repose, after I'd made my way through it.

I know I'm supposed to interpret my sexual past as symptomatic addiction, evidence of an ignored "inner child" who by not admitting to his sexual sickness makes it clear he doesn't want to grow up; as proof that I am a male whose desperate emptiness is quenchable temporarily only by the conquest of women again and again; a man without a self. I know everyone says that's what philandering means. But I can't bring myself to contribute another thousand words to that pile of shining theory.

It's true that sexual anticipation and arousal was its own safe place, one of the few reliable feelings I had. However lost I felt, I knew where I was when I was turned on. The tiniest bell set it off: a direct look, hazel eyes, a ready laugh, the slope of a breast in a sweater, a pair of legs so long I thought I could see the future between them. It made me breathless, like being punched in the chest, but at least it was reliable territory.

It seems callow to me now to have used women as little more than sexual pacifiers. But neo-Freudians and orthodox all-intercourse-is-rape feminists and moralists and we-can-save-you-from-yourself-if-you-bark-at-your-inner-moon therapists, not to mention I myself when I'm at my most sanctimonious and revisionist, all ignore the obvious: the power of sexual adventurism as a way of divining ourselves, as a psychic Etch-a-Sketch.

I remember a day many years ago when I slept with a girl I believed I loved in Boston before breakfast, flew home to Toronto, had a high-calorie dinner with an old girlfriend, and then spent the night with my new girlfriend. It didn't happen often, but it happened. Today, I find my behavior that day unbelievable and thoroughly appalling. I am full of remorse. I am a disgrace and a heel, a moving target. But at the same time I can't apologize with any sincerity. In the end, what I did affirmed some shadow in me: it said, yes, this is me, this is me, this is me.

Is that so surprising? Neo-natal specialists claim neither boys nor girls distinguish between themselves and their mothers for the first three months of life. As far as the kid's concerned, they're one and the same being. When a girl finally figures out she's not part of the mother ship, but a satellite on her own, she looks up to see what she must become.

But a boy? A boy is likewise born of a woman, undifferentiated, and then nurtured and raised by that woman. At least he was in the fifties. But when a boy finally looks up, he doesn't see his own kind. He sees what he was, and is no more. If he's lucky, he breaks away from his former mooring, his mother, the Mother of All Women, to become something entirely different—a man. I will give Robert Bly and the Forest Dancers this: in a culture where fathers tend to be at work all day and remote at night, often resented by mothers and children alike, where the only steady influence is a maternal one—how does a boy locate his manhood?

Is it any wonder sex becomes an answer—that becoming a man is like trying to find your way out of a blizzard, where the only visible landmark is your own erection? Sex transforms us: the first act of intimacy we knew—being suckled, at the breast, lips wrapped around a nipple like a tiny elastic waistband—suddenly recedes before an act of greater intimacy, in which we're no longer taking, but giving; not for survival, but for pleasure. Things grow clearer: intimacy becomes a choice, a desire rather than a need, active rather than passive.

Sex told me for the first time where I began and where I stopped, where my outline was and wasn't.

I suspect sex is a man's first encounter with power—the power to exist as himself. I suspect it's true, alas, that the desire to control the world is somehow masculine; because the desire to control the world springs from that early male sexual desire *to be* the world. Have you ever longed to be with someone who didn't return the longing, loved someone on and on in the face of their rejection, and then, finally, found yourself having sex with him or her? Do you know the sense of power I mean? That sense—not of conquest, but of self-possession? That desire suddenly to shout: I made it! I'm here! With her (or him)! I'm the first person on the moon! To me it felt like my body was laughing. The will to self-possession lies at the heart of a man's love of sex for sex's sake. The act is linked like cause and effect to the act of being. This may be true of women, too. But for women (I sometimes tell myself) the consequence can be a body growing within them. For a man, who has no continuous bodily link to a fetus, sex can more readily be an end in itself. This makes men and women natural antagonists. I sought out new bodies, new physical geography, new maps to discover my own whereabouts. Sometimes I revisit those women in my mind. I always forget someone, and I'm always surprised when I do. How could I forget her? She was *that time.* Using women to locate my self made them exist sometimes only in relation to me; and in that there was a dose of misogyny, or at least of a potentially demoralizing mistrust of women as themselves. But there I was. Jobs come and go, prospects build and fail, marriages sharpen and blur, children love us and hate us, money fills us and denies us: but at least for this man sex, the simple cosmic form of physical identity, lives on.

I admit I was never lonelier or more desperate. As soon as I was there, in the humid zone from whence I had come, I wanted out again, the cycle of all life told again and again, never boring, a retellable story. Why else, in those days, did my friends and I never tire of recounting our sexual adventures? Because it's the eternal tale: becoming something new. This is what you are like, each woman said to me: this is what makes you afraid; this is where your heart is now, and now, moment by moment. I found new landmarks in the darkness, woman by woman. They fixed me against the latitude of affection and the longitude of wariness, only to spring me free again, to lurch blind to the next encounter, where I could be lost and found again. This search seemed more important at the time than the feelings of the women I disappointed with my inevitable departures.

There are surely other ways for a man to define himself. But is having a baby one of them? That's what I needed to know.

Osterman's stag was being staged in Rhode Island. He was having one of those East Coast stags, one of the expansive generation-soaked traditional rites Wasps are so good at: thirty Establishment boys surrounded by concentric circles of family, wives and ex-wives and ex-ex-wives, endless baseball and golf and lobster, all set in a seaside town where the entire clan has "summered" all their lives, and where you can distinguish between a townie and a "summer person" at a single glance, from the wattage of the tan or the cut of the hair.

Osterman's friends were in their late twenties; all but two were single. They were shy. They talked about past adventures made more memorable as their circle split up, grew apart, lived in more distant places.

For two days we drank and smoked and drank and played baseball and visited and drank. By the third day I knew why the Professor had invited me to his relative's bachelor party: he needed company, a fellow mourner. We were there to bury something. As well, this was his old zone, where he'd grown up before he moved to Los Angeles. We'd become friends, and he wanted me to understand his past.

The third and last night of the stag, Osterman and his friends gathered on the beach in front of the family's boathouse, lit a fire in a brazier, and roasted the groom: stories about his rambling stories, stories about sexual conquests or road trips or backward townies who infected their summers on the shore, stories that linked them all in their manhood. They all had nicknames: Osterman was Toad, someone else was Howdy, Petey, Sicker, and so on, the Seventeen Dwarfs. The nicknames dated from their private schools, Groton and St. Paul's and Choate, where dreaming up nicknames was a high art and allowed the men—it seems the wrong word, but let it stand—to express otherwise impermissible tenderness.

Finally, Tuna Boy, a fat, vivacious guy who wrote commercials for Fox and seemed to model his style on that of Oscar Wilde, told his story. He was standing in the first row around the brazier, and the light from the flames lit his face in shadows. The thought of fat Jimmy dancing his naked Shadow Dance started into my head. Someone, the literary type from their old high-school crowd (he was now writing sitcoms on the Coast), had just read a long funny poem. Everybody had been waiting for Tuna Boy to speak. He had a reputation.

Tuna Boy's story recounted the first time Toad asked Bitsy, his future wife, out on a date. Bitsy was dating Toad's closest friend at the time. "So Toad phoned Howdy, and he said, Do you mind if I date Bitsy? And Howdy said, Sure, go ahead. And Toad, he says, No really, do you mind? And Howdy says, No, it's okay. And Toad says, No, really: is it okay if I ask her out? I really like her. And Howdy says, For Christ's sake, Osterman, it's okay. And so they went out, and the rest is *l'histoire*. All of which just goes to show you why the Toad's our friend: because for the Toad, his *hombres*, his guy friends, are more important than *chiquitas*. And that's the way it should be." I thought Tuna Boy was going to cry.

What the roast reminded me of was my father-in-law's funeral. He was crazy by the time he died, his brain overrun with cancer; as much relief as grief was felt at his passing. But standing around his open grave on that chilly Pennsylvania hillside, watching him lowered into the ground, fifty people joined arms, and I suddenly realized why: We linked arms to hold on, to prevent another from slipping into the darkness of the open hole.

Osterman's stag was like that, as all stags are: a last stand against change and what seems like loss. Even I, a married man, sensed it: as if women had become the enemy, for snatching away another man before we had a chance to tell him all the things we never found words for. We wanted him to be happy, to go on to love and the rest—we really did want that for him—but he was our surrogate, and we were afraid our adventures with him were over. "I hate stags," one of the kids said. "Especially when there's no talent." He meant strippers. "All my friends are dropping, getting married. It makes me sad as hell."

"You're right," another said. "And I hate it when guys get married and then you never see them again. Or when they have kids and they disappear out of your life. What does that say about the friendship you've had?" They were all in mourning for Osterman. Insults and crude remarks were coasting through the night air, but the message was otherwise: don't forget us. Don't forget you felt this way once, you asshole, who are leaving our dry, quick, nervy cause. You're abandoning us for her and them, for the cause of settling down. Don't forget whence you came, don't become polite and tame, don't forget the color of the dirt you crawled in, with whom you first became a man, don't let them push us away. To us you are still dressed in that crumby green sports jacket you wore in tenth grade. But now you've abandoned us and made the compromise of death-and-convention seem that much more inevitable. We loathe you for that, resent you for it, want to make you feel bad. We want to taunt you with naked women to make you regret your decision. We don't want to be reminded that you have to make a choice, that the choice has a price, whichever way you go. So pay up: don't forget us as you disappear from our sight, how much we needed you, how we held each other up, and spat upon the world. Take this evening, your stag, as a last memento of the sweet romance of our friendships, as you embark on your solitary married expedition, your paltry retreat inwards, where you must stop breaking away and find yourself in joining.

Don't forget who you were, and who we are still, standing out here on the edge of the sea by a fire in the night, wandering and still unformed.

IO

My Wife Is a Wave

*Delusions of male persecution vs. things for which
men have actually been blamed – Night talk –
A sex scene – An unexpected development –
Paradise lost on a surfboard*

I had promised Johanna, my wife, that we'd start in earnest on a baby on
her thirtieth birthday. The closer the day came, the more exercised I grew.
I seemed to believe I was the victim of a plot to promote universal
motherhood at the expense of men. Women wanted to control my
life—and hadn't they always done a good job of it? No wonder I was
worried! Women, always distracting, were now overwhelming me.

My conviction that I was the victim of a plot made me debate my
wife, argue with her friends, and harangue women I barely knew. I carped
incessantly about the sexual politics of child-rearing. I worked out

infinitely complicated arguments that collapsed under the weight of their own impressive logic. I took the anthropological tack (males have always been warriors, raising offspring is counter to their nature); the biological tack (if women didn't have a more "natural" role to play with children, why did their breasts leak milk?—that wasn't social conditioning); even the economic tack (women entering the work force had weakened the middle-class standard of living by reducing demand for workers—a fabulous theory for which I even cited studies, though I actually didn't know of any). I pointed out *ad nauseam* that women—Margaret Thatcher sprang to mind—ran the world no better than men did. I even kept a notebook of all the terrible wrongs for which various women said I was responsible by simple dint of my manhood. I was blamed for sexism; the Vietnam war; all racism, and the economic oppression of all races but my own; the nuclear arms race (boy toys); rape (who else?); sexual and economic harassment of women; the poverty of single mothers (men not making support payments); advertising (created by men and insulting to women); alcoholism (men can't face their emotions); the proliferation of guns in society (more power toys, necessary because men can't talk about their feelings); violence (a male thing); the fact that I wanted to protect my wife and sisters against physical violence (my patriarchal mindset); boring football on TV (stupid guys); male bonding (excludes women); capitalism (controlled by men); pro-abortion rallies (irresponsible men, never facing the consequences of their urges); anti-abortion rallies (men trying to control women's bodies); the fact that there were so many single women who couldn't find guys (men can't commit); the fact that my sister couldn't do math (guys get all the attention in school); homophobia; and on one memorable occasion, the incarceration of women by mother-hood (because I had no breasts).

I never believed any of these positions, or their opposites; I simply was desperate to find a reason for my own terror. Men's "needs" were ignored because over-valuing maternity guaranteed the status quo, perpetuated the system for the ruling powers, and kept us all prisoners—oh, I tell you, I had the whole thing figured out.

At other times, when Johanna woke up in the middle of the night, I lay awake to keep her company. I liked talking to her then: the darkness hid us from ourselves, and we opened, like nocturnal orchids. We'd talk about when we were teenagers, the details of how we met, old lovers, things we misunderstood as children (I thought horses and knives were male, cattle and spoons female); about the way she could remember the lyrics to almost any song; about a weird old lodge we stayed at one night in South Dakota; about insignificant things we remembered because for some reason they made us stop and notice where we stood and what color the buildings were and who we were at that moment. Mostly we laughed at each other's stories; sometimes, when tenderness overcame us, we made love.

With me in high anti-family dudgeon, things often didn't go that well. One night—it was one of those fall nights in Los Angeles when you can feel the breeze off the ocean ten miles inland—Johanna recited poems and sang rhymes she had memorized as a girl in seventh grade. Then we had a fight. On television that evening, some researchers had declared that men and women had very different brains. Women's brains were capable of doing five things at once, while male brains were distinguished (in the phylogenetic sense, at least) by their literal "single-mindedness"— male brains could do only one thing at a time.

"So this explains all sorts of things," my wife said. "Why women nag, for instance. It's just their brains, thinking about five things at a time, and trying to get the male brain to think of more things than it can."

"Yes," I said, my eyes closed. I was nearly asleep. "That's why nagging is unavoidable. It's never going to accomplish anything, and it's never going to stop."

"Well, it's understandable." She was touchy about nagging. "Women have been doing all these things around the home, and in the last generation they've been working, too."

"I'm not sure you can say they do everything." I was touchy about not meeting my responsibilities.

"Studies I've read say they do everything."

"Studies you've read? What studies?" Five a.m., and she was citing studies she'd read? "Surely you mean you've read articles, generally by women, in magazines read by women, complaining that they do everything. That doesn't mean they actually do everything. There are other studies, in any event, that say just the opposite. That doesn't mean men contribute less." I was wide awake now, staring at the ceiling. I was speaking louder than was strictly necessary, given that my wife was eight inches away. "I mean, there are more ways to be around than picking up socks. A woman often spends more time with her children because that's who her children—especially her very young children—need to be with. Oftentimes she just has no choice in the matter, especially if she wants to breast-feed. What can a guy do about that? Grow breasts? Force the children to spend more time with him? The only sure way to avoid having her entire life colonized by work and children is not to have children. Wasn't that why many women wanted reproductive freedom and the right to abortion, to be in control of their own bodies and biology? In any event, there isn't a lot a man can do about that, either. But somebody has to compensate the woman for her discomfort and her second thoughts, which is where nagging comes in. If the brain theorists are correct, dissatisfaction is a biologically unavoidable fact of modern family life."

I was interrupted by the sound of my wife's breathing. She was asleep.

Strangely, my attitude had no effect on my wife's desire to have a child. Procreation was unstoppable by my puny inventions of logic. Motherhood was a gigantic steamroller: I could see it coming for miles, I fired my cannon at it, but I couldn't seem to get out of its way.

One day a friend invited me out for lunch. "I married the wrong man," she said.

"What do you mean, you married the wrong man? He wasn't the wrong man when you married him."

"No," she said, "you're right. I married him because I knew he should be the father of my children. No one ever says it, but it's true: women are drawn to certain men because they know they have to have children with those men. And once they do, then it's over. The man has served his purpose. I know it's awful to say, but it's true."

That wasn't news. Our friends Melanie and Peter were on the verge of divorce. Peter could barely stand to look at her after eight years, and yet Melanie still wanted to have another child with him. Why? To lay claim to a piece of him and his time and his attention and his money, for as long as he lived—even if he wasn't around? That's what he thought. Or because she couldn't help herself—because her body was ordering her around, telling her not to fail in its mission, no matter what the consequences?

How could I resist a force that strong? And how could I ignore it? My ambitions—my "work"—seemed paltry and futile next to the destiny of fathering a child, but my work was critical to the feeble sense of self I had.

I knew how pallid my plight sounded next to civil war or world hunger or even the disappointments of couples who couldn't have children. But it was exactly that built-in, no-questions-allowed rectitude of "parenting," not to mention the inevitability of becoming a parent, that left me livid. I'd fallen in love with my wife, she fell in love with me. But then—kapow: feed my womb, big boy. The sperm lotto was underway.

And with that all my private hopes were . . . second-rate. Now I was mere material (genetic, and occasionally journalistic). Queen Biology has taken over, and would you please get out of the way? Because, hey—this is life we're talking about, La Concepción. If you were a smart man, or a lucky man, or a "healthy" man, you told yourself this is what happens in life, it's a sign of maturity, you will simply find your new self-definition in your child. It's all for the good. Society appreciates the vote of confidence, pal.

That was the machine of motherhood. I protested, but something kept me in its high beams. It was like running out of gas on the highway. You keep looking at the gauge and see E looming larger and closer, and yet you keep thinking you can make it another thirty miles. And then, when you finally do run out of gas and have to walk three miles in the middle of the frigid night to some flyspeck gas station where fuel is $150 an ounce, you're shocked. You can't believe you didn't do something about it.

I couldn't step out of the way. Maybe I knew what might happen if I did. One night I stopped at my local bar for a drink. I drank there sometimes when I didn't want to talk at home. It was a Mexican place with a wide-screen TV in the corner and a huge aquarium built into thick sienna walls. Jorge, the bartender, was serving a story about his partner Jerry when I arrived. Jorge was hilarious, a big guy in his forties who sometimes wore a ponytail.

"Jerry's got himself in big trouble," Jorge said. "Big trouble. Because he came on all romantic to this chick. 'Ooooh, baby, I want to take you away for the weekend,' that sort of shit. But you don't come on all romantic to a chick on the rebound. You come on hot—sure. You come on wanting sex, fine. Because she wants that. But not all romantic. But he did, and now he's got all these troubles with her wanting him around all the time. Because chicks are like that: they just want to own you, man. They do. They just want to own you. They come on all loving and saying they want you, and then they get you, and once they own you they just disdain you. Disdain you and measure out their pussy. Just measure that pussy out and the rest is disdain. Don't tell me, man. I know women. I got me one like that myself. But I ain't havin' any of it."

Maybe there was some truth in what Jorge said. But there was bile in it, too. *Pussy, chick, own you*: it was the patter of transformation, magic words used to change someone into anything but another human being, to put her at a distance, to make her go away.

In the midst of my full-scale revolt against the dictatorship of parenthood, I did a bizarre thing: I gave Johanna her long-promised thirtieth birthday present. We began to make love in earnest, *sans* condom. After a weekend with a bunch of guys in Las Vegas (where I attended a Grateful Dead concert, won $900 playing craps, and generally behaved like an ass), I impregnated my wife. It was thrilling. I was a god, and she was, too. We made love three times a day. I called her at work in the middle of the afternoon and told her to come home.

Afterward, of course, lying awake at night with her sleeping soundly beside me, I was a puling wiener of doubt. How could those two states of being co-exist? Something happened during sex, some strange backflip took place, as if we were turning ourselves inside out and into one another. Did she emit some kind of pheromonal nerve gas that knocked out my logical capacity just prior to our sexual congress?

A week later she came home with a pregnancy test. The container was slim and pink and had an opening at one end. "Come and help me do it," she said from the bathroom. I stood in the door and watched the ritual, a delicate dabbing of urine. The result required a minute's wait. I stepped into the bedroom. I closed my eyes and prayed the test would be negative. I wasn't ready for this. Then I regretted the thought and tried to pray in the opposite direction. I stepped back into the bathroom. A small pink cross had appeared. Johanna was pregnant. I was petrified. I was ecstatic.

Why did I change my mind? In the end, my mind had nothing to do with it. I think what happened was that at the last minute I realized I couldn't stop the steamroller and wouldn't survive a flattening, so I jumped up into the cab.

From that point on, I watched Johanna swell and become inhabited by an alien. We called it the Plant. The days passed so slowly I had to time-lapse my attention to perceive any progress at all. Bolts of fury still struck me at random, and I still devoted entire days to building huge, beautiful, uninhabitable monuments of logic to the unattached heart. I still do. But they seem less resolute than they did. They're like a favorite old joke that never works again after you see some idiot tell it on TV.

Her pregnancy seemed to knock out whole sectors of my memory. What I can't forget—I sometimes wish I could, because the memory touches me too painfully—is the night she sang the rhymes of her girlhood in our dark bedroom near the sea.

I was to be a father, was I? My own father hit seventy three days after I turned thirty. We were eating breakfast at the short-order joint across from his squash club in downtown Toronto.

"So," I said. "I've heard forty is bad, and thirty feels tough. Seventy is thirty plus forty; you must feel terrible." It was a lousy joke.

"Actually," he said, "fifty was the worst. I thought, at the time, half a century! That's old. But I haven't noticed any change in the past twenty years."

I didn't know if that was good news or not. "What would you have done if you hadn't married and had kids?"

"Me? Sailed around the world."

"That would have taken a year or two. What about the rest of your life?"

"That's what I mean," he said. "I would have taken off forever." A beat or two passed. "But to have a son who's thirty—now that's something!"

Years later a woman suggested I ought to have been hurt by his remark. It never occurred to me. I understood perfectly. What might have been was very different from what was.

I remembered that conversation over a brace of Mai-Tais in Harry's Underwater Bar. It was a Thursday afternoon. Harry's was found—literally—in the subterranean parking garage of the Outrigger Reef Hotel, on Waikiki Beach in Hawaii. The Outrigger didn't approve of Harry's (hence its location, on level P1) because the bar's picture window was imbedded in the wall of the hotel swimming pool. Harry's patrons drank to the sight of headless, unsuspecting swimmers floating by.

Johanna and I were celebrating the conception with a trip to Hawaii. It was July: the climatic ambience of the islands resembled that of a large commercial laundry. We spent mornings visiting pineapple plantations and extinct volcano craters and reconstructed Hawaiian villages; in the afternoons we lay on the beach, and I watched my wife's breasts and belly grow. It was like a distant storm approaching; you know it's going to pour like hell, but you want to catch as much sun as you can while it lasts. Every few hours a thirty-second rain shower broke the silence and then stopped. It was hurricane season. Afternoons, Johanna took a nap, and I dropped by Harry's.

I liked Harry's. It was refrigerator cool, for starters, and dark and empty and completely private—the complete antithesis of the beach at Waikiki, where our room was perched above the exhaust vent of the kitchen's french fry machine and opened onto a panorama that had been described by my travel agent as a "partial ocean view," which in fact was ninety percent concrete wall. Down in Harry's, on the other hand, sunlight from the pool dappled a dolphin blue through the room; human forms in the pool were neatly upholstered in their fluorescent skin, more graceful than they ever are on land.

By now I had been staring through the window at the bodies in the pool for a long time. I was thinking about Paul Gauguin, who emigrated to Tahiti from Paris to find his natural soul. I was wondering if that was still possible, or even a very good idea. You never know what you might find.

"The right girl and the right music," said A.J., the bartender, "and it's just like watching MTV."

Yes, even this bar could be paradise. Paradise is privacy. As this thought breaststroked through my mind, a young girl swam into view. She was eleven, maybe—still fat, small proto-breasts still forming. She hung on the edge of the pool, showing her body to whoever was watching below.

She knew we were there. I felt rather nervous. She played with her bathing suit, snapping the elastic.

"A little older, she'll be okay," Santa said. Santa—so named for his long white beard—was in his eighties. He was in Harry's every afternoon between four and six. "People say I'm a dirty old man. I don't care. I am!"

I stopped drinking at Harry's.

The North Shore of Oahu was deserted. In a month's time bad-tempered storms and twenty-foot waves would press in from the North Pacific, and amateur and professional surfers from every shorebreak in the world would converge here on three infamous beaches—Waimea Bay, Sunset Beach, and the Pipeline. The North Shore was the village green of international surfing, international surfing technique, surfboard design, surfing everything. It wasn't uncommon for even a moderately stoked waveman in these parts to have seventeen surfboards racked on his front porch. But in August the surf was small. Families and flocks of children bobbed in the waves on boogie boards, rising and falling, rising and falling. In August on the North Shore, the ocean held no menace.

I was eating breakfast in the Haleiva Café, where all serious surfballs eventually chowed, with Duncan Campbell, the café's owner. Campbell was famous. When Duncan was fourteen, he and his sixteen-year-old brother, Malcolm, invented the three-finned surfboard. They turned surfing inside out. Until the Campbells came along, surfboards were beefy fifty-pound, twelve-foot-long full guns in the Hawaiian tradition. The Campbell bonzer (Australian slang for "crazy") was six feet long, thin, light (ten pounds), and—because of its three fins and contours—wormily maneuverable, especially on small waves. Surfing became gymnastic, which meant more television coverage, which created professional surfing and the surfing business. Companies such as Body Glove and Gotcha (whose president, Mike Thompson, still surfed every day from his home on the North Shore) began to sell $100 million worth of surfing shorts a year. California glamour surfers like Christian Fletcher now modeled their hairstyles and their attitude on those of Axl Rose, the rock star; endorsements followed them like wake. Rebellion and anarchy were selling well. Even *Esquire* had run an article about surfing—except that it was about glamour surfers in California, which is another way of saying it was not about surfing at all.

Campbell despised all of it. If anything united the hard-core surfers who lived within the hermetically sealed world of North Shore surfing, it was their distaste for capitalists and the way they tried to colonize surfing.

"Surfers were always guys who didn't want to join," Duncan said. He was boyish, slightly heavy for a surfer, and congenitally relaxed. He spent a lot of time these days painting. "Those have always been the people attracted to surfing. At school if you were a surfer, you looked different. And you were different. . . . But now, suddenly the whole country is looking like the rebel the surfer once was. And the surfer says, hey: I don't want to be status quo. I'm not wearing that stuff. And then your core pulls out. You see, the monetary thing really defeats the true experience of surfing. It's really a life experience. It's about the environment, it's about relationships that develop when you're waiting for a wave."

Duncan stopped talking, and considered. I knew what was happening: he was experiencing the Heisenberg principle of the true surfer, who never wants to belong to any club he can describe. "In the end," Duncan muttered, "surfing is the constant. It doesn't matter whether it's short board, long board, knee board, body surf, it's all about riding a wave. You can use it as a life lesson, or you can use it to get girls. But when people put it out there to change the world, or use it as a lit candle to show the way, it's just bullshit. It's just one thing we do. It's just . . . surfing."

This much is true, though: surfing was about paddling out into the ocean by yourself, on your own board, and waiting for your wave, and standing up and riding in on nature's most powerful muscle, the sea that never stops flexing, by yourself. The terrors and thrills of surfing belonged only to those who surfed. Jim Jones, who lived on the North Shore and was one of the few men ever to survive being crushed by a fifty-foot wave (he almost quit surfing after it happened), once said waves were "the music of the ocean. And the surfer is trying to find a harmony with that wave." The intensity of that thrill made surfers greedy for it, and that in turn made them unreliable. You could make an appointment to talk to a surfer, but the odds were at least even, if there were waves around, that he wouldn't show up. "Surfers as a rule are not good providers," Duncan Campbell said. "They're really selfish, self-centered people."

I couldn't blame them. Surfing was about coming ashore from the ocean, the watery amniosis from which all life first waded. Surfing a wave felt completely original because it was about being born, over and over and over again.

What never changed were Hawaii's waves—the pulses of water that built, uninterrupted, from the Aleutian Islands 2500 miles to the north before they erupted, booming and hissing, on the North Shore. The heart of surfing was still the big wave, just as the true heroes of surfing were still the big-wave surfers.

Big meant anything over twenty feet. There was some debate on the North Shore as to whether anyone had ever surfed a thirty-foot wave: *Surfer Magazine*, the thirty-three-year-old bible of the sport, claimed thirty-five feet was now the "unridden realm," whereas most big-wave surfers wondered whether anyone had ever ridden a true twenty-five footer. But big wavers liked to underestimate.

However big "big" was, it was always horrifying. The waves that approached Waimea Bay in winter advanced like regiments of mountains, huge and black and incessant. For starters there was the problem of paddling out through the oncoming waves to reach the break, which could be half a mile distant: even the wash-out foam, or wake, of a spent thirty-footer was six feet deep and instantly deadly, and the waves came every ten seconds.

Then there was the problem of catching a wave that moved at thirty miles per hour, and the problem of standing up on a nine-foot fingernail of fiberglass while screaming down the jacking 80-degree face of six tons of water—a face so large, in the case of a thirty-footer, it had waves of its own.

Then there was the problem of wiping out. Roger Erickson, who'd been surfing big waves for more than twenty years, said, "You just gotta be good enough that you don't," although that didn't explain why Erickson had permanently separated ribs or why Peter Cole, another famous big-wave surfer, was blind in one eye. A shredder (surfer) who did get beefed (crushed) by the ax-curtain (the descending crest) of a thirty-foot monster (aka pounder, loomer, heavy, or Mack) needed to be able to scuba (hold his or her breath) for a full minute—and not just one minute, but one minute, followed by a single breath, followed by another minute, etc., all as he was being boiled alive in the soup, until he could swim to safety, wherever that was. The good news was that a single big wave could spit you a hundred yards closer to shore: the bad was, such waves liked to dribble fallen surfers along the bottom, where there was coral and pitch darkness. It wasn't uncommon for surfers who fell in truly huge surf to be stranded between shore and the break, requiring rescue by helicopter.

And yet: these huge killers, which were so dangerous, also had undeniable appeal. I had never surfed, but whenever I saw even a photograph of a vast wave, I experienced a stab of fear in my chest, as if a small rodent were trying to burrow its way out of my lungs. But another, bolder urge also made me want to try one. This, as Johanna pointed out, was a dangerous urge in a man about to have a baby; still, I set out to find Roger Erickson.

I found Roger at his post at the lifeguard tower on Lililani Beach, home to the infamous Pipeline (formerly the Banzai Pipeline), where massive waves formed perfect cannoli tubes. The sound of surf crashing was incessant there. Two or three people "maki out," or die, at Pipeline every year: the spiky coral reef is three feet below the surface. Roger surfed Pipeline until the day a twenty-foot tube skewered him on a pinnacle of coral, shattering three of his vertebrae. That was twenty years ago. Now Roger surfed only the big ones at Waimea Bay.

When I finally found him, he and Michael Chau, his life-saving partner, whose specialty was windsurfing thirty-foot waves, were lamenting the death the previous day of the Marlboro Man: lung cancer. The news was traumatic for Roger, who was trying to shake a thirty-year smoking habit in time for the Eddie Aikau Invitational Big Wave Tournament, which was held on the North Shore every January provided the waves were at least twenty-five feet high. The top prize was $50,000, which would have been nice for his wife and two kids, as Roger was at that moment earning $9 an hour as a lifeguard. So far, Roger had only ever won Best Wipe Out category.

Roger was the epitome of the 1950s-style Hawaiian "waterman," someone at home on the ocean, no matter the conditions. He was wearing red lifeguard trunks and a red lifeguard cap, reversed, and his eyes were sweeping back and forth across the shorebreak like a metronome. Roger was forty-five, but he had the body of a very fit twenty-year-old, the body of a transplanted Californian who had been surfing since he was nine, who had come to surf in Hawaii at nineteen, which he did alone while his buddies were in Honolulu getting girls; the body of a Vietnam war hero who trained for big wipeouts by filling a heavy bag with rocks and then swinging the bag and letting it crash into his sides. ("Sometimes I work out on the bag," he said, "and sometimes I let the bag work out on me.") Roger surfed Waimea back in the days when you called someone up to go with you. "You wouldn't want to call someone now," Michael Chau said to me. "Because it's already too crowded."

What Roger liked about surfing big waves was the camaraderie. "It's just so much of a stoker to be out there with such good surfers," he said. He spoke as distractedly as you can speak and still be understood by other humans. "I mean, you get out there, and they look at you, and you can see the feeling in their eyes: hey, you paddled out, you're one of us." He figured he could surf Waimea or Sunset until he was sixty, "if you were fit, and as long as you had the balls. Because it takes tremendous courage. You can't even imagine how much courage it takes on the very very biggest of waves."

For Roger and most other big-wave men, surfing was still as pure as it had been in the late 1950s. Professionals, endorsements, attitude . . . none of that existed. "I think this new generation, they're all affected," Roger was saying. "Although I shouldn't say that, because it's prejudiced, and I'm not. But it's like the chameleon effect. They're trying to be something. They're trying to be men. I mean, we're all trying to be men. But that's image. Surfing is—it's the ultimate freedom. There's nothing like it. I've yachted, fished, canoed, everything. And surfing is freer." Pause. Wave scan. Hat adjustment. "Of course, there's no such thing as ultimate freedom. You have to eat." It sounded like Roger was still learning that lesson.

To my surprise, these thoughts resonated in me, and I began to think, insanely, that I had a lot in common with Roger. Maybe, I thought, maybe the big waves are not so impossible after all. That was when Roger called out to a passing friend, a man with a handlebar moustache. "Hey, man," Roger said. "I was on the Big Island the other day, on the sixth floor of an office building, looking over a balcony. And looking down, I got the full take-off elevator rush."

I recognized the phrase: the elevator rush was what big-wave surfers called the initial free-fall on a twenty-five-footer. I was once on a ride at Six Flags Magic Mountain Amusement Park in Valencia, California, that simulated the effect. It was called Free Fall, and its plunge was so intense I experienced heart palpitations and a splitting pain in my anus. I vowed I would never ride it again. And yet here was Roger saying, "It was such a rush, imagining what going over would be like. I just wanted to go off the balcony, man, over the edge. It's like a dog with a ball, Pavlov. You just can't help stoke up."

That was when I knew there was a difference between Roger and me.

I looked at a really big wave and saw something that could kill me, whereas Roger looked at it and saw something that made him feel alive. Shortly afterward, I took my leave of Roger, and shortly after that I signed up for a hula lesson with four other tourists and my wife and learned to impersonate the rain and the trees and the wind and the sun with my hands.

The next day I kiss my wife good-bye and leave the North Shore. I drive through the red-dirt interior of Oahu, through the somber light of the cane fields and the pineapple plantations that seem to hold so many secrets, whose colors are so much darker and more serious than the pinks and limes and whites of the coast at Waikiki where I am headed.

My plan is to learn to surf a few small, manageable waves, just dinky ones, and so to find Paradise on an offshore board. No thirty footers, no heroics, but a wave nevertheless. The first thing I see as I step out of my hotel onto Waikiki's two-mile-long, vastly overpopulated—but fun!— stretch of beach is a guy in a fluorescent orange French Foreign Legion kepi standing waist deep in the ocean and strapped into a metal detector that resembles a penis extending from his waist. His name is Pat and he's from Alaska. He's been in Waikiki for a week and is staying another. "So far I've found eighty-five cents and a cheap gold band," Pat says. "My wife gave me the metal detector for my birthday. Keeps me out of trouble. Keeps me from looking at the bikinis."

The metal detector makes me want to disappear, never to be found by my loved ones again. It's shocking, the idea of metal-detecting as leisure activity. Still, I'm not here to grow depressed for a premagnetic Waikiki I never knew. Hence I make my unsentimental way down the beach, past the Royal Hawaiian Hotel, the famous pink ornament now stranded among skyscrapers on the beach like a souvenir my great-aunt left behind; past sun-baked old babes in royal blue muu-muus and real cat's-eye sunglasses and matching royal blue turbans; past thongs and luaus and the enjoyable illusion that paradise still exists; and eventually, on the beach in front of the Moana Surfrider, before a gentle reef known as Canoes, I enquire as to the whereabouts of Gabby Makalena.

Gabby, it turns out, is working the surfboard rental stand next to Lifeguard Tower Four. This is about as specific as the directions in Hawaii get. Gabby's a beach boy—the spiritual son of Duke Kohanamoku, former movie star and patron saint of surfing. Duke's surfboard, a seventy-pound redwood full gun with his name carved into its chest, sits in Honolulu's Bishop Museum. Duke's fellow beach boys are in their sixties now, another endangered Hawaiian species. They too make me sad. Lost hopes, spent youth. From a distance, dispensing beach towels and umbrellas and rides in outrigger canoes, they look like very busy, glossy chestnuts.

Gabby has been teaching idiots like me to surf since 1946, the summer of the great tidal wave. The police that year called everyone in off the water, but the surfers, predictably, stayed out. "I said to myself," Gabby says, "if they can stay out there and it's not that dangerous, I want to surf, too."

The lesson proceeds almost too quickly. Gabby explains the board, the principle of paddling, the technique of getting to one's feet, the equation of balance. Within ten minutes we're in the water. Within half an hour I'm surfing. True, they're small waves, and the surfboard's the size of a barn door, but I am still surfing. Only later do I learn Gabby guarantees this sort of progress.

Every day for nearly a week afterward, I surf twice a day, once at seven, once at five in the afternoon. The waves get bigger—three and four feet—and I get better.

On my last day in Hawaii, I paddle out to the farthest break a quarter mile from shore, where a dozen surfers are sitting on their boards, waiting in a crowd for waves. There are sixty-year-old women out here, and seventy-year-old men, and lots of guys in their forties. They don't smile as I paddle up, or welcome me into their hallowed club of bravery. They don't talk about waves and ax-curtains and the elevator take-off. Mostly they talk about their weight. "I used to weigh 165 in college, and 185 in the service," one man says.

"I hit 240 when I was married," his companion replies, and then spins to catch an approaching wave. He misses it.

Still: I like it out here. Out here, waiting for a wave, I find a moment of repose, an instant when what I want is no different from what I have. By now I know I'm never going to surf the really huge waves; by now, I know I don't want to. I'll keep surfing, and I'll get better, and one day, I've promised myself, I will surf a six-footer—a wave no bigger and no smaller than I. For now, however, I'm as content as I have ever been.

The only thing I can't figure is why I can't stop thinking about big waves. I see them in my mind, feel the push and pull of my fear and my awe, a dozen times a day. Why I should miss something I have never done and that would be virtual suicide is beyond me.

All I know is this: whenever I see a big wave, I remember a scene in the movie version of *From Here to Eternity*. "Too bad they got to get you sooner or later," Burt Lancaster says to Montgomery Clift. By "they" he means the Army, and the way it eventually makes you buckle under, but he also means life itself. There are rules, after all.

It seems to me, as I sit on my surfboard, waiting for a last slight wave before I head home to the mainland, that surfing, especially big-wave surfing in Hawaii, is one way to keep them away, to keep them from getting you, to break the rules you never agreed to, to keep some small corner of the world yours and yours alone. But to get there, you have to be willing to die trying, to risk everything. If you can't do that, you stick to the small waves. You stay safe, and alive. But every time you hear a big sea pounding, you hear your dreams crashing on the shore.

II

Toby and Jim, Jim and Toby

An unforeseen detour – Feeding the falcon –
Strange ways of a gun dealer – Treachery – Hunting
and being hunted – Arms and the Man –
How to disappoint a friend

I called Jayne from a motel in northern Arizona. From my room I could see RVs turning north to the Grand Canyon. There was a spot on the eastern rim of the canyon where the old parked their trailers, unfolded their lawn chairs, mixed cocktails, and sat in semi-circles to watch the sun go down.

I'd known Jayne in Winnipeg, never intimately. She was a sophisticated, well-read woman. Once at a party I overheard her describe the toilet in a monastery run by some Basilian monks. "That's a lot of monks," I said, and there was real surprise in her laugh, the kind of surprise that makes you remember someone.

Jayne had moved to Oklahoma City and married a gun enthusiast named Jim. Her friends were shocked. Jayne was hip, urban, and politically righteous. But her girlfriends, when they finally met Jim, all said he was the perfect Western man: an outdoorsy, un-ironic guy who knew what he wanted. I told her I wanted to talk to her husband about guns. I envied him before I even met him.

"Before you do," Jayne said, "you should meet my friend Toby." Toby was a hunter, too, and a photographer. He lived, Jayne said, in a small town in Arizona. Since Jim was hunting deer in south Texas and wouldn't be home for a week, I headed for Arizona. Later I learned that both men had been in love with Jayne; that they'd stalked her from the moment they met her; and that their affections had turned them against one another. I never did figure out why she sent me down there, and I suspect she hasn't either, but that's the sort of behavior men tend to find irresistible.

By the time I crossed into Arizona, the country had become so remote I could drive for three hours and not see another car. The roads were like seams across acres of tan cloth. The only thing I could pick up on the radio was the Navajo station. Whenever the announcer had a community message to send out, he'd say, "Now listen carefully," and then, chanting, all *heys* and *yas*, smooth and improbable, he filled the air in my truck. It was a beautiful sound, but I had to conclude I wasn't an Indian, just as I wasn't a gun lover or a principled noble Western man. I wanted to be, in the warm attic of my fantasies, but what I really was was a man who lived in the city and read the newspaper. Then I came up over the mesas, and soon I was driving through thick forests. The stars were so matted in the sky that I stopped my truck and lay on the roof and watched them. An hour went by that way.

Toby's town had one intersection and no traffic lights. Toby himself looked like a cowboy: longish gray hair cut locally, black jeans, boots. But he didn't live or talk like one. His house, a small stone square off the town's one cross-street, contained a de Chirico, a painting by Russell Chatham (the well-known Western artist), and an original print or two by Audubon; two rifles and a shotgun; a Colt .45 on his dresser; quite a few pairs of cowboy boots; a couple of fly rods; subscription copies of *The Paris Review*, *The American Rifleman*, *Gray's Sporting Journal*, and *Saltwater Sportsman* (among others); a TV; a dog named Leo; a small flock of exotic Spanish pigeons; a good book collection; and, in a back room, in a travel box, a small merlin falcon with whom Toby had been sharing his kitchen for a week. The house had the thoughtful, measured feel of a place full of artifacts—in this case, of a certain timeless idealized Western male life style. There was no telephone: Toby used the phone at the local corner store, where the owner took messages.

Toby was forty-two years old. He had lived in the town for eleven years. He never planned to stay. He'd grown up in Provincetown, the son of an Italian-American engineer. He dropped in and out of college, studied some biology, and when he finally realized he wanted to be a writer, enrolled at Dartmouth to study English. He was thirty-two years old and drinking when he decided to move West. "I think I was bored with not having a role for myself out East," he said. He talked between bites of a huge breakfast of eggs and toast and sausages and coffee in one of the town's two cafés. "Another reason this place is a good place for me to live is that the West is very tolerant. You can be almost anything you want here as long as you don't shove it in somebody's face."

He was a brainy guy. He talked about "the tension between the contrary impulses of connoisseurship and nomadism, the impulse to acquire objects and knowledge versus the impulse to narrow it to essentials." He also liked his cranky Suburban because it was just big enough to carry everything he owned. The town was too small to care about fashionable photographic styles, offered year-round hunting, and was surrounded by wilderness. The wilderness reminded him that everything he did had a consequence.

Within two years of moving to town, he'd taken enough photographs for a book about ranchers. His plan was working. Then he fell in love.

Debra was ten years older than he was. She was, as Toby described her, "a WASP adventuress, a mordant wit, a smoker." He'd worked on that description, I thought. They were both private-school graduates. The decade difference between them was no trouble, and they talked effortlessly. "One of the things Debra and I shared was a sense of the past as illuminating anecdote," Toby said. He'd used that line before as well.

Then Debra suffered a stroke and died. He published another book about that, photographs of church altar rails and phone booths and other places where people felt protected against danger, and where the safe feeling was an illusion.

"Five years, less than a month ago, November eighteenth," Toby said. He was suddenly crying, right there in the café. "I never get over it. But hey—I'm just an emotional Italian. I left town for a year after she died. I couldn't face looking out the same window. Although it's just occurred to me I've changed where I sit since she died; I used to sit by the front door, and now I sit at the counter. I am finally, again, after the aching loneliness of having shared my life with someone who died, reasonably happy again being alone. I was lucky once. Maybe, maybe, I can be lucky twice. But trying to plan your life to fit in that piece of the jigsaw puzzle—I don't know if that's possible."

For Toby, living in an isolated hamlet amounted to a form of discipline. If you were the susceptible type who took on the coloration of everything around you, the town was a way to narrow the range of your temptations. It was the opposite of L.A., in other words. A lot of male writers and artists of Toby's ilk, the Chathams and the McGuanes, had taken to the West for that reason, among others. Never mind that the rest of the world was hundreds of years removed from the dry interior: at least in the West things stayed the same a bit, and what you loved one day you could be forgiven for loving the next.

"I don't want to consciously adapt to be successful," Toby said. "I want to be successful doing what I want to do. I have a lot of friends who get along, but who dwell in this slightly depressed state of compromise."

We walked back to Toby's house and fed the falcon lunch. The falcon, a gift from a breeder in Idaho, was a prairie-raised merlin, the smallest of the hunting falcons (gyrfalcons are the largest, peregrines in between). Lunch was a piece of raw meat tacked to a leather spindle. At first the bird wouldn't go near it.

"We're just going through a difficult period," Toby said. "He's a wild bird, after all."

Toby walked over to a closet and began to fish around in a box. We talked about Jayne, and he came out of the closet carrying a sheaf of her letters. He'd saved all of them. Jayne's husband had burned all of Toby's letters to her; burned them, and then spat on them, one afternoon in Oklahoma City.

Jim and Toby had met Jayne the same day: at Toby's wedding to Nora. Jim was Toby's best man. Jayne was a friend of Nora's. Toby was marrying Nora in the aftermath of Debra's death. It was all extremely complicated. Toby had even dedicated part of his photo-memoir of Debra to Jim. They were pals. Then they fell in love with Jayne.

In keeping with his Old West literary habits, the newly married Toby wrote ten to twenty letters a week. A lot of them were addressed to Jayne. He knew Jim liked her, too, but Jim was married to MaryLee and had two children. Toby liked the way Jayne spoke, the mocking suggestiveness of her voice. He knew his marriage to Nora was doomed. When he finally divorced Nora six months later, he pursued Jayne. They met whenever they managed to find themselves in the same part of the country.

Still, Jim was his friend, and Jim was smitten with her, too. Toby wanted Jayne to tell Jim she was involved with Toby. Jayne said she would. In the meantime, she wrote funky little cards to Toby's dog. A card might feature a drawing of a chicken looking fondly at a dog, say, and in a bubble above its head the chicken would be thinking: "Cosmopolitan."

A year went by that way, and Toby concluded that Jim and Jayne were just platonic pals.

Toby was completely shocked, then, when Jayne told him she was going to marry Jim. On TV it would have seemed overwrought, but as reality it was deadening. Not that Toby ever wanted to have kids with her. He figured he was too old to have kids, and besides, being a photographer in a tiny town in remote Arizona was no way to afford them. But he loved her: there was no doubt about that. She liked his photographs, for one thing.

But Jayne's betrayal of Toby felt like nothing compared to the business with Jim. Toby had trusted Jim, and between them, with their twin fetishizing of the old Western values, they'd practically raised loyalty to godliness. Plus Jim was married! So Toby hauled out his letter paper and wrote Jim a letter. There was some debate about the exact wording, but the sentence everyone remembered afterward was the one in which Toby called Jim "a lying shit without honor." That was the way they talked: hyperbolic frontier honor talk, musketeer gunslingers demanding satisfaction or death.

Toby sent the letter. A year went by with no reply, and then one day there was a knock on his door. Jim. He'd ridden a motorcycle a thousand miles out of his way to face Toby.

As Toby remembered it, Jim was the first person to speak.

"Take your best shot."

Toby looked at him. "You gotta be out of your mind."

"I was offended that you called me a lying bastard without honor."

"Lying shit, actually."

It went on from there. Toby said he'd been in love with Jayne. He said Jim ought to have known that. He said Jim ought to have told him of his own plans. He did not apologize, though Jim claimed he did. He did say they should forget it and be friends.

"I don't think I can be friends with a man who slept with my wife," Jim said. Then he turned away, climbed on his motorcycle, and rode home to Oklahoma City.

Toby watched him go. Part of him wanted to laugh. Jim seemed to think his life was a novel. He'd been on his way home to Oklahoma City from Montana, by motorcycle, and turned a thousand miles out of his way to settle a question of honor. There was definitely a part of Jim that was lunatic. But it was the sort of craziness that made you believe he loved his friends for all he was worth.

Neither one of them thought to blame Jayne. There was an argument to be made that, if there had to be a culprit, Jayne was the one. But she was their obsession, and a man in the West never blames his obsession. It's not . . . Western. The Western manly thing to do is to put the woman on a pedestal and mistrust other men.

Nearly two years had fallen away since Jim and Jayne's wedding, and Toby still thought about her. But he was learning to forget her, too. A year after I met him in the diner, I called Toby back. He'd finished a novel about a rancher who introduces predators to his ranch. One of the characters "shares some speech patterns with Jayne," Toby said, "but that's it."

I figure he got some of what he wanted from her, in any event: a woman who made him remember part of himself. He was dating someone new up in Montana. He struck me as a civilized man.

I said good-bye to Toby in the middle of the road that afternoon and headed to Albuquerque. The light went from hard to soft. A few hours later I was sitting in a fancy bar called the Fire House, browsing the clientele—tall, tanned men and women who seemed to have no inhibitions—when a woman about my age sat down beside me and told me I looked sad, but that I certainly didn't look like I came from Albuquerque. I took it as an insult.

Her name was Lucy. She was treating herself to a few drinks for courage before a blind date. "I don't know whether to blow him off," she said. "I'm afraid I won't like him." She had black frizzy hair and a long face. I wondered what it would be like to go home with her, to her big body and an apartment where she lived with her kid and no more husband. But when I imagined being with her afterward, and imagined how much I would want to get away, and how there would be too many extension cords running across the carpet and how the lightbulbs would seem too bright and everything would have an unfamiliar smell, like vinyl or some unidentifiable food stored too long, and how I would look down and see my naked chest angled weirdly in the lamplight of a raw room and feel like a stranger even in my own body, and how we might disappoint one another, and how unlikely tenderness was—then there was no doubt I didn't want to go home with her.

I told her to go and meet the guy; she could always leave. I imagined she would spend the night with him. She was getting ready to go when she asked me what I did.

"I'm a writer," I said.

"You look like a writer," she said. "Writers are always drinking too much and smoking too much. But mainly writers are always wishing they were doing something else."

"Have you known many writers?"

"None." She drained her rum and Coke and had ice cubes still in her mouth when she said, "Stick around. I'll probably be back." I left immediately, heading for Oklahoma.

Jim had been back from his hunting trip a couple of hours when I knocked on his door. It was early afternoon, and Jayne was still at work. He'd bagged three deer and a Spanish goat on the trip. The goat's head was boiling in a pot on a Primus stove outside the back door of the kitchen. Jim wanted its skull boiled clean and white, in the European taxidermic fashion.

I expected a tall, thin, silent, wiry young man, but Jim was stout, wore a moustache and baggy jeans, and talked endlessly. He looked like a good old boy. His hair was brown, but his moustache was run through with red, giving the impression that his mouth was on fire. He was thirty-three.

For three hours straight, he leaned against the fridge and drank beer and talked. "Do you ever read some James Dickey poetry?" he said at one point. "'The Last Wolverine'? That's kinda my own personal credo. No Rick Bass. I hate that guy. He just pushes buttons. He pushes buttons like a pornographer. He reminds me of a Clark's Wallabee shoe. It's kind of a soft, comfortable, outdoor-looking thing."

A stuffed seal's head had been mounted above the fridge, a reminder to anti-hunting types that every meal was a transaction with nature. I counted seven other animal skulls mounted on the walls of the kitchen alone.

I asked about the bandage over his eye. This produced a long story about a bar fight he'd participated in after one of his partners insulted a mother-daughter duo in a bar. It was a complicated story, and I was never sure who won. From Jim's account, I gathered the highlight occurred when one participant said to an antagonist, "You just came to a chair fight with a bottle."

Jim didn't know his real father. He was by his own description low white trash. After he was adopted as a young teenager, one of his many uncles and surrogate fathers taught him to hunt. ("The finest man I ever met," Jim said. He was always saying hyperbolic stuff like that.) Instead of a .22, the gun that children traditionally learn to shoot with, his uncle gave Jim a Winchester Model 94, a center-fire deer rifle, for his twelfth birthday. Armed with this gun, Jim and his uncle would lie in the woods all night, hunting coons and fox. "Taught me all kinds of patience," Jim said. "I learned to hunt even when I wasn't killing anything. Eventually you learn that." For the first time in his life, he felt like he belonged somewhere.

When Jim mentioned "real guns," he meant $75,000 English-made guns, implements of exquisite destruction best employed with $20,000 hunting dogs. But he wasn't a snob about hunting. "If you really like guns, and you really like to hunt, then it's just a more perfect weapon. Beautiful game should be killed with a beautiful weapon. I've stayed out all night with coon hunters, and I've been with vice presidents of Shearson Lehman who've shot pheasant in Denmark. And they were all gentlemen. They didn't express it the same, but they were. And I guess what bothers me is guys who don't care—I guess you'd call them middle class. Middle class in the very sense of the words—neither higher nor lower. These guys who just want to latch on to something. Because that's not hunting. It's not just a passing fad. It's a passion. You just gotta do it about to the exclusion of everything else, save God and family."

He was holding his beer in his hands. "And it's the same for hunting itself. The only reason I ever killed something is because I wanted to get closer to it. And hold it and touch it and own it. That's really what it's all about. People say, I've got my moose. And other people get offended by that. But it *is* yours. Every time you think about it, it's like you own a piece of that country. It's like you locked it up. And some people are offended by it. But you *love* it. I was hunting a while back, going after a predator, a mountain lion. That's always interesting, because you are one, too. A predator, I mean. Anyway, I heard this branch snap. And I wished to be quieter and quieter, and to be able to move soundlessly. I was just wishing I was more of an animal. More of a mountain lion. You can't want something till you know it."

"Or vice versa," I said. I felt like a character in a Hemingway story.

"You can only pay homage to something by wanting to have it so bad that you'll hunt for it. That's what life is about. Earth is a proving ground. This place is a proving ground for a higher place. And it's up to you to prove yourself." He often declared what life was all about. It's not a habit I have much enthusiasm for, life being in my opinion nonsummarizable.

Jayne arrived home and immediately set about cooking some venison steaks. The last time I'd seen her, Jayne was an urban artist sort working for an art gallery. Now she was frying venison steaks in a mansion in Oklahoma City and working for the Voice of America.

At the table, after Jim said grace, we talked about Sooner society. We were using the heavy silver—"the divorceware," Jayne called it, left behind by

Jim's first wife. The house had huge gaps in it, spaces where furniture had stood when Jim and his first wife had owned it.

Jim was sitting at the head of the table. Jayne was sitting across from me. I found her quite attractive, in an eccentric, slightly loopy way.

"I'd shoot a man who had an affair with my wife," Jim said.

Jayne rolled her eyes. "That seems a bit extreme."

Jim liked things clear. He didn't like anything he couldn't control. He had no time for men who slept with other men's wives. Jim was the sort of guy who would probably forgive such transgressions if they were unavoidable and love-caused, or if they were done openly and the consequences were faced, but he didn't go in much for doing it and then hiding the fact and then doing it again. At the same time, he found his views on the subject to be extremely campy. He was a subtle, complicated man.

The phone rang, whereupon Jim excused himself and left the table. "I hope you're keeping notes about all this," I said to Jayne, after I heard his voice in another room.

"About what?"

"About life amongst the civilized savages of upper-class Oklahoma City. I always assumed that was part of why you came down here."

"It was at first," she said. "But Jim and I talked about it. He said that living something to write about it was different from living it because you were just living it. If you're always planning to use what happens to you in a book, your life is automatically one step removed from real passion. I think he's right. I think that's one of the differences, for instance, between him and Toby."

After dinner Jim invited me up to his study for cognac. The glasses were about the size of the Stanley Cup. Stuffed animals, elks, and other big-headed creatures stared down at us from the walls, their eyes popping out. One side of the room was occupied by floor-to-ceiling safes.

"Jealousy's territorial," Jim said. He was sitting behind his desk, leaning back and smiling, semi-drunk. "It's really about being an animal."

"Like the animal you hunt to own?"

"Jayne and I argue about this all the time. But I'm not trying to own her. I tell her that in my own backward way I'm just trying to protect her. Men see a look in another man's eyes that women don't see. To her it's a compliment. But to a man it's a slap in the face. It's encroachment. I understood exactly why that fucker strode up in the bar the other night. We were encroaching. We were encroachment men, slob men that night."

"Middle-class men, who just want to jump on a bandwagon, be somewhere or do something for less than passionate reasons," I said.

"Right. Anybody that's not in your party is an asshole. You're playing golf, that foursome up ahead taking so long to play? They're assholes. That other football team? They're assholes. It's just that old war-party philosophy of life."

"But we're not just animals, or assholes," I said. The cognac had separated my head like an egg. The yolk felt as if it had just splattered on the floor, which was why I was picking an argument with a gun lover. "Do we have to behave that way? And why condone it? There could be a higher consciousness than violence and intolerance."

"But that's how it happens in reality," Jim said. He was defending his idea, but he was still leaning back in his chair and smiling. He liked to fight. "Encroachment, the desire to encroach or protect against it, comes upon you *just because you're an animal that walks on its hind legs*. We're just human animals. And everything you feel, if you boiled it as stock, and simmered it down, it's all animal. That's why I like to hunt, that's why you like to have sex. Because it's what we are."

I think Jim hunted because he needed to know why he was put on this earth, what his presence meant. His hunting looked like cruelty, but in fact it was his philosophical method: He wanted to know how it felt to be hunted down to the point of surrender and complete fear, the only place where nothing is an illusion. He hunted to stalk his own soul, to learn the clues to his own behavior. It was a matter of balance, of understanding both sides. Hunting a cat to the end of the canyon was like falling in love and marrying a woman and having two kids, and then, one day at the wedding of your best friend, falling in love with another woman, and deciding to pursue her, even if it meant the end of all you had lived for.

Anything that tried to make Jim less than he was, for better or for worse, struck him as encroachment. To keep his fierceness at bay, he was adamant about manners, the way Southern men often are. "I can tolerate anything or anyone if you got manners—which I guess is just another word for consideration," he once told me. Consideration was another word for letting people be. Anyone who was unmannered enough to try to prevent you from being what you were was to be guarded against—with a gun, if necessary.

He loved guns the way someone else loves a lake or a job or a painting. The more polished a gun was by sensibility and care and history, the more he considered it a work of art. He talked about Holland & Holland, or James Purdey & Sons, the great English gun makers, as if they were close friends of his. He described their guns that "come into your arms like a welcome woman." He had just sold his own Purdey and ten other "good guns." I could tell it hurt him.

He knew all the rules. He knew that if you were invited to be a guest at a good Texan's quail hunt, you were expected to show up with a good gun. He knew TR—Teddy Roosevelt to non-gun owners—shot a Winchester, and that Hemingway used a Griffin & Howe. He knew Americans had become the best riflemen in the world because they had the opportunity to hunt on the open range. He knew not only what a buffalo rifle was, but which buffalo rifle from what maker in what year, at a glance.

He defended guns all the time. He often sounded like an ad for the National Rifleman's Association, and like most NRA members he explained the killing of innocent people as a fault of people, not weapons. To Jim's mind, a law that banned guns was a personal affront, offensive because it outlawed a part of his own self—the part of him that knew he

189

was capable of behaving responsibly with a gun, the part of him that earned and deserved his freedom, the part of him that tried to control his fate and that therefore made him noble, more than an animal. Dignity was a function of choice, and guns were a way of showing you knew how to choose. It was an argument of great antiquity, and it was tough to answer, even though Jim was sometimes intolerant, afraid of doubt, and the sort of man who occasionally said things like "One day I'll be shooting at a can, but the next day it might be a Mexican."

He pointed to the safes along the side of his study. "These are kinda all my shooters here," he said. He opened the safes and began to pass guns to me. There were dozens of them. It was like being in an exotic temple. One of his favorites was a .338-caliber Winchester-action Griffin & Howe. He kept a gun in the car, and another in his briefcase. He kept a 12-gauge in the bedroom ("the sound of high performance," he called the sound of a shotgun being cocked in the dark), and he left a .44 on the bookcase in the bedroom for Jayne.

He used them, too. Shortly after he married Jayne, he'd been celebrating his daughter's birthday when he heard a tremendous racket out front. He jumped up and ran onto the wide front porch of his house. Three "Mexicans" were driving their car in circles on his front lawn.

"What in hell are you doing, you stupid son of a bitch? There's kids here, you could hurt someone!"

The car stops instantly. One of the Mexicans gets out. "You want to fight?"

Now, Jim's a guy who learned to ride a motorcycle at the age of thirty-two by driving a Honda Trans Alp with a 600cc V Twin engine from Montana to Texas through Colorado, some *5300 miles in sixteen days* (including the detour to Toby's to demand satisfaction), and who said of the experience, "It was like having a .44 magnum right here, at my forehead, loaded and cocked, for the first two days, until I figured it out. Then it was great."

"Sure, I want to fight."

The Mexican smiles. He pulls back his shirt, which is white and hanging loose around his black pants, and pats his waistband. It appears he may have a gun.

What does Jim do? *He grabs his crotch.* Jim knows that a fistful of *cojones* is the single gesture most certainly guaranteed to drive the Mexicans into a rage. It is the equivalent of saying, Your balls do not exist.

At this, the Mexican is joined by two of his buddies. They have broken bottles in their hands. Meanwhile an older man named Stogie steps out onto Jim's porch. "I'll call the police," he says.

"Too late," Jim says quietly. "There's a gun under the seat of the car. Get it, and very slowly, hand it to me."

Jim starts to back up very slowly, toward Stogie. By now the Mexican fellow thinks he pretty much has Jim over a barrel. He thinks Jim—this pasty, slightly overweight, obviously soft and overprivileged gringo in a pair of tan chinos—is trembling and thinking, Dear Lord, what've I gotten myself into? He thinks Jim is about to start jabbering about how he didn't mean it, and please, Mr. Mexican, won't you please leave me alone?

Finally, Jim feels Stogie slip the gun into his outstretched hand. He quickly jacks one into the slide, aims the gun at the lead Mexican's leg, and fires, pulling off-target at the last moment so that the slug burrows into the ground a few feet from the Mexican's foot.

Suddenly a lot of things happen at once. The Mexican's friends peel off in the car. Stogie calls the cops. Jim runs down his antagonist—he's a teenager, it turns out, but Jim figures he'd better keep one of them, as a hedge against retaliation—and pins him face down with the gun pointed at his head. It's a scene from *Lethal Weapon*, except that it actually happens, and in one of the best neighborhoods in Oklahoma City, as an old couple shuffles up the sidewalk and the old man says to Jim, "That car that just drove away, that's our neighbor's car."

By now Jim's feeling pretty foolish. The kid is telling him who he's tangling with. His friends are gang members, they'll be back. "*Señor,*" the kid says, full of respect. "*Señor*, my friend, he's going to come back and shoot you."

"Well, if he does," Jim says matter-of-factly, again straight off a script, "you're not going to see it. Because if he even approaches me, I'm going to shoot you. And you'd better explain that when he arrives." *Señor*.

That's when he spots the carful of Mexicans on its way back, reloaded. They're a hundred yards away, and Jim is telling the kid to explain the circumstances, when finally the police show up and chase the carful of Mexicans off. The last time I spoke to Jim, he'd just run into the Mexican again in a McDonald's, four years after the run-in. Did Jim run away? No. He ordered his Diet Coke and sat down *at the table next to the Mexican fellow* and waited for something to happen. But the Mexican fellow didn't recognize him.

This is why Jim is never, ever going to give up his guns. You can give him all the anti-gun lobby reasons that exist, how guns increase the incidence of violence, how gun play is a form of psychological acting out, *ad infinitum*. But they don't make any difference, because odds are you've never had to apprehend a bottle-wielding, family-threatening hoodlum on your front lawn. Jim had to. He was the man.

Sitting in his study that night, telling his well-carved story, surrounded by priceless guns and other touchstones of the sad and noble history of American violence, Jim was in his element. It's only when he steps beyond his own home that everything changes. Out there, for instance, ragging on Mexicans is unacceptable. Nowadays the moral sanctity of self-defense is cloudier and much too male for the prevailing ethical orthodoxies, which are domestic rather than warlike, and men like Jim wear their steady confidence privately, with more than a few resentments.

Downstairs, the goat skull had boiled dry.

After Toby's wedding, Jim couldn't shake Jayne out of his mind. That very day, he thought: I'll marry her. I don't know how anyone who's married can be definite about such things, but Jim claimed he was. He couldn't say why he couldn't forget her. They were both rangy blondes, but he could take things further with Jayne than he could with MaryLee, who was practical and had a tendency to shut crazy notions down. He still loved MaryLee, but it was different. "I loved Jayne for me," he said, "whereas I loved my first wife for our children." Jayne seemed to have known him all his life. He could slip into her skin like a jacket. So he wrote her, and she wrote back. He knew some of his letters were pretty insane. But he wanted to say it all, get it out of him.

He knew Toby liked her, too, but he thought it was temporary, because Toby was still fresh off Debra's death, not to mention married to Nora. He also thought Toby wanted to be in love with Jayne because he, Jim, was in love with her. Toby seemed to need to ape him, to catch hold of some of Jim's trueness.

Before long Jim's preoccupation with Jayne was showing up at home. He was short-tempered, touchy about insignificant things, a malcontent, all the usual signs. MaryLee finally figured it out. "You're in love with that girl, aren't you?" she said. He couldn't lie to her.

The only people he told were Toby and another friend. "I love Jayne and I want to marry her," he said, once.

"Why don't you just stop doing that, Jim?" Toby said.

"I'll stop when she tells me to." It felt as if someone had tried to pump too much air into the room. But then they said to hell with it.

Their lives rambled on this way for some time: Jim wooing, Toby wooing, Jayne writing them both. Finally Jayne was commissioned by some bridal magazine to write an article about wedding gowns in Mexico City. She had a three-day stopover in Oklahoma City. She called Jim.

They stayed in a hotel. He didn't touch her until the very end. That was the first time they slept together. When she got to Mexico, he called her at her hotel and said, "Now will you marry me?" She said she would.

Shortly after that, word leaked out at the law firm where Jim worked. It was a conservative place, so rumors started to fly: Jim was getting a divorce, Jim was using drugs, Jim had a pony tail and had bought a motorcycle.

So Jim resigned before he was fired and went from making $100,000 a year to making nothing. That was when he started his own firm. He'd been buying and selling guns, including some of his own "to save my own company," he told me, very late one evening. He liked talking at night. When he first read Dickens, he thought it had all been written at night. "To save *us*."

Then Toby learned about the wedding and wrote Jim the letter about being a "greedy lying shit with no honor." Jim knew that wasn't true; he hadn't lied to Toby. He didn't write back, but Toby wrote occasionally to Jayne, asking if they couldn't be friends, and finally, a year later, one of those letters precipitated the thousand-mile detour by motorcycle to the small town in Arizona. Except Jim remembered it differently. The way Jim told the story, Toby welcomed him at the door and offered to shake his hand, and Jim refused. The way Toby behaved, it was like nothing had happened, which was not the case in Jim's mind. He didn't take lightly to having his honor impugned. Jim went to Toby's for either an apology or a fight and claimed he not only got the apology, but offered one of his own. Toby wanted to be friends again, but Jim said he couldn't see that. The worst part was that afterward, Jim didn't miss Toby much. That made him wonder if they'd ever really been friends at all. He worried that his judgment had been bad, and he wondered why that might have been so.

In any case, they hadn't spoken since. Jim had lost his best friend, his wife, life as he had known it with his kids (the most painful part), and his job—all because he stepped out after his heart. It was an expensive little tour. He prayed to God for guidance. "Do you know that the Father, Son, and Holy Ghost are one?" he said to me. "Because that's what your instincts are: God talking. You *know* what's right and wrong."

All I could think of were the big gaps in the rooms downstairs, ghosts of furniture.

During the days we went to Oklahoma City's gun stores. The stores were always the same. There were shells and guns and tins of artificial buck urine scent, Inside the Pant holsters, telescopic sights and scope cones, Paint Ball supplies, and all manner of implements of destruction and finesse, all dedicated to one end: giving you the edge over Nature. Meanwhile the conversation fluttered back and forth, kept male and undiluted by the mere presence of firearms:

"Jayne never had a dog. She says it always seemed like having a real stupid human being around. . . ."

"Oh, he's tough as nails. And funny as shit. And he's a great buck hunter. . . ."

"There wasn't anything of that motherfucker left. Vaporized the cocksucker. . . ."

We were in the last store, a small, well-lit place, when I saw a beautiful rifle. It was a little Remington .22. The fore-end underhold had split and been repaired, and it was secondhand, but it was a sweet gun, made with great care. The hatching on the stock was gorgeous and carefully cut. The owner, a friend of Jim's, wanted $300 for it.

I'd never owned a gun, but I wanted this one. There wasn't much hunting in my neighborhood in L.A., however, and a single-action .22 was not going to stand up well against an Uzi were I to find myself in the crossfire of a drive-by shooting.

"You should buy it," Jim said. "Go on. You know you want it."

"I don't have a permit."

"I have a permit," a stranger said. "I'll buy it for you, and give it to you."

"I don't need it," I said.

"I wouldn't be driving around the country without a gun," Jim said.

I came very close to buying it. I wanted to do something definite, to behave in a way that someone could spot and identify. I needed a symbol! If I bought the .22, I reasoned, I'd nail part of myself down: Someone who owns a .22, a fine old Remington to boot, he's a man who doesn't change with an unpopular wind. He's a *man*.

But then I thought about driving around the country with an unlicensed .22 in the back of my truck. I'll get stopped for speeding and the cop will discover this gun for which I have no permit, and I'll end up in jail. So I didn't buy the gun. For a while I regretted it. But I didn't want to live that way.

Afterward, we went to a café. Jim told me his "goal in hunting is by the time I'm fifty to have hunted all twenty-seven species of North American big game. I've got about fifteen so far. I try to kill one a year." He needed a polar bear and a jaguar, although he had no desire to bag them while they were endangered. He claimed the eleven-percent excise tax he paid on guns and ammunition provided far more money for conservation than did my contributions to Greenpeace or the Sierra Club. "I just want to say to some of these anti-hunting guys, just how much money have you spent on conservation in the past year? Twenty-five dollars for a newsletter? I spend thousands of dollars."

We ate our hamburgers quietly. There was a level of exhaustion in our conversation. He'd offered to fight in the Gulf War but was told he couldn't unless he enlisted. He didn't want to enlist. He didn't think he'd be much good at taking orders. So he planned to move to Wyoming or Montana or Idaho or Alaska. Now was the time. "In fifteen years you probably won't be able to own a handgun in this country, either," he said, and he seemed truly sad at the thought. They were wiping him out slowly and surely, the people who didn't understand.

We were about to go when he said the most surprising thing. I'd been talking about Patagonia, and how much I wanted to go there.

"I'm planning to ride my motorcycle from here to Patagonia," Jim said. He was excited. "Do you want to go?"

"What do you mean, do I want to go?"

"Do you want to do the trip with me?"

"I don't know how to ride a motorcycle."

"You could learn. It's not hard. Would you like to? I can't think of a better way to see it."

It wasn't the motorcycle, though. "I'll think about it," I said, but I knew I wouldn't. It would've been fun, terrible, frightening fun. But I imagined my (pregnant) wife's reaction, and everyone else's, too, how they all would say the same thing: bad idea, it's not your thing, you'll kill yourself. Jim, of course, knew this was a possibility; that was one of the attractions. Hunting, motorcycles, they were the same: he was chasing himself.

It was only after I left Oklahoma City that I understood he wanted to be friends. I suppose the trip would have done it. Jim valued loyalty because he needed it so much. He thought I was loyal. He wanted *from another man* what all men want and have a hard time finding, especially from other men—simple compassion. Not just compassion anyone can agree with—compassion for the hungry and the infirm and for kids who have only weeks to live and whose one desire is to go to Disneyland to say "I love you, Mickey Mouse!"—but the more difficult variety, for the greedy and the faulted and the mean and the angry. I think Jim thought he might get that from me.

I left that afternoon, after we got home. I packed quickly, threw my things in my truck, and walked into their kitchen to say good-bye. Jim and Jayne were holding each other under the seal head, talking. I knew right away I wasn't going to kiss Jayne good-bye. I wanted everything in plain sight.

"He almost bought this beautiful little .22," Jim was saying to Jayne. "He almost bought it. I was so proud of him."

Jayne wrote me a couple of weeks later and told me they'd named my bedroom "the I.B. Memorial Room," and that Jim often said, "You know, I miss old Ian Brown."

Of course that was before things got mixed up. In her letter, Jayne also thanked me for not telling Jim that I'd been to see Toby beforehand at her suggestion. "Thank you for not revealing a sordid little secret not worth keeping," I believe she wrote. But I wasn't sure what secret she was talking about, and I thought I'd better find out, so I wrote her back and asked. Jim was home when the letter arrived, and he opened it. Apparently they had a big fight. He said I'd lied about knowing Toby. Jim said he'd asked me outright if I'd met Toby. He said that I'd said I hadn't. I don't remember lying. I just never said I'd been there. I kept my mouth shut, to protect Jayne. I did what Toby had done, what Jim had done, what most guys eventually do, one way or another: I sold out a man to protect a woman.

I wanted to blame Jayne, but what was the point? If a guy wants to be your friend, you should either be one or not be one, and you should make clear which you are. After the Patagonia overture, I should have recognized the signs. It's a funny thing, a man's need: it sits there, silently, and never says a word, but gradually, unless you point to it and say it's there, it crowds you out of the room. Two guys trying to get to know one another: honestly, it's like some bad comedy routine, nearsighted deaf-mutes trying to shake hands and say hello.

12

Fishing and Marrying

*Ducks at dawn – Pursuit of the mysterious permit fish –
The role of the twenty-year-old swimsuit model in the
life of middle-aged man, and other questions of slavery –
A whale of a time*

"Coming left," Marshall said, and swung his gun up at some ducks. The
barrels coughed twice. From other blinds, I could hear other shots, distant
oofs in the wind.

"Too fah," Theodore said. "Too fah, man. You never hit that duck."
His voice was thick and quiet, a hedge of sound. He was invisible against
the black of the early morning sky.

I was sitting in a punt watching Marshall hunt. He was thirty-one, and
in a week he was going to marry a twenty-year-old woman he'd met
eight months earlier in a remote fishing camp on the Ventuari River, a

tributary of the Orinoco in Venezuela. The woman, a former Venezuelan model, didn't speak English. I'd asked her what she modeled, and she'd said, "Bathing suits and earrings," which was a charming combination. Body and face. She was back in Key West, where Marshall lived.

The punt was floating in a blind of reeds on thirty thousand acres of blackwater canals owned by the Edisto Club, a private hunting preserve in low-country South Carolina. The canals had been built back when Edisto was a rice plantation; only the guides like Theodore, third- and fourth-generation descendants of the slaves who had worked the paddies, knew how to regulate and navigate its waters. The guides and the former slaves shared the same exotic oyster names—Dillguard and Maniogault and Swintou and Bluette. Theodore had worked at the club for seventeen years. He was somewhere between thirty and sixty and parted his hair down the middle.

Twenty minutes later, Marshall bagged a hooded merganser in two shots. It was small and blue and had a hairy head.

"A duck," Marshall said, "hard to shoot." This was not true. "But no points at the dinner table."

The excitement dissolved him. His cheeks sagged, and his face lost its outline. I think it was the killing that took it out of him.

I could hear other hunters laughing. Fitz, our host at the Edisto Club and an old friend of Marshall's, said that once you'd done enough of it, hunting was less about the hunt than about everything that led up to it. Daybreak made all the men feel our own dawns again—not nostalgically, but as a thing itself, as, say, morning damp, or the cold of a shotgun stock against a cheek, or even, in one case, the smell of a pre-dawn cigar. All those sensations were a way of feeling young again, or at least a way of getting back to feeling something that hadn't changed.

I counted the shells. Twenty-three in the bottom of the punt. But now two gadwalls flew over. Boom, boom. The female stalled in the air, leveled again, not realizing she was hit, and dropped from the sky. She was still alive, hit behind the wing. We could hear her splashing and drowning in the water. The male flew on.

Theodore squawked his duck call. A minute later the male returned, looping over the blind to find his mate. Marshall hit him clean in the head. He was dead by the time he smacked the water, killed by an act of loyalty.

Theodore poled us over to get the ducks. The female was still upright, her head dipped over, as if asleep or drinking. Theodore threw her in the punt.

"Would you like a candy bar, Theodore?" Marshall said.

"Yes, suh," the black man said.

"Baby Ruth or a Mars bar?"

"Baby Ruth, suh."

"There you go."

"Thankee, suh."

It was light now, and the air was clean, save for lovely puffs now and then of spent gunpowder. The ducks were piled into the boat at my feet. The gadwalls were brown on brown, duns and caramels and grays like a fine old fall coat, with russet in the wings of the male. The female's bill, resting on my boot, was shut tight, a shiny black spoon upholstered in patent leather, very finely made. In the early days of the club, in the twenties, a party of six often took 175 birds. Now members were limited to three. The members were Southern businessmen from Richmond and Atlanta and the like. Most were back at the lodge already, playing cards and talking about why Sam Nunn would make the best president, and how treacherous sexual harassment had made their world. They had a specific view of things. It was like talking to a set of antique chairs.

We floated in. The lodge was surrounded by angel oaks draped with Spanish moss that in the early morning hung still like guilt and fear from the branches that reached out there. I was climbing out of the punt when Marshall said, "Theodore. Do you like duck?"

No reply.

"Theodore."

"Umm."

"Do you like to eat ducks?"

"Oh, yes, suh."

"They're yours. You can have these ducks."

"Thank you, suh."

No smile, no visible resentment, just a blank. A space behind the eyes. A black man saying "Thank you, suh" as he and his family had been saying thank you to white men for centuries. Marshall saw it too, and I knew it made him feel unsteady. He admitted the South was still widely bigoted. He'd been raised there and thought blacks and whites got along better in his part of the country; they weren't as violent in their distrust of one another as they were in the North. On the other hand, he admitted economic dependency had a way of taking the spunk out of anyone. "I wouldn't hesitate to say there are still slaves in the South," Marshall said. I agreed. I wasn't a Southerner, but the drive through on my way to Key West had shocked me. In town after town I saw no blacks until I went around a corner, down a road behind a bar, and found them all there, living on two streets, in shacks. The men stood still and silent and peering in their rutted driveways when I walked by. Theodore was one of perhaps four black men I had met and talked to at any length in the two years I had lived in the United States. It was not too great an exaggeration, in other words, to say it was possible to be a forty-year-old white man in the United States and not know a single black man well.

Marshall's pals George and Fitz are out on the water beyond the Marquesas, twenty-five miles due west of Key West. Hemingway probably liked to fish here. George and Fitz are arguing about where they're most likely to find permit and tarpon. Taken on a fly, tarpon are arguably the most thrilling game fish known to man. Ichthyologists theorize that tarpon migrate across the ocean bottom and eat crab and cuttlefish as they go. The trouble is, no one knows where they migrate from, where they migrate to, or even if they actually migrate. They may just go offshore a bit for the summer, like rich guys in yachts. As for permit, which are almost as exciting as tarpon but even more difficult to find and hook, no one knows anything at all about them. Permit are the Garbos of the fish world.

Fitz, the one with the silver hair, is in his early fifties: George, rounder and red-haired, is a few years younger. George was a national champion motocross racer not so long ago and liked to hunt coyotes from a helicopter. Or he'd load an extra-powder elephant gun, climb on his 750 cc Husqvarna motocross bike, and wheelie off across the desert to blow up prairie dogs. George would line up one of the varmints in the gun's massive telescopic sight; take aim; squeeze the trigger; and then watch through the sight as the prairie dog suddenly became a cloud of pink vapor. But all that was when George was younger and less mellow.

Nowadays he and Fitz are content to fish for tarpon or permit about a hundred days a year—in part because fly-fishing for tarpon and permit is to fishing what a three-point shot to win the game with half a second left is to basketball, except that with permit the excitement can last fifteen minutes and with tarpon up to half an hour, provided one is as talented a fisherperson as George and Fitz are, which is unlikely. On April 1, 1993, for instance, Fitz landed a 195-pound tarpon, obliterating the previous world record of 188 pounds. This is the end to which Fitz's entire life has been dedicated; it's a measure of the sort of man he is that he released the fish into the water, thereby depriving himself of the formal official record, which requires a fisherman to kill his catch.

The other reason George and Fitz are fishing is to test the permit fly George designed. The fly is called the McCrab and sells for $7 in George's tackle shop in Livingston, Montana. He makes them on the premises when he isn't taking George Bush fishing.

The McCrab, not surprisingly, looks exactly like a rubber crab. But the McCrab is more than a mere fishing fly. It is a meditation on the form of perfection, because a fly that attracted the mysterious permit would represent one of the pinnacles of accomplishment of the human fishing mind—that is, it would signify that George was able to *imitate prey better than anyone else.* As in some love relationships, this is pretty much the major point in fly-fishing.

There's only one problem: the McCrab doesn't work. It doesn't attract permit with ease or regularity. The only fly that does that is the Del Brown yarn fly, so named after its inventor, who has used it to catch 218 permit, far more than anyone else. Fitz and George have about twenty-five apiece. The Del Brown fly is a long whiff of tan and green yarn sewn with chartreuse thread around brown tail feathers and white rubber legs. It does not look like a crab. It looks like an earring an eight-year-old made in art class.

"There's an extraordinary difference between this fly and George's fly," Marshall says, holding a Del Brown. He should know: Marshall makes his living as a fly-fishing guide in Key West. "An extraordinary difference. With this fly the permit starts shaking and gets all nervous. Whereas with George's fly, it's more, 'Uh-huh.'"

Marshall has known Fitz and George for years; Fitz is almost a second father to him. Marshall poles his boat over to theirs. Marshall's boat is a Hewes Bone Fisher, a low flat skidder seventeen feet and ten inches long—"ten and a quarter when it's wet," Marshall says. It draws six inches of water under power, eight when poled by hand, making it perfect for tarpon and permit, which like to tool about in the coral shallows and grass flats that surround the keys.

But nothing's happening fishwise. Overhead someone appears to have strewn clouds like balls of trash across the hot sky. Marshall is standing on the boat's platform, a raised bridge across the stern that lets him pole and scan for permit and tarpon. He's wearing polarized glasses. So am I, but I can never see the fish he says he's seeing.

This, Marshall says, is because I'm trying too hard. It's a problem I have. The secret to seeing fish is not to look for them directly, but rather to scan and let yourself be diverted until you spy one out of the corner of your eye.

"The trick is to meditate until the images appear," Marshall says. "That's how to spot fish."

I try to meditate. I try to imagine mysterious permit I have never seen. I imagine my shoes smell of fish from standing in a whaler full of angry permit, slithering across the bottom of our boat like lusty wet babies. I imagine we're heroes when we pull up to the wharf. I wait for the fish to appear on my indoor screen.

Nothing. *Nada.* I open my eyes. The whaler doesn't smell of fish. There isn't even a drop of bilge in the boat; it's as dry as bone, as dry as the hot salted air of Key West in the winter. Even the sea seems to be laughing at me, its wetness a taunt. I can't see the fish.

"George," Marshall says, "there's something large and white and about twelve feet long out here in the middle. . . ."

I look. I see nothing. It's hopeless. My mind wanders. I try to imagine what it's like to spend a lot of time with a twenty-year-old earring and swimsuit model. It's almost as hard to imagine as it is to imagine permit.

"Marshall," George says, watching the water, "will the 'cudas go for the yellow permit fly?"

Why does he want to know this? Does he want to catch a 'cuda? Or not catch one? It's impossible to tell. The answer is one of ten million jigsaw pieces of fisherman logic Fitz and George have been fitting together since they first threw out their lines as boys, fishing for catfish on cane poles.

"No, probably not," Marshall says. "But I had a big yellowtail hooked once on a yellow permit fly."

"Ummm," George says. George and Fitz are not interested in yellow-tail. They're interested in permit, and maybe 'cuda. If you don't have any information about permit or 'cuda, you have nothing to say.

Marshall can see George and Fitz are too hung over to entertain us. We say our good-byes, kick up the motor, and head around to the other side of the Marquesas. The boat buzzes over the flat water like a big fly. Marshall keeps looking out over the horizon and changing course; I'm not sure what he's following.

By now it's two p.m. The sun's whacking down, the water looks like a sheet of paper.

Suddenly things happen.

"Over there," Marshall says. "See that disturbed water? That's a school of permit. Quietly, move up to the bow and cast that crab in front of them. About ten feet. But be gentle. They spook at anything."

The surface of the silver blue wetness is flashing dark crescents, slander hinting over the water. It's hard to see the permit except when they dive, when an edge of steel-blue tail fin knifes out of the water like a T square. Permit surfacing! There must be ten of them. You can see them, but you can't see them. Very Zen.

My crab hits the water with a smack, and the permit vanish. Then they come back. I blow it again. They disappear and reappear again. This time Marshall tries, but even his cast spooks them. That makes me feel a bit better. Then Marshall says, "That's generally considered to be the hardest thing to do in angling, to catch a permit on a fly," and I feel like a dope once more.

But this encounter with the permit spirit is enormous, emotionally. Two hours have flown by. We turn around, spent, and speed straight across the water for Key West, as if, having come almost too close to the unseeable, the ethereal permit, the unnameable answer itself—having come so close, we need the firm feel of land. We've had some kind of close encounter. We're as spooked as the fish.

I watch the sun begin its fall to the west. The yellow sky is like the first coat of an abandoned painting. All the sunsets in Key West are like that, as if to say, this painting doesn't have to be completed: there'll be another sunset tomorrow, and another the day after that. We have no ambitions, and for the moment that feels like freedom—the great strength and weakness of all places where the sun shines most of the time.

When I first met Marshall, he'd just graduated from college. He studied classics. In those days, he described himself as having three interests: repairing motorcycles, fly-fishing, and translating ancient Greek poetry. I admired each pursuit—the hands-on mechanical expertise on the bike nicely setting off the braininess of the poetry—but it seemed a suspiciously perfect combination until I realized Marshall was simply trying to get laid. He admitted as much, which I thought was to his credit. Apart from that, he was tall, brown-haired, and big-jawed, in the manner of Southern nobility. His mother's family were Cubans and, according to Marshall, had most of the verve.

After college, Marshall went to work for an entrepreneur who published magazines about horses. Marshall was twenty-three, financially successful, and living with a co-worker from Connecticut. He still liked fly-fishing, poetry, and motorcycles, but he spent most of his time studying spreadsheets.

Then he disappeared. The next time I saw him, he'd quit his job, moved to Key West, and was making his living as a fishing guide. "Up north I felt like I was living in school, in a police state," he said. "It was no way to live a life." Now he signed his letters Capt. Marshall Cutchin, worked long hours and countless fishing competitions, and sang the glories of fly-fishing for permit and tarpon. But his girlfriend was unhappy. "She misses the horses," Marshall said. She was leaving him.

For a while after that, Marshall turned up intermittently on the East Coast, generally in a happy state of disrepair. At one party a tall Italian girl named Maria was hanging off his neck. She finally swanned off to the bathroom, and Marshall dragged me into a corner. "I keep saying to these women, can you promise me you'll be faithful to me? But they always say no, I can't. So then, for me, it's over."

I thought he meant it as a joke, but it wasn't. He was willing to be faithful for life, and he wanted the person he married to want that too. In any event, I said, "If you're looking for a woman who can resist other men, Maria's not exactly a great choice."

"I know," Marshall said. "But I have a fatal weakness for someone who keeps reaching for my crotch." It was only years later that he admitted he was paranoid about faithfulness because he was so unfaithful himself.

Now, in Key West, he seemed happier, closer to the ground. His skin had lost its poochy pallor from his horse magazine days. I told him I'd been hanging out with car thieves, researching face-lifts, and dancing in the woods with a bunch of fat naked guys.

"The men's movement," Marshall said. "That's pretty much for forty-two-year-old attorneys who belong to national associations, isn't it?"

"Many of them have managed to get this far in life without having a single introverted thought, yes."

"Well," he said, "I'm getting married."

Her name was Anaitz. Twenty. I couldn't seem to get that detail out of my mind. He invited me to the wedding.

"Are you happy?"

"The difference between a twenty-year-old woman and her thirty-year-old counterparts is mind-boggling. Another planet. The older women suffer from this idea, an old idea, of who they should be at thirty, professionally and otherwise. Anaitz is younger, so she can wait to have kids. I wasn't ready any earlier."

In the fishing camp on the Ventuari River where they met, Marshall and Anaitz had a conversation Marshall found difficult to forget. "You are all I need," Anaitz said. She looked delicate yet healthy, brown hair and brown eyes and tanned skin and darting ways. She resembled a small sleek otter.

"Well," Marshall said to her, "I appreciate that. But you're young. I know what I thought when I was twenty; I had very definite opinions. And my views have changed considerably. Yours probably will, too. And you should recognize that. I just want you to admit it."

"Yes," she said, finally. "I know. But all I need is you anyway. You've already given me more than I need."

She said he was a genius, agreed that life would change, and then insisted it wouldn't because he was who he was. Marshall believed her. Who can blame him? "I knew she might leave me," he told me. "Because she was younger. But I knew my interest wouldn't change. And that's what was reassuring."

I was surprised how physical Marshall was with Anaitz in public. Then I remembered he'd always been that way with women, and that it had always surprised me. I've always envied men who could touch women easily and gracefully, but on Marshall it seemed like a hunger. He could be so analytical and abstract, but when Anaitz walked near him he wrapped both arms around her waist. He pressed her brown skin against his face and closed his eyes. Every morning he walked half a mile to the Cuban bakeries to buy bread she liked. She had made him more emotional, plugged him in.

I worried Anaitz would be bored in Florida. She never spoke English, although she seemed to understand it. Marshall said she did it to keep her distance until she came to know Anglos better. In that I thought I saw stubbornness, willfulness. But she touched Marshall all the time, fingered the hairs on his arm, the hem of his shirt. She was like a little breeze playing around him. She also spent hours watching dance programs on television. She stared directly at the dancers, never blinking, mesmerized.

She was doing that one afternoon when I left Marshall's house and walked down Duval Street to the center of town. I was almost there when I discovered I'd forgotten my wallet. I turned around and walked back. Marshall's house wasn't far, but I was tired, and I walked slowly.

I stepped into the house, and there was Anaitz dancing alone, still in front of the television. She was standing in one spot, her arms fanned out, hands tilted up, her short white skirt swirling. I excused myself, found my wallet, and rushed out again. Anaitz, who never stopped moving to the beat, waved good-bye.

On the walk back into town, I wondered: how long could Marshall keep her desire and yearning at bay, this slim twenty-year-old dancing woman who lived on music fed into her chambers through an electronic tube? A woman with her own desires, separate from any man, desires she could aim in any direction and at anybody and satisfy or not satisfy at will. I think he loved her because she hadn't been corrupted by orthodoxy.

But anything can rush into a blank space. Of course no one could hold that against her.

That evening, we ate in Key West. It was a locals' place, a Cuban restaurant, with varnished golden wood booths and red leather banquettes. Marshall told me that one afternoon at the fishing lodge on the Ventuari, he was approached by a Yanomami tribesman who walked straight out of the bush. The Yanomamis were one of the last tribes on earth not to have had contact with "civilized" man. But they learned fast. The Yanomami who came into the fishing camp wanted to trade his daughter for a job.

Anaitz was sitting on a bench beside Marshall, looking sweet. She kissed his shoulder while we talked and Marshall translated. Occasionally she said something in Spanish about the wedding.

Anaitz's girlfriends all thought Marshall was a real catch. "They thought he was handsome, and an American," Anaitz said to me. "In Venezuela, being American means you have lots of money."

"What else did they think of him?"

"They can't get beyond that," Anaitz said.

"Did you think he was rich?"

"Oh, no, I knew he was poor."

Marshall laughed.

"Well, no, it was nice, he was an American. But I liked him, too. He was *muy macho*, and smart. He talked. Not like most."

"Do you want to travel?" I said.

"Oh, yes," she said. "New York. Oh, yes. And Europe."

"And Sweden," Marshall said. It was a silly joke, and I laughed, and then Anaitz asked him to repeat it, which he did, and they laughed together.

We went home after that, and I went to bed and thought about Marshall and Anaitz. Months later, when I told anyone about Marshall, about this thirty-year-old white guy who was marrying a twenty-year-old Venezuelan who didn't speak English, a funny thing happened. A lot of women who heard the story grew incensed—incensed with me, for telling them the story, and then incensed with Marshall, a man they didn't know, for what they called "taking the easy way out"—taking as his wife a woman who was younger and "less of a challenge," someone he could "dominate" in return for bringing her to America, someone whose main virtue was her youthful fetlocks. These possibilities crossed my mind, too, but to me they seemed unlikely. "When you put it on paper, it's easy to think you see premeditation," Marshall explained when I mentioned these doubts. "But at the time, when it's happening and you're falling in love, you're so caught up, you don't have the time or the energy to premeditate anything. Unless you're a genius, which I'm not. One of the appeals of Anaitz was her lack of any of the usual premeditation." Anaitz didn't seem like a pushover to me as I lay in my bed, thinking about her; I hadn't seen Anaitz making his supper or doing his laundry. She seemed if anything to have Marshall in her thrall, and she seemed to enjoy it. Maybe Marshall *was* Anaitz's ticket out of South America. Maybe that was one of his attractions. But maybe he knew that. Maybe that was one of the attractions she held for him: she was someone he could save, be useful to, be needed by. I decided it was none of my business.

But I still couldn't sleep, so I got out of bed and went to find a book. I was brought up short at the foot of the stairs by Marshall, hugging Anaitz fiercely in his arms, and swirling her across the living room. He must have gone around three times. Then they saw me, but they didn't break apart. I felt like a dog in a room where it's not supposed to be. From my bed for a long time afterward I heard them laughing. They couldn't wait to be alone.

Before he met Anaitz, Marshall had been dating a woman before whom "I prostrated myself," he said one day. "I got lower and lower. Finally, I got so low she told me to get lost." Enter Anaitz, twenty, with no English.

"So Anaitz is easier than an American woman your own age?" I said to Marshall one afternoon.

"Well, maybe," he said. "But she teaches me as much as I ever learned from any other woman. She's amazing, how open she is. I found a woman who had real feelings instead of just a set of philosophical principles."

Everything Marshall thought and did boiled down to his passion for fishing. For Marshall, life imitated fishing. There was a print of tarpon feeding on other fish in his bedroom, alongside others of a fishing hole, fishermen, and boats. His toilet seat had lures imbedded in its Plexiglas. The rod rack in his study held thirty rods, a lacrosse stick (I thought of Spence, that absurd lie he told in the club in Palm Springs; I could still see the woman's blank, disbelieving face), pheasant feathers for tying flies, a model of his first permit taken on a fly, a fencing foil (he was fencing for a while in Key West, but fishing made a regular schedule difficult), tarpon flies, and a copy of *The Mortal Hero: An Introduction to Homer's Iliad*. For Marshall, fishing was about dropping a line into a habitat other than your own and seeing what you came up with.

"I don't think we fish to catch fish," he said one afternoon. We were drinking beers on his back steps in front of a stain of purple bougainvillea growing up the cedar shingles of his garage. "I mean, we can approach it from a different angle. Why does the Pope wear the ring of the fisherman? Why do they call the Pope the fisher of men? And in the Grail legends, the man who guards the grail is the Fisher King. Why is the fish the symbol of all the Christian Church? It's all about the idea that fish represent a subconscious element of the human personality—an element that needs to be lifted up and elevated to a higher place."

"You mean, like, the soul," I said, swigging my beer.

"Yeah." Marshall waited a moment, then continued. "I think it's a wistful attempt to capture an emotional experience that's not normally accessible to a lot of men. It's sublimated, in the Jungian sense that human beings tend to sublimate feelings that are unwelcome in their culture. Their bloodlust, for instance. But that's only one thing. They could be sublimating their own self-questioning, which is always an unacceptable, disruptive thing."

"From what Fitz's wife was saying at dinner the other night, even fishing is too disruptive." Martha, Fitz's wife, maintained tarpon were a penis substitute—for Fitz, but not, alas, for her, unless the catch was good, in which case Fitz came back more gung-ho than usual.

"Women have something that's comparable, maybe," Marshall said. "Maybe it's the sacrifice of their body to the creation of another human being."

Women fishing in their bodies for babies. That was interesting. Briefly, I thought about my wife back at home.

Do you know what I remember most clearly about the time I spent in Marshall's company? I remember a night Marshall and I shared a room at the Edisto Lodge. We were about to turn out the light when Fitz stepped in to say good night. I remember he was wearing striped silk pajamas; I thought that was pretty elegant, for a hunting lodge. Then Fitz noticed a pair of Anaitz's underpants in Marshall's bag, alongside Shamu, her stuffed whale—"so you don't forget me," her note said.

Fitz held the whale up. "What are you supposed to do?" He paused for effect. "Is this some form of substitute?"

We laughed, which I suppose sounds harsh. But we weren't laughing at Anaitz. We were laughing at our own susceptibilities—three men drawing the wagons around ourselves in the absence of women. Tenderness was a dangerous and frightening thing to a band of men alone in the woods, and we did our best to scare it away.

13

The Leather Man

Death and friendship – An investigation of shocking
darkness – Left vs. right, pitching vs. catching, and other
lessons in submission – Terror and fear of the
heterosexual Author – Dog collars and manacles –
Sadness and consolation

By the time Ryan looked out the window of his Manhattan office for
the twentieth time, rain had been falling for twenty-four hours. Why did
it have to rain the weekend he moved Hans into the new apartment?

Eighteen stories below in Penn Plaza, the streets were black and
shining. New York's war cries (the incessant whining of trucks backing
up, the shouts and sirens and brakings and accelerations, the sighs of taxis
washing through puddles) seemed louder in the rain.

The rain would make the move tougher. Twenty years' worth of Hans's books, and all those slippery steps.

At least the new place didn't have any stairs.

The move was Hans's idea. The new place would be easier to navigate once he went off his medication. Three of Hans's friends were coming over Saturday to help. What were their names, anyway? Ryan barely knew them. That might be bad, a day with strangers, moving his dying lover. Tuesday Hans would come home from the hospital. He'd signed a three-month lease, but a week was more realistic.

Hans didn't want to die in his old apartment. The Sufi group he met every week in the Village might have planted the idea. Hans had lived in the same building for ten years. He'd been in New York for sixteen, arriving from Paris, full of plans to dance and write plays. The men in Hans's life changed, his projects changed, his body changed, but the place where his books were, where his work had been done, stayed the same. Two years had passed since he'd been diagnosed with full-blown AIDS.

Hans had been positive for ten years. Ryan still tested negative. It was a fluke, because he'd done everything. After the first year, Hans's virus went into remission; the lesions went back where they came from, into his body. Hans began to write another play, about Patient Zero, the Canadian airline steward alleged to have been the first carrier of AIDS. Hans let Ryan read it, and Ryan thought it was the best thing Hans had written.

Then a week before Thanksgiving Hans lost the use of his right arm. He had a lesion, the AIDS specialists told him, on the left side of his brain. He had a hard time getting out of bed now, and wore six intravenous tubes at once. He lost fifty-five pounds and had full-blown pneumonia. His sister paid a round-the-clock nurse. Ryan traveled as little as possible.

Ryan kept Hans's illness in a box in his mind, and he tried to keep the box shut. Nearly all Ryan's close friends had died from AIDS, ten in the past year alone. He deliberately tried, as if he were memorizing directions, not to feel much about them. Loss had become a routine, a schedule.

Hans's dying had been stuffed in the box in Ryan's brain so long it was almost a relief to know the whole thing was nearly over. Ryan felt guilty for feeling relieved, guilty for surviving. Both forms of guilt were common.

Only when Ryan wanted to talk, and found the person he wanted to talk to no longer there, did all the deaths depress him. He forgot they were gone, and then when he remembered it was like banging into something at slow speed in your car. He didn't try to control these sensations: he let them roll in, he let them bleed away. The disease and everything about it were unpredictable, like some wild drunken uncle: the way it worked, the way you reacted, the sorrows and sometimes even the painless hole you felt when somebody died. Anyway, it was Thanksgiving, and Christmas was coming. He had plenty to think about.

And it was the weekend. He could go out. Ryan always went out on the weekend, AIDS or no AIDS, Hans or no Hans. He'd go down to Rawhide and the Eagle and the Spike, the leather bars in Chelsea, tonight and again tomorrow night after the move, and on Sunday, too.

Sometimes when the box popped open in his brain unexpectedly he didn't want to go out, but that was rare. It sounded callous, but one thing about being a gay man in the time of AIDS: you didn't have to buy that solitary remorse crap. You didn't have to believe anything or agree with anything, which created a strange liberation at the center of the tragedy. You could admit you loved going out, loved the attention you got at the bars, the way the looks from other men made you feel desirable, admit that it made you feel alive when all around you there was death. It was almost a political stance.

Ryan had always loved a party. He refused to stop. He worked long hours and traveled half the year as a senior vice-president for one of the world's largest travel conglomerates; he needed the release. The irony was that this week of all weeks, the week Hans was likely going to die, had been one of the luckier ones of Ryan's life. On Monday in London, after his appointments, he'd picked up two tricks in a leather pub and almost had to fight off a pesky third suitor. Wonderful inventions, leather pubs: the ambiance of Olde England, in a contemporary leather codpiece setting. The next day, in a sex club in San Francisco, he scored twice. Not bad. Almost as good as four in a day, his old record, which dated way back to the days before everyone started to die.

I'm shocked by Ryan's cavalier behavior while his boyfriend dies. Then I run into Jaffe, who's in a complete state. He's so ashamed of himself he can hardly speak. "Oh, God," he says, "I am such an asshole. I am the world's biggest asshole."

Jaffe has just returned from visiting his best friend's wife in a hospital in Vancouver. She's thirty, and she's dying. An exotic disease of the lungs. Jaffe has known her all his life. He dated her once or twice.

But this morning when he walks into the dying woman's hospital room, her best friend, Theresa, is sitting at the foot of the bed. Theresa's clever and athletic. She's a very specific kind of woman that every guy knows: a woman you know fairly well, and admire, but whom you can never pursue because you've known each other too long. You have no illusions about one another. Still, she's the kind of woman who wears cable-knit hunter green cardigans that do good repressive things to her lively body, and which you imagine unbuttoning, to her vast relief, in your fantasies, which tend to occur after your second glass of wine at brunch when your friends are over.

Anyway, Jaffe has always had a secret thing for Theresa, and there she is at the foot of her friend's hospital bed. Jaffe sits down in a chair, and says hello, and he and the dying woman get to chatting. Death is close; she has a month to live. Thirty years old.

Then Jaffe notices Theresa's combing her hair. Theresa's slim hands, almost silvery in the cool air-conditioned hospital. He can't take his eyes off her combing. It's turning him on. And bingo—he has an erection! Right there in the hospital room! At the foot of the bed of his best friend's dying wife! He's beside himself with shame, but I understand, and I understand Ryan, too: unquenchable life in the face of unavoidable death.

Ryan didn't go out of his way at work to hide the fact that he was gay or that he had an extensive leather fetish. He didn't hide, but he didn't brag.

If Ryan had been less competent, he might have worried about the professional consequences. The truth was that by the mid 1980s, he was convinced his homosexuality was an asset: the fact that Ryan was openly gay was a sign to his boss that Ryan could be counted on to tell the truth. Anyway, the travel business was easier on gays, unlike the financial services industry, where most of the gay men he knew were still in the closet. Brokerages were packed with them.

He didn't look rough enough to be a leather freak. In the mirror at the Ferrante Salon, submitting to his fortnightly clip, he looked like what he was: a senior vice-president for corporate strategy. He traveled the world, which made the prospect of Hans's death easier to bear.

Though in truth, Hans was the one who pulled away. Hans had said as much, and Ryan had talked about it with his friends. Hans wanted Ryan to be free of him. That was like a dominant, when you thought about it: dominants, or tops, as they were known in the leather community, liked to think they were in charge. Hans was putting everyone at a distance, Ryan included. Maybe Hans saw death as an island: you waited for everyone to leave for the mainland, and when you were finally alone, you died.

Maybe the haircut was a mistake. Erica, the hairdresser, had to pinch Ryan's hair close to cut it. Still, in a leather bar, your hair could never be too short. It was easier to wear a hangman's hood. Hoods were great, especially the ones with the zips over the eyes and mouth. There was the element of surprise, for starters, and somehow eliminating the senses above the neck enriched the ones below the waist.

He watched Erica hover about his head, reducing him. No, by day, in a charcoal suit and a tab collar and tasseled loafers, a striped shirt and a peacock tie, he looked like every other executive in Manhattan. Maybe his hair was a bit shorter, maybe he was a bit fitter. He eyed his beard. His cheeks were going gray in a quite becoming way.

At the hospital that evening, Hans was barely registering. Ryan kissed him good night, drove back home, and changed into his leathers while he waited for John, who was in New York from Detroit for the weekend.

At Rawhide they drank eight beers and eight shots of root-beer schnapps. The shots were free: the bartender always threw one in when Ryan ordered a beer. He never knew why, unless it was because he was such a loyal customer. By eleven he and John were feeling rabidly uninhibited. They left Rawhide and staggered to the Eagle.

After two more beers, Ryan and John left the Eagle for the Spike. The Spike was in the next block, hard on the waterfront, and one of New York's premier leather bars.

Ryan relaxed visibly in the Spike, as he always did. He could feel the packed bodies emanating their heat, the energy of the looks he attracted pouring into him, making him feel wanted and rooted beneath the buzz he could feel in the surface of his skin. Every man in the Spike dressed to be masculine: black leather pants, leather chaps, leather shirt, leather tie, leather cap, leather vest, leather bandolier, leather jacket, all backed against the wall to create a gauntlet for newcomers. The ideal was a stereotype of masculinity, but that was the point: it was a pose, an ideal, the way a statuesque and beautiful woman is an ideal to any number of men.

This was where he'd first seen Hans. He remembered the night clearly. It was a Thursday. He was standing in the corner, in his circle of friends. Everyone tried to commandeer this, the best cruising spot in the bar: you could see everyone coming and going through the door, and you could see the back rooms as well, not to mention the doors of the toilet.

Hans sat at the bar, in full leather, including leather shirt. He talked to no one. Ryan's crowd noticed him: Hans was gorgeous. Then he left. Saturday he was there again, same spot at the bar. Only this time Hans walked over, parted Ryan's friends with his hands, and introduced himself—to Ryan. He was tall, with a muscular dancer's body. He looked like a man in every sense of the word, and he took Ryan's breath away. They went home, but from the start it felt like more than a trick.

Ryan looked at his watch. It was two a.m. John had brought some amyl nitrate. Poppers: Ryan hadn't used them since . . . well, at least since the Mineshaft closed, or maybe it was after it was falsely reported that poppers caused AIDS. They were great. He loved the rush, the high swoop.

Ryan could hear John chatting up a former paramour. Christ, John could talk. "I hope they don't show the Mr. Leather America contest videos," John was saying. The Spike played videos all night on its TV sets. "That would be awful."

John had been in the contest. John was Mr. Leather Great Lakes 1992 and had advanced to the Mr. Leather America finals in San Francisco. A photographer asked him to pose for a photo spread in a leather magazine. "Okay, West," the photographer said, shooting all the time, very glamorously, just as John had imagined he would, "show me what you've got! Make it hard! Make it big and hard!"

"It is hard," John had said.

"Well then, turn around, show me your butt . . . that has to be better."

The next day, Saturday, moving day, Ryan was hung over. He was paralytic. But the moving went quickly. Hans's three friends turned out to be decent guys; they made jokes about Hans's thirty boxes of books. The phone rang every half hour, and it was always Hans, calling from the hospital. He was about to die, and he didn't want them to leave anything behind.

There were so many things to do when someone was going to die. Like a baby, really, in reverse. They'd put Hans's house in the Catskills up for sale the week before. The cat had been given away. Funeral homes, invitations to families and friends.

By the time they finished moving it was four o'clock. Ryan thanked everyone and went jogging. He tried to go every day. Afterward, he drove to the hospital, calmed Hans down about the move, drove home, went into his bedroom, opened the closet, and set about deciding what to wear out to the bars.

Hans owned twenty-three pairs of boots, and each pair ran to $300. That was just the footwear. He'd bequeathed it all to Ryan. Clothing was what separated serious leathermen from jaywalkers and voyeurs and the vanilla couples and the breeders taking a holiday stroll in the wild.

Leather pants. Yes. But not chaps, they were too hot. Leather shirt? Ditto. A black T-shirt was better . . . and a leather bandolier, this thin one, to formalize it. Yes. Knee-high boots. No cap, not tonight. The leather jacket with the pads and the lacing in the back . . . oh, yes, a thin black cord, fashioned into a garotte, for neckwear. A nice touch. . . .

He bought most of his gear at The Leather Man, Inc., on Christopher Street. In the late 1970s, Christopher Street was the spiritual main street of New York's gay community; now, to the extent it was gay at all, it was tourists and teenagers visiting sexual Disneyland. The clerks played it up, too. "You want to see anything," a clerk said to me the first time I walked into the store, "I'll show it to you."

In The Leather Man that was no empty threat. The shop was two stories of leather sexual paraphernalia. Upstairs, street level, were $300 leather pants and $600 leather jackets and chain-mail bras and four sizes of cock rings, condoms, hitches, straps, and even stuffed animals (Sir Bear, dressed in leather). Downstairs the more erotic specialties reigned: $65 full latex hoods (latex was big, especially the flesh-toned latex T-shirt that made its wearer into a mannequin, which was the whole point: with AIDS everywhere, the just-off-the-morgue-table feel was in vogue), Iron Duke Servus Rubber Co. waders (for pee-fests, a big deal in New York, where golden shower dominatrixes did a thriving trade advertising late at night on community access cable), ball gags (to suppress shouts), slings (to suspend) "lifelike cocks with swinging balls," speculums to dilate the sphincter (yahhhhhhh!!!), ball stretchers (leather thongs to wrap around the scrotum), eighteen-inch-high black leather boots with full cordex lacings, leg irons, hand and neck manacles ($386 in chromed iron), zippered leather or metal scrotum pouches, spiked and studded codpieces and dog collars, leashes (these were common at night, even on the street in New York), penis pumps, and two clerks watching an explicit pornographic gay videotape on a TV at the counter.

Cock rings were the best-selling item in the store. The penis pumps (often known as enlargers) were almost as popular. They were manufactured by the San Francisco Pump Co. For $138—a sum of money gay men parted with more willingly than straight men did, a clerk informed me—the system consisted of a Plexiglas tube with a valve at one end that attached to a suction pump. "You should get the two-and-three-quarter-inch-diameter size if you've never used it before," the clerk explained. "You should get it a little larger so you can get it off. Then, as you progress, you can move up. Easy does it every time. Feel a good pressure, but don't overdo it. Pressure should be relieved every few minutes or so. Allow about forty-five minutes to see any results. We recommend a two- to three-hour session." The effects, the salesmen in The Leather Man were too eager to explain, were "long-term temporary." One man had pumped up regularly most days of the week for a year and a half and had gained an inch in length. It seemed like a lot of trouble.

The trick was to place the tube over one's penis, extract the air through the valve, and watch one's member fill the vacuum. You could do this alone, or you could dress up in your leathers and go down to Cellblock 28 in the Village on Pump Night, some Tuesdays, and stand in groups of two and three around communal pumping machines and get off, by hand, on the pumped-up largeness of yourself and your co-pumpers. Afterward, guys liked to sit around drinking coffee until they became aroused again, their tubes still hanging from their engorged but detumescent members, albeit unattached from the communal pump. This gave Cellblock 28 the appearance of a science-fiction porn movie set. Or maybe it was the fake "dungeon-like" cobwebs in the corner. A lot of men who dropped in on Pump Night were in their forties and fifties.

Ryan didn't spend much time analyzing his sex life: analysis was considered infra dig, unmasculine. While straight men retreated to the forest and pretended to be Vikings or Iroquois, gay men wanted to be Marlon Brando in *The Wild One*. But when a leather devotee did judge his sexual habits, it was always by the degree of intimacy they revealed. Ryan said he did what he did simply because it felt good, but the deeper appeal of being tied up and masked and gagged—his particular fondness—was the way it proved he trusted his partner and could be trusted with his fantasies in turn. They were intimate, even if they'd met an hour earlier.

Fantasy was everything. The point of the gear and gags and gizmos was to lure fantasy to the surface. If your particular mask or darkness was to be overwhelmed by a man, and raped, then you could act that out with, say, manacles. It was a common enough wish for a lot of gay men whose sexual desires had once been a source of shame and who fantasized being "forced" into sex. If you longed for sex to be anonymous, or to be nothing but sexual, if you wanted to be all cock or no cock at all, The Leather Man had the hood or the dildo or the cage for you. Every sexual eddy and current imaginable—the wielding and yielding of power, the most detailed obsessions, passing fancies—could be magnified and transformed into a concrete event, acted out, made real, seized and owned and controlled. You felt like a conqueror, you could be one. You felt like a crotch-sniffing dog, you could be that, too.

If the get-ups were sometimes laughable, the intention was most serious: to be masculine, you had to be your true self, cock rings and all. A real man was honest and true to himself. Is that such a bad definition? Some sexual practices seemed faintly preordained and somewhat intellectual for my white-bread tastes: in my experience, good or exciting sex meant going somewhere in your heart or mind you never expected to go, which seemed difficult if you were already dressed up as, say, a charioteer. But that was just my opinion.

And if you didn't have a personal kink you needed to iron out? Not to worry! The leather world was like a tux rental shop: time-honored classics were also available. In addition to the daddy-son fantasy, there was the more garden-variety master-slave arrangement; the bear-cub scene (men who sported great forests of body hair, and men who wanted them); the circumcised-uncircumcised split; various penis size *aficionados*; "chubby chasers," who liked fat people; nipple and chest enthusiasts; piercing addicts (those who preferred their nipples, penises, glans, scrotums, vulvae, navels, tongues, and sacral fundi pierced by metal hoops, Prince Albert rings, leather thongs and bolts); and the boot and uniform lovers. Uniforms were considered extra-disciplined.

The full array of possible gay sexual fetishes was like the number of stars in the universe: unknowable, and potentially infinite. There was a box of colored handkerchiefs on the front counter in The Leather Man. Next to the handkerchiefs was a chart entitled The Partial Hankie Code:

Color	Left Pocket	Right Pocket
Black	Heavy S&M Top	Bottom
Gray	Bondage	Bottom
Navy	Fucker	Fuckee
Red	Fister	Fistee
Light Pink	Dildo fucker	Dildo fuckee
Purple	Piercer	Piercee
Light Blue	Wants head	Expert sucker
Yellow	Pisser	Pissee
Hunter Green	Daddy	Son
Beige	Rimmer (oral analist)	Rimmee
Brown	Scat top (fecalist)	Scat bottom
Charcoal	Latex fetish top	Bottom

COLOR	LEFT POCKET	RIGHT POCKET
Orange	Anything top	Anything bottom
Light Green	Humiliater	Humiliatee
Robin's Egg Blue	69er	69ee
Rust	Cowboy	His horse
White	Masturbate Me/Novice	M'bator/Novice
Kelly Green	Hustler	John
Coral	Shrimper (foot fetish)	Shrimpee
Lime	Dines off tricks	Dinner plate
Lavender	Likes drag queens	Take a guess

Ryan folded a gray handkerchief neatly and tucked it into the right rear pocket of his jeans. He checked himself in the mirror. He was ready.

He checked himself in the store windows on the way to Rawhide, too. He was lucky he was tall, because the competition was fierce. Every leather freak in New York wanted to be a bottom, the submissive one. The most aggressive, in-your-face city in the world suffered from a surfeit of sexual submissives. By day they were executives like Ryan, making decisions that affected the lives of thousands of people. By night they were desperate to have someone tell them what to do. In San Francisco, where everyone was much more laid back at work, bottoms were a minority.

Within twenty minutes Ryan was engulfed in the warm human soup of Rawhide. He thought about the week to come and his schedule and suddenly the box opened in his head and he remembered he was going to Boston on Wednesday, to Newton, the wealthy suburb where he'd grown up and where his mother and father still lived.

His father was dying of cancer.

He didn't want to go, not with Hans just back from the hospital and alone for the first time. But his father was dying of cancer.

Pretty soon Ryan was talking about his father. He said he hadn't really spoken to his father in eight years.

"But he's your father," I said.

"But he wasn't. That's the point."

Ryan had grown up in the Newton debutante scene, dating girls, even sleeping with them. He thoroughly enjoyed heterosexuality. Only after he graduated from Haverford College and finally slept with an acquaintance who came on to him—the second time, Ryan said yes—had he understood he preferred his own kind. The intensity of the passion convinced him, the physical sensation that he was returning to a deeper, more ancient longing, as if he were grasping the root of himself.

Now his gayness was a part of him and he part of it. He really almost loved Rawhide, its dark wood and American flags, its pool table and the motorcycle mounted on a block in the middle of the room. He stopped by every weekend. For all its leather-clad toughs, Rawhide was much friendlier than any straight pickup bar, where men and women were snappish and hostile. Men whistled to one another, sang to new prospects, hugged, kissed, and gave each other nougies—head rubs performed with the knuckles. At Rawhide everyone knew why he was there, and no one felt ashamed.

Dennis, a tall, thin blond man with several days' carefully tended growth on his face, came over. "Remember Rick?" Dennis said.

Ryan looked at the newcomer. He was a short, heavyset but powerful-looking man, black, and he had a moustache.

"Sure," Ryan said, and smiled.

"You'd better," Dennis said. "He fisted you for lunch last fall." It was a joke.

Ryan was thirty-nine years old, and he'd slept with five hundred men—in his experience about average for a gay man. He never much liked anal sex and being penetrated, and to that he attributed the fact that he was still alive. He'd had serious love affairs, too, which ran like a disco bass line under all the tricks.

Hans didn't mind. They were friends and companions first, sex partners second. They solved the fidelity-boredom conundrum by having sex with other people. Ryan had sex with a stranger, mostly guys he met in bars, at least once a fortnight. It was a regular thing. A survey in *The Advocate*, the gay weekly, claimed only one in ten gay couples was monogamous. On the other hand, Ryan figured, they were probably a lot more honest about it than straight men. Infidelity always complicated things, but complication was part of its charm. Sex was almost a hobby for Ryan, like cooking or jogging, even under the shadow of AIDS. Ryan never had trouble being friends with his former sex partners, the way straight men did; most of his friendships had begun as sexual encounters. He had sex with someone and realized he was better suited as a friend than as a partner. Sex didn't threaten Ryan's relationship. It just wasn't always linked up to love. He knew the difference between love and an orgasm: having one with one man didn't affect having the other with someone else.

The real question was, how could he keep it hot? A new person was hot and erotic; if you'd done it a hundred times, it wasn't. A new man reminded him he was desirable. The narcissism of being attracted to those who seemed to be attracted to you was not just an observational feature of gay life: in Ryan's mind, it *was* life, the machine that drove his own.

Tonight Ryan knew a lot of the faces he could see at the Spike. Odd, recognizing most of a room of five hundred people, weirder still to have slept with a lot of them.

In the old days—the seventies—when wearing leather implied you knew a lot about sex, whole floors of clubs were devoted to particular practices. You could be chained to a wall on four, or peed on in a bathtub on six, as if you were riding the elevator in Macy's. An air of continuous erotic abandon prevailed. Nowadays an evening at the Spike entailed standing around talking and drinking and eyeing the crowd. Sex was private, for later. Nowadays, safe sex ruled, within a wide frame of what was considered safe. You decided what level of risk you were willing to take on and went from there, rather like skiing a glacier. Masturbation was back in a big way. Oral sex was considered safe at this point in time; fisting less so, but it was said to be possible to fist safely. No one talked much about specifics.

What hadn't changed was the importance of sex, even with the specter of the plague everywhere. Sex was Ryan's last hedge against terminal respectability—especially the respectability AIDS had ironically brought upon the gay community. Sex was still mysterious. It was always a draw. What else was there, really? Ryan had never wanted children, and without them there seemed little reason to be domestic or even heterosexual. The gay men he knew—in New York and London and Provincetown and San Francisco—were his family.

I watched Ryan move through the crowd. I was leaning against the heavy door of the Spike's beer locker when a bartender edged past me and disappeared into the frigid room.

"I could go in there and kill him."

A short, stocky troglodyte—all chest and no legs, shaved head, wearing leather chaps and a black leather sleeveless vest and a leather peaked cap—was standing next to me.

"That's true," I said.

"I'd make him drink the case of beer and then kill him. Be the best fifteen minutes of his life."

"You can't be that bored." I was scrambling. He sounded like a psychopath. Then I realized he was inventing a fantasy. I was supposed to play along.

"In this place?" he said. "All these little girls standing around in their outfits, I've seen every one of them before." This phrase I had heard before: S&M was often known as Standing and Modeling among the hard-core leather fiends. They had no time for their passion as a fad. "I haven't seen you here before."

"My first time."

"Standing around, doing nothing, dressed up in their leathers for their mirror parties. The frustration of not having sex must be more satisfying to them than actually getting fucked." He took my left hand. "Married?"

"Yes," I said with relief. I wanted to declare my loyalties. It was a peculiar sensation, being a straight man in a gay bar. Every time a man looked my way, my indignation rose. That wasn't supposed to happen . . . if only these sick pigs could control their . . . I realized, with a start, that I was staring into the source of my own homophobia. You ought to be flattered, I told myself.

"How long?"

"Three years."

Now he was the one to relax. We fell to talking. His name was Joseph. He had a Ph.D. in English literature from New York University and wrote murder mysteries. (Hence the bartender fantasy.) He was literary, pleasant, and without doubt extremely dangerous.

"Why are you into leather?" I finally said.

"I like to tie guys up and fuck them as roughly as I can."

"Why does that appeal to you?"

"I like the aesthetic. They look so beautiful." It wasn't only sex he was after, but a metaphor, meaning, emotions he could name and interpret— art, in other words. He tied his lovers up and violated them for the same reason Robert Mapplethorpe photographed his gay friends fisting one another and submitting to pain and pushing their fingers up a glans: he wanted to formalize his lust, its itch, its dirty stirring, establish it in a knowable, recurring scheme. That way, even lust lasted.

"Well," I said. "I have to go."

He gave me his card and told me to call. During the day, he taught high school in the Bronx.

Across the room, meanwhile, Ryan wanted to leave. He wanted to walk back to the Eagle and talk to the fireman. The fireman liked him. Ryan could tell. The fireman had definitely been cruising Ryan. He walked by, back and forth, three, four times, as if he were a model train on a track.

He wasn't easy to miss. The fireman was wearing knee-high Wellingtons and a huge black rubber New York Fire Department slicker with reflective yellow stripes on the sleeves and carrying a black fireman's hat in his hand. Never mind that Ryan was dressed up like a leather knot himself, and that the man he wanted to go home with was a grown man dressed up like a fireman. Never mind that this was what they did every weekend. What made them feel wanted made them feel like men. We were no different that way.

I thought my foray into Ryan's world might have ended there, but I was wrong. One afternoon in The Leather Man, I leaned on the counter and listened to a man named Bolton describe a fisting.

He was in full flight. Bolton had faint sideburns, light blue eyes, a red goatee, and a dirty brushcut, giving him the washed-out quality of a piece of fabric left to fade in a patch of sunlight. He spoke wetly, occasionally spraying his words, as if his tongue was too thick for his mouth.

I found the act he was describing difficult to talk about, think about, speak about, contemplate or even write about. I knew I was being squeamish. Plenty of books, including several popular guides to male heterosexuality, urged women to explore this dark but promising land and claimed prostate massage was "a pleasure not to be missed in life." The Kama Sutra insisted fisting was one of the most sacred of acts. It was definitely compelling.

But I can't bring myself to describe it, not that, not the way Bolton told it, in loving detail. I can't go into detail about the black sheets over the plastic ones, or about the tubes of this and gloves of that, or about the three-way cock-and-ball toy that was as complicated as an airport freeway exit system, or about the spanking fantasy beforehand in which Bolton reprimanded Ted, his boyfriend, at the "office," or about the removable tattoos Ted sometimes wore to surprise Bolton, such as the eagle flying toward his anus. I can tell you this: a fisting took four hours. "It's the sort of thing that doesn't always work out a hundred percent of the time," Bolton said. "You really have to listen to your bottom." He meant Ted, of course. "But the whole thing is very satisfying on a spiritual level, because it requires an enormous amount of trust."

Afterward, exhausted by the debilitating exposure of soul that fisting demanded, by the oiling of the terrifying machinery of their lust and the progress of their shame, Ted padded off to have a shower, and Bolton did the laundry. It was his gesture to Ted, a nice thing to do. *I'll clean up, honey—you made the dinner.* After all, that was why they did it. They loved each other. By that act, their submission to one another was total. It reminded me of another act of complete physical submission—the birth of a child. After such knowledge, forgiveness.

I tried not to flee the shop too quickly that afternoon.

The rain was on and off in New York that day; water squawked and boomed against the underside of the cab I finally found, but ticked softly down on the roof. Johanna, my wife, was in town, in our hotel room. She'll be asleep by now, I thought.

I looked out the window at the city in the rain. Traffic was bad, and we lurched uptown. Strange, the way I'd left the store so suddenly, as if it were a mine and the air supply had given out.

Maybe it was a mine. The same thing had happened a few nights before, after I wandered into a club in the Village. There didn't seem to be anyone there; a few men by the bar, nothing more. I wandered through a passageway, down a stairway. Disco music was playing. Then I was standing in a concrete bunker under a faint gray light, the light of dreams. Then I saw: I was surrounded by pairs of men in one another's arms, strangers, heads together, coats open, hips apart, kissing and shaking. That was when I turned and fled. Fled, not because of what they were doing, but because my isolation was finally overwhelming. Because that was as far as the road went in the opposite direction from women and children: it ended in that daring, ghostly basement of men; you could get no further away. The taxi dropped me and I ran up to the room where Johanna was asleep. I undressed, and lay in bed, and reached my arm around her, and felt the tight drum of her belly, swollen under the white hotel sheets like a surprise.

Hans died five days later, on a Thursday. The following evening, Ryan hit the bars as usual.

14

Cahl Jooniah

Lamaze and the degradation of the male soul –
Revelations concerning the passage of wind – The list –
Why women control men's lives

There are twenty-four of us in Lamaze class, twelve pregnant couples in our thirties. In Class One we introduced ourselves and volunteered our impressions of pregnancy. (Lamaze class is nothing if not voluntary.) The guy with the brown hair and the Filofax said, "I've been smoking a lot of dope and I started going to topless bars." For two and a half hours every Thursday night throughout the Lamaze class, he roots in his Filofax. I can't tell if he's trying to schedule his baby into or out of his life. Strung out in a circle, we resemble a fleet of blimps and their mechanics.

Each week the teacher writes out what we'll be covering in class:

Introduction
Names
Due Dates
Discuss Names
Other Children
Other Facts
Self Work

The categories terrify me. Names I can do, but Other Children seems premature, and I become unpleasant if Johanna broaches the subject. She wants to talk about having more; I think we ought to see what one is like. "I'd rather have had none than just one," she says. I didn't know that at the time.

The Lamaze method, the teacher explains, entails psychoprophylaxis, "the prevention of physical pain through psychological means." Which is to say, a form of brainwashing. We'll use formal breathing patterns to "interrupt the fear/pain/tension cycle." The lessons are full of unfamiliar, medieval words: the bloody show, crowning, the almighty fundus. In the instructor's diagrams of the pregnant uterus, the babies are always huge and orange.

The woman to my left hands me a plastic chart the instructor has passed around. The chart consists of ten gradually enlarged holes: this is what will happen to my wife's cervix. The first stage, at one centimeter, is a tiny disk smaller than a dime. Ten centimeters is a dinner plate in some California restaurants. The instructor holds up a rag doll that is attached to a rag placenta by a rag umbilical cord. She asks the men questions. "Coaches," she says, "what do you do in the first phase of labor?"

"Go and play pool," someone says. It is a man, of course. It is impossible for a woman to be flippant during a Lamaze class.

The instructor is a short busty woman with long dark hair. She's a neuropsychiatric nurse with a master's degree in sociology who became a birthing coach because "I had such a wonderful birth experience." She has three children. She is exactly the sort of overeducated walking amnesiac I was afraid would be running the Lamaze class. Her name is Magda. Perfect.

A week later. Actually, I realize, Magda's quite attractive. She makes eye contact.

The women like to catch up on each other's physical news at the beginning of class. They jaw about cramps and gas and bowel movements as if they were discussing stories in the newspaper. The men listen in amazement, gazing upon a new species of talking tomato plant. We are "the coaches"—never men, or husbands, just coaches. I'm certain this is to desexualize us, to make us safe for fatherhood, but I'm wrong. Some teams aren't married, so Magda uses the politically correct term.

Anita, the blabbermouth in class, had a half-hour contraction last night. Every week it's something new with Anita. I know more about her cervix and vagina than I do about my own testicles. "I don't think I'm going to make it to the last class," she says. She describes herself as "an entrepreneur" who makes "vintage baby clothing."

My mood is a car on a slick road, front-heavy and unpredictable. I veer so often between panic and the overwhelming urge to sleep that panic seems familiar. Sometimes I imagine getting up, walking out of the class, throwing my skis in my truck and disappearing for the rest of time. I keep remembering in starts, the way we usually remember bad news, that I am about to make a huge self-sacrifice. It is as if I am willingly throwing myself on an altar to be burned. But when I put my arm around Johanna, I immediately feel calmer. I have no idea why. It never used to happen this fast.

But sometimes, another, even less familiar calm overcomes me: as if finally, in becoming a father, I have a destiny I can't avoid. This idea has been creeping up on me. Marriage, real estate, work, writing, country, friendships: all these I could leave, I presume. But I'll never not be this child's father. Why doesn't that feel like prison? Why does it calm me?

At break, all the men rush out to buy coffee in the vending machines. I tried to memorize the numbers. J2, espresso. J3, coffee with whitener. I still drink coffee at night. I think: I still make unpopular choices. This brainless idea actually passes through my head.

"Who's afraid of the episiotomy?" Magda says. I raise my hand. I am the only person who does. Then I realize this was a question for the women.

But it's true: the episiotomy terrifies me. I see it, vivid and red in my mind, at night in bed. The episiotomy is a surgical incision made in the rear of the vagina to widen the birth canal. This vagina was my private place, and now some person I don't know plans to build an extension onto it. Not that her vagina was ever mine, but she lent it to me, and me alone. Well, not any more. Everything belongs to everybody now. These days when I read the paper, I find myself more sympathetic to capitalists. Suddenly I want to own something.

Wednesday, several packets of stool softeners arrive (by courier, no less) from Celeste, a friend of my wife's. Later Celeste telephones. Apparently the stool softeners were extras left over from her last pregnancy, and hey—why not share them?

"You'll need them," she says. "I can't believe they didn't tell you about that. Don't you have hemorrhoids? No? Well, you'll have them afterward. You'll really need those stool softeners."

Like a lot of ambivalent mothers (name one who isn't), Celeste is routinely driven berserk by her three children. "Having kids turned out to be so much less romantic than I imagined," she once confessed to me in a moment of desperation. But to admit this to anyone else would be to admit that motherhood is something less than the greatest accomplishment mankind can ever know. Having recently promised the next twenty years of her life to proving this proposition true, she can't afford to say it might not be. So she eats her terror and becomes a walking booby trap of resentment. She makes everyone discuss "poopy" for hours. Poopy is as diabolical and intractable a dilemma, apparently, as peace in the Middle East and starvation in Somalia. You may not know much about poopy, or even care much about poopy, but in Celeste's company you don't have any choice: poopy is all. "Having kids is going to totally change your life," she said to me the last time I failed to sidestep the conversation. She bored the words into me, drilling into my brain with the heat of her temper. "Whatever you think, it's going to be different. They're great, but your life is going to be totally different. I mean, totally different."

But Celeste wants to have another baby. Sure. Does Celeste have a vacuum at the center of her being, a terrified hole that keeps collapsing on itself as she tries to find some purpose? From within the hole, having children seems like the easiest way to fill it. Having kids is the thing to do. "Everybody has kids," she says, and it makes me want to yell at her. She thinks her motives are selfless. Not long ago I saw Freddy, her husband, for the first time in a year. He said hello, shook my hand, and began unstrapping giant cartons of baby clothes from the roof of his Volvo wagon. He carried them over and dumped them, one by one, into my arms. "These are for you," he said.

The longer the baby clothes lay around his house, the longer Celeste would whine about another child.

Every class, Magda repeats everything we've already learned, but I can't remember anything. This is why two and a half hours of information are stretched out over six weeks: Lamaze classes are baby-sitting for adults during the most stressful weeks of their lives.

I'm dissociating like an amoeba. When are we supposed to call the doctor? After two hours of thirty-second contractions that are five minutes apart? Or when the contractions are five minutes long and thirty seconds apart? No one else seems to write anything down. Plus, my minor crush on Magda has now become a major distraction. She is more than attractive. She's a sex goddess.

Johanna, on the other hand, is now quite large. Nevertheless, I experience waves of lust for her whenever I can get near her. She sleeps surrounded by no fewer than five pillows. One supports her leg, another her back, another her breasts. It's like sleeping with a refrigerator wrapped in moving quilts.

Every class kicks off with a game. One night we split up into two groups, "coaches and moms," and make a list of our likes and dislikes about pregnancy.

We separate. The men aren't bashful. They want to talk; they just don't have words for what they're trying to say. It's like listening to chimps.

"I worry that I won't ever read another book," I say.

"Right," someone else joins in. "Plus gaining weight myself."

"One of my dislikes," says the only black man in the group, "is her mood swings."

"No sleep."

"My wife has to stop working."

"Child-care costs, health care."

"I feel like I finally have a destiny I can't avoid," I say. This is my contribution.

"Right, that's the worst."

"I meant it as a positive thing."

"Guys," says the man writing the list down. He's heir to a vast sports fortune. He won't have any goddamn problems affording a kid, the spoiled creep. "We need a few positives."

Silence. "Well," says the fellow with the Filofax, "there's the extra tax deduction."

"Sex is not the greatest," someone says. "I mean, there's desire, but that stomach doesn't exactly make it easy."

"But," says the Filofax man again, ever the optimist, "you get more blow jobs."

"That's true," says a guy who's a talent scout for a record company. "Now you get them whenever you want."

More blow jobs goes on the list. In fact, it is the only positive fact of pregnancy, on which the men are unanimous. After fifteen minutes, the men's list is as follows:

LIKES

A destiny you can't avoid
Can get on first on airplanes
Feeling the baby move
Talking to the baby
Solidifies relationship
Father's Day
Buying toys
Feeling of luck
Teaching
Sharing
Someone to pass things on to
The chance to try to do better than your father
Wife's happiness
Choosing a name
Closer relationship with in-laws and parents
Excitement of family members
Additional tax deduction
Blow jobs
Big breasts
Excitement
Pride

My favorite is "Feeling of luck." But our list of dislikes runs longer:

Destiny you can't avoid
Wife's mood swings
Male weight gain
No time to read
Lack of free time
Unable to sleep through the night
Wife not going back to work
Decisions (child care, health care, pediatricians)
Financial worries
Repetitive questions from wife and others about the pregnancy
Not being able to party with one's wife
Drinking alone
Going to bed early
Worry that baby won't be healthy
Sick of shopping for a crib and baby bumpers
Cost of day care
Competency of day care
Choosing a name
In-laws, parents around more
Hassled to read about pregnancy
Sisters, friends saying "Just wait"
Lack of paternity leave
School decisions
No sex
Cutting back on selfish activities (skiing, vacations)

We break and return to our seats. The women have their own list. This is a conservative crowd: all but one couple are married, and all but two of the twelve women have taken their husbands' names.

LIKES

Feel baby moving
Creativity increases
Energy increases
Ultrasounds
Going to the doctor
Better hair and fingernails
Hearing the heartbeat
Don't have to clean the house
Your husband helps more
More help from strangers, who are nicer
Excitement about having a living baby in you
An excuse to buy clothes
Bigger breasts

The women have many more dislikes, too, most but not all of which
are physical:

Breasts too big
Scared of labor pain
Size of body
Clumsiness
Heartburn
Sleeplessness
Leg cramps and back spasms
Can't sleep on stomach
Constant peeing
Nasal congestion
Fear of stretch marks
Fear of death

People asking too many questions
Always feeling warm
Bitchiness, mood swings, crying, depression
Bad maternity clothes
Big ugly underwear
Restricted activities
Shortness of breath
Strangers no longer find you attractive
Limited shoes and clothes
People giving advice
People's expectations of what sex the baby will be
Lack of concentration, spacing out
Acne
No glow, never feeling sexy, lack of desire
Financial worries
Fear of never getting one's body back
Life as you know it is over

"And flatulence," the woman reading the list says. "Not just having a lot of gas, but also the fact that our gas seems to give our husbands tacit permission to fart at will as well around the house." She pauses. "Actually, that was our only unanimous observation."

The men look at one another. The thought speeds across our foreheads: *so, you fart around the house.* Not that pregnancy was required, but now everyone knows. Pregnancy could never be called cerebral.

Listening, I suddenly know what has been left off the guys' list: pregnancy has made me fall in love with my wife again. Is that what I am feeling, love? A warmth I am half-ashamed of? Like admitting that I enjoy sitting in the bath? Or, more precisely, like sitting in the bath, replacing the hot water every once in a while, and not getting out, and—this is the part that I think may be love—not telling myself that I should get out of the bath and do some work, not telling myself that I'm losing my self-discipline if I don't, but instead sitting there and saying, *Don't freak, it's okay to sit here in the bath simply because it feels good?* Can somebody please tell me if that's love?

If it is, none of us thought to say so. Maybe we didn't have the words for it. The closest we came was "your relationship is solidified." *Charmant, n'est-ce pas?* Or maybe that's what Peter, the big guy with the moustache, meant when he said "talking." He works as a TV editor at a big network. I smiled when he said it, and he thought I was mocking him. "No, you know," he said. "I mean, talking in bed and stuff. Just stupid stuff." I knew what he meant.

Before the third class, my mother calls. My mother is seventy-eight and cannot believe I am enrolled in Lamaze class. "Why do you want to be there at the birth?" she says.

I'm not sure I have an answer to this. Once I heard a woman on a TV call-in show say that it made for "kinder men." The best reason I have heard so far, though, was a remark in one of the birth films we have been watching. It was made by an older man in his fifties. "I found out there was more to life than just golf, or fishing, or other things that I just love to do," he said. "I discovered I can generate some of that love right here."

But my old ma is not buying this. "Do you think your father attended these classes? Not on your life. Do you think he watched your birth? Not a chance. I think it would have put him off sex for the rest of his life, gazing up somebody's hoohaw."

This possibility has occurred to me. The sheer thought of a head passing through my wife's vagina—an act, I have read, that some women say is the most erotic sensation of their lives—turns my forehead to rock. The pain! Sex, her vagina, is no longer simply pleasurable; it has consequences, and the consequences will be indelibly indented on my sexual focus. I think this is what my friend Stephen, a three-time father, means when he says, "Stay up at the head. Don't go down and look."

And what will this child look like? Will it have my wife's features or mine? It could be a real nightmare, if it lands my eyes and nose and teeth. And how much will it look like me? How many times did Henderson call me that first year of his daughter's life, hissing into the phone, trying to keep his voice inaudible to his wife (the woman was a German shepherd; she could hear smoke wafting through the air): "I love the kid, but I want her to have a few of my features! I want some Henderson in her!" Strange wild pride of the father.

And what about the baby's appearance right out of the tunnel? How was I going to react to that? It wasn't exactly a limo ride down Birth Avenue, and the journey left its mark, Magda reassured me: stork marks on the face, coneheadedness, cradle cap, enlarged scrotums, molded heads, sucking blisters, crossed eyes, vernex, vaginal discharge, or (truly blessed child!) a slick coating of meconium, high-density amniotic supershit. . . .

Not that it could ever be as bad as it had been for McManus. Poor McManus. He was a Maritimer, a handsome man, with ruddy cheeks and ruddy manner, the great hope of a long line of Prince Edward Islanders. McManus was going all the way with the Lamaze birth trip, sitting in, coaching his wife. Eighteen hours she was in labor, with McManus running out every eight minutes to phone the clan and broadcast news of any progress all over their tiny island. And finally the great moment occurred, and the fruit of his loins slithered out into the doctor's rough hands, and McManus leaned over to see it, and there beheld –

Jesus Christ! What the hell was it? It was a miniature gorilla! Baby-sized, sure, but covered with thick dark hair, all over its arms and legs and chest and tiny backside and face! "I've given birth to an evolutionary throw-back!" McManus's mind gasped. "My child is King Kong!"

And through the thickening wall of his shock he heard his wife's faint, exhausted voice . . . "What's he like, Tommy?"

And McManus, true blue that he was, said "Oh," *we've given birth to the Wolf Child, the brat's a monster*, "he's beautiful." Three days later all the hair fell out. By then someone had told McManus about the common newborn condition known as lanugo.

The women control the tone of the classes, not to mention the moral high ground of the entire subject of birth. This is because pregnancy is submission, because being a mother is a life of sacrifice, because only women can give birth and life, much to their annoyance.

But it's also because labor, as Magda says, is no picnic. We coaches should be direct, verbal, and supportive—not my best side. Direct, verbal, and supportive are in my experience mutually exclusive modes of communication. "Don't take anything she says during labor personally," Magda says.

Magda says the transition between labor and birth will be the worst. The contractions will be ninety seconds long, excruciatingly painful, and only thirty seconds apart.

"How long does that phase last?" someone asks. There's panic in his voice.

Our job as coaches (and therefore as men), Magda says, is to serve our wives: fan them, massage them, remind them (to empty their bladders often, to move about), count their breaths, bring them ice chips. I am the birth butler. The prospect alarms me. I despise servitude. But that is what becoming a father is all about: submitting, obeying, being tamed. I can't find the grace therein, not yet.

I can hear the infant cardio-pulmonary resuscitation class in session in the next room. Downstairs in the lobby of the hospital news crews are camped out, awaiting word on the teenager shot this afternoon in class at the high school a few blocks from our house. This is the world I am bringing a child into, a world of choking and massacre.

But Magda's talking about enemas. Enemas are not required these days, because times have changed, and birth is natural, not to mention a woman's prerogative, and largely sacrosanct. In any event, women in labor are encouraged to pass more than just the child these days.

"I'm going to shit," a woman sitting next to me says to her husband. She thinks she's whispering. "I hope you'll be prepared for that."

He turns his head and looks directly at her. He owns a construction company. He makes his living adapting to unforeseen problems. But tonight I can see raw yellow terror in his eyes. This terror is a question: *And what, exactly, do you want me to do about it?*

I raise my hand, as if I were in grade school. I'm ten years old again, apparently. "Tell me," I say to Magda, "have you read this latest news that Leboyer, who invented the underwater birth, has changed his mind and now says fathers have no business attending birth?" I read it in the newspaper.

Instantly the mood of the women in the room floods against me in a massive tide. I am a traitor and a pariah. It's almost as bad as the class where I asked if people really did eat the placenta to ward off post-partum depression. I read that in the newspaper, too.

"Oh yeah?" Anita says, staring me down. "So where is this guy Leboyer now? Having lunch with Salman Rushdie?" She was fierce.

On break I buy a J3, and sit by myself in the empty classroom. Everyone else is out in the hallway. The door opens, and the CPR instructor walks in from next door. She's a knockout, with red hair and a slim body.

"Can I borrow your strength?" she says. She wants me to carry some mats. Of course. Isn't that what I was made for? I give you my strength, and you give me a little attention.

By now Magda's charts are more alarming:

Thoughts about medication
Fears
Partners' feelings
Types don't want/Types acceptable
Feelings tonight

Feelings tonight. I am trapped inside a Barry Manilow song that is being played over and over again on the oldies station that has enveloped my life.

Tonight we see a film about The Important Job of being a birthing coach. It's mostly wide-angle head-on shots of babies being squeezed out of vaginas. From what I can see, being a labor coach consists of being a physical presence but not getting in the way.

The lights come up, and one of the men, an agent at a major Hollywood agency, can barely speak. For three weeks he has said nothing in class and been more or less unconscious. He always shows up late, and I thought he rather disdained the proceedings. Now he's having a nervous breakdown. His eyes are gaping, he's sucking air like a dying fish. "So," he says, "uh, so, like, how far contracted are we at this point?" *Feelings tonight.*

I visit Dr. Katz, my wife's obstetrician, on one of her appointments. He's younger than I am, a pleasant, capable, goofy guy. He has three partners, all women. A modern guy. The white walls of the waiting room are covered with pictures of babies. Women, bulging upright drumlins, waddle about with their hands on their hips while their husbands speedread back issues of *Time.* Every time I catch the eye of any nurse, she smiles at me as if I were four years old. This is what happens when you go to the obstetrician: everyone treats you as if you're the baby. Maybe you are. Maybe that's why my wife likes going to the doctor. She gets to be three years old again and spend half an hour with a man who actually knows what he's doing.

Katz shows me the ultrasound picture of the baby. I see my child sketched in gray and white streaks on a video screen. I could be looking at a dozen passing thoughts made real. The baby is now eighteen inches long: I can see its spine, its feet. I am hot and dizzy with excitement, and faint with worry and fear: until now, I had no real idea how many things could go wrong. The heartbeat sounds like a toilet flushing again and again very quickly. A squishy heart.

I decide not to visit the doctor's office again. This thing is alive.

On the weekend I have to turn down a game of golf to buy a crib. My resentment is pooling in my shoes. At home afterward I retreat to my study. I open several beers.

I make a list of what I get out of my marriage, and what my wife gets. Under my wife's name I list the baby, love, the fact that she is living where she wants to live. Under my name I list one other word: book. I get to write a book.

My greatest fear is that I have stupidly, thoughtlessly given my time and therefore my life away; made myself, as Bacon wrote in his essay "On Marriage and Children," a "hostage to fortune." Sometimes these thoughts ambush me, and I feel defeated and betrayed, and then, in a crack of fury, I want to break whatever I happen to be holding. These moments pass quickly.

I come to class four drunk. Adrienne, one of the women, is lying on a mat on the floor. Her blood pressure is up on the roof, and she has to spend her days and nights prone. A nightmare.

Another couple, a new pair, are attending this class because it's about Cesarean birth. Their baby, their third, needs an operation on its brain, and so the doctors will be performing a planned Cesarean.

The German guy and his wife have a tiff in class. He's a movie producer. He's counting off her breaths, but she's not following him.

"It's my breathing," she says.

"It's my rhythm," he says. "I'm the coach."

"The coach," Magda says. "Not the boss! Partners!"

Anita's baby is induced this week. During class we take a tour of the hospital and visit her. She's not talking, which is a miracle. She looks empty, and slightly green. Her husband, on the other hand, who barely said a word in five weeks, glows as if he has a 10,000-watt bulb in his head. He can't shut up. He's holding their baby in his arms in the hallway, a small, scowling ball of piss and puke and sleep and yowl. He even cut the cord. Magda considers this "a very positive sign."

"You're in for an amazing experience," he says to me. Blasts of a weird yellow sour smell—what is it, that vapor of babies?—are rising off the kid. But why is he talking so directly to me? There are other guys standing around. But he's looking straight into my eyes. Have I really seemed so reluctant?

"Before, I thought, ah—me, in the birthing room? I don't think so. But now I see: you have to go through it, and then you understand why. I bawled my head off when the baby came out."

Afterward in class, everyone is amazed. "David seems like a changed man." I would say that's an understatement. I would say David looked like he'd been kidnapped by friendly little blue men.

But we have to rush back to class to see another film. This one's called *Hello Baby* and features three couples from Boston, all of whom are giving birth. All the birth movies we've seen bear marked similarities to pornographic films. The action is about as varied, the characters are even less developed. The sound tracks are comparable, too, heavy on women moaning. We watch them for the same reasons: to focus our imaginations, to cut out external stimuli, to find the source of our desires.

One of the couples in the movie, a lout named Carl (or Cahl, in Bostonese) and his wife, are complete buffoons. Cahl's wife is suffering dull agony; the only place she can bear the pain of labor is in the shower. She can barely tell Cahl to stop fanning her head, and Cahl is not the sort to pick up on things. Cahl is supposed to be soothing her fears and pain and apparently volcanic heartburn. But all Cahl can say is, "Mustah bin dat hoagie you ade dis ahftahnoon, huh?" Everyone finds this extremely amusing. And yet when the baby finally fights its way out, and Cahl is leaning over watching, and his lip starts to quiver, and he says, "Ohmigahd, honey, it's Cahl Jooniah, Cahl Jooniah is heah!" and the tears burst from within him—well, I know it sounds idiotic, but all around me, on blue mats in the dark, men and women are crying.

One night toward the end we rehearse labor in class. We have to inflict pain on each other to prove that the Lamaze breathing techniques work.

They seem to, which is encouraging. What's even more interesting is how seriously the women try to hurt their husbands. I suppose they don't have the opportunity often.

"If that's as bad as it gets," the guy with the Filofax tells his wife, who's gripping his thigh with all her might, "you have nothing to worry about."

"Okay then," she says, "maybe I'll try gripping a little higher." By now everyone's nervous, even afraid. Everyone, man and woman alike, wants to blame the penis.

We celebrate our last class with a potluck supper and an exchange of phone numbers. We've become a family. I am appalled to find I'm strangely thrilled: I imagine the reunion, and all those babies. At last I will belong to something, I think, even as I tell myself my brain is turning to aspic.

"Let's talk about what this is really going to be like when you go home with your baby," Magda says. "Because sometimes it's like. . . "

Magda stalls. She can't quite find a way to say this bit. For six weeks she has glorified childbirth and family life, but this is harder.

"It's a wonderful life-style change, but sometimes it's hard to get used to. Your relationship definitely changes."

She pauses. She has been saving the worst for last. "You can't come home on Friday and say, Let's go to Palm Springs for the weekend. And the big question here is, Is there sex after birth?"

"No," a woman says instantly.

A few minutes later Magda dims the lights and leads us through a "guided visualization." We lie on the floor in the darkened room on our blue exercise mats, blue the color of a big summer sky. Magda tells us to breathe . . . and to imagine a park . . . where we can relax . . . and where we have three balloons . . . each of which represents our worst fears about birth. . . .

"Let each balloon go," Magda says. "Watch it float up out of sight. Okay, now let the second one go."

My first balloon hasn't disappeared from sight yet. The balloon is my fear that something will be wrong with the baby. I can't stop being afraid.

During the potluck supper, the women pack around Magda like seals and talk about breastfeeding: duration of, when to stop, developmental considerations. "A friend of mine says she stopped when she saw her son lumbering toward her to feed," my wife is saying. "He suddenly reminded her of her husband. She said that was it."

Isn't that just how women understand men? They see us, and if they don't run, they laugh.

The men prefer the perimeter of the room. The German is telling me about the Berlin Wall. He used to live right beside it. He never expected it to fall.

15

Death and The Professor

*A long journey – Various reminiscences – The habit of
backseat driving – Danger at night – An upset*

I thought if I kept driving and stayed away from home long enough, some
sign would show itself to me, and I would have the answer about children
and wives and family life. I'd know, one way or the other. But I was just
waiting for something to happen, something that would make up my
mind for me.

Eventually I went golfing in Wyoming with the Professor. It was a last
spree of purposelessness before the arrival of the baby. My game had
improved a little, especially since I'd started following all the way through
on my shots, but I still didn't play anything close to reliable golf.

The Professor was driving. It was easier that way, and much more
relaxing for both of us. The Professor was Mr. Inside—the guy who always

knew how to light a match in the wind, where to find cheap tickets, which restaurant served the best crab in the city, the fastest lane on the freeway, which hotels would comp us in Vegas—and he drove me berserk on the highway with his incessant suggestions. The Professor was the kind of guy who liked to push in the cigarette lighter *before* he took a cigarette out of his pack. I wasn't sure what he did with all the spare seconds he saved, but his routines seemed to give him an almost reptilian unflappability. Perhaps it was his way of preserving his fast-paced, East Coast, Harvard-educated background now that he was working as a semiotician in California, where leisure seemed to expand endlessly, reducing the pace of life to a well-tanned soporific glide. Or maybe he used all those precious saved seconds to think; in the three years I'd known him, I never once said anything he hadn't thought of first. He was a good guy to hang around with.

It was a long way to Wyoming from Los Angeles. For the first couple of hours we talked: people we knew, plans we had, projects we were considering. Then we went quiet, and after that we talked in bursts, more or less about single subjects. Sometimes he talked about his father, or how much he hated teaching at a university. In the long pauses between bursts, I wondered whether the Professor was pulling back from our friendship, in anticipation of the baby's arrival. I noticed it sometimes; he was busier with other people now, he was afraid to ask my wife how she was feeling. I thought the whole prospect scared him. At other times I thought he was just the same; it was me who was scared, even paranoid.

If I wasn't worrying or talking, I watched the scenery. I saw a flock of sparrows bombing the highway the way they do, expanding and contracting like a lung. I noticed that, traveling east, the night fell first as mist. Sometimes I saw something by the side of the road—a taxidermist's sign, in this case—that reminded me of something else, such as one night in December in Texas when I bought some firecrackers and stopped for the night in a bare town that was nothing more than two highways crossing. Before I went to bed, I set the firecrackers off in a truck lot next to my motel. They were green and spun wildly across the truck yard. I was afraid they'd hit a truck and ignite its gas, so I hid in the shadows and watched, and as soon as the show was over I ran sneakily back to my room. I'm nearly forty, you know. The next morning, I woke up and thought the fields and the cinder banks of the railway beds were covered with frost. It turned out to be thousands and thousands of bolls of fresh-picked north Texas cotton, fallen from hoppers on passing trains. I couldn't figure out why I remembered those details, and not others: why instead of recalling what my wife had said over dinner, I remembered firecrackers and cotton bolls on a cinder bank when I was by myself. I supposed it was because I was the only one there, and the crackers and cotton bolls were my proof, mine and no one else's, that I was.

Then I started to remember people I'd met the last time I'd been up that way, toward Wyoming and Montana. I met a man who sold socks and knives, period. I remembered another man in the Bitteroot Valley in Montana, who walked from Oklahoma to California with his family during the Depression, picking fruit and unloading watermelons. "Do you know the book *The Grapes of Wrath*?" his daughter had said. "Well, we were part of that." The whole family, four generations, lived on a ranch now, and the old man couldn't believe his offspring were so prosperous. Life was pleasant. How unbelievable! He'd grown up in Indian territory, before Oklahoma was a state; it gave me a charge just to be in the room with him. His father had harbored the James brothers when they needed to lay low. Now his grandson, Fred Joseph, was in his fifties. He was the local fireman. "What else is there but family?" Fred had said to me. I could see his point. But I also wanted to say: freedom, privacy, work, sex, wandering, and lightness.

By the time we crossed the state line into Wyoming, I was feeling pretty lonely. That could happen even with the Professor in the car. I remembered a blizzard in North Dakota, and the way the fresh snow looked like huge white sheets tucked into the earth, and the way the towns poked up out of the flatness reluctantly, like prairie dogs forced to tend to some matter in the middle of hibernation. I thought about my wife's hips, and her upper arms, and the light caramel of her skin, and the way it drew me, and that helped. But that got me thinking about some other woman's paler skin from years before, or how someone else wore so many bangles in bed it was like making love in a Balinese temple, and that made my loneliness worse. Then I worried the Professor could somehow tell I was thinking about sex. I was disturbed to realize that I got along well with my wife when I was on the road. I needed to be alone, but I needed to know I had somewhere to return to, some home, as well. I wanted to belong to something, but it had to have a back door and an ejector seat. Selfish and unfair, but true.

I also thought about what an unexpected landscape the terrain of North American manhood had been. In California, I expected to find drum-happy circumcision-reversing Earth Worshippers at every turn, but I also found the most literal manhood of all. The dreams of men in Los Angeles *were* their lives: if they wanted adventure they built it and filmed it, if they wanted women they made them out of plastic, if they wanted to live forever they sucked the fat out of their necks and tied the flaps back. Their "inner children" were not metaphors but actual beings they felt they could contact at once on psychological car phones, preferably while naked in the woods. Sex was pornography and pornography walked down the street. West Coast men existed and breathed in the present, in the hard literal.

When I moved inland, I fell back into a more traditional time, or at least into a time where experience was in the past, and hope lay in the future, and each one kept its distance from the other, if possible. Cause and effect were more obvious on the plains, in ways they never were in California.

It was on the East Coast, where I had expected to be rebuffed by busy, skeptical, and unemotional men that I met complete pagans, pantheists who wanted to deify and see meaning in everything, whether it was a sauna, leather, a fish, a poll, wilderness, wearing suspenders, or someone else's anger.

But no matter where the men I met lived, no matter what they did or how they passed their time, no matter whether they argued for a living or drank incessantly, one question rolled around their heads like a pea in a gourd, one thought always rattling: what's next? Even the Professor, who was addicted to sports on television, wanted as much, because each game held what he sought: an adventure whose outcome he couldn't predict. I remember looking over at him as he drove and thinking, that's it; that's what men want, from the moment they leave their mothers' arms.

We finally arrived in Jackson, Wyoming. We checked into a cabin and had an unspecified number of drinks, and I suggested to the Professor that we ford the Snake River.

It was late, around two or three in the morning. The Professor was not entirely enthusiastic. "Come on!" I said immortally. "It'll be great." I wanted us to have an adventure. I wanted the trip to be memorable, more memorable than just another couple of fairways, so that if the baby did change things, at least we'd remember this time.

"You're fucked," he said.

"No, really, we'll have a good time."

"I will not have a good time."

I began to pick my way across the river, by stone, thirty feet to the other side. The water was only waist deep; it wasn't like shooting the Fraser or anything like that. It was cold, though. It isn't inconceivable that something drastic might happen, I thought to myself. This is exactly the kind of stunt that leads to tragedy.

I was getting wet. The Professor hung back; he'd put anything into his body, but when it came to physical adventure, he was cautious.

I made it to a gravel bar. It was September, but the water was higher than usual after that spring's bumptious runoff. The moon was full and so bright I could have been standing in the parking lot of a suburban super-mall. It reminded me of the nights in Palm Springs, playing golf in the desert, how Spence had been revealed by the moon. The gravel bar was chalky white in the moonlight. The Professor stood on the bank, watching me. I could see his bald spot gleaming.

"I've got an idea," I said. I wanted him to join me on the gravel bar. I wanted that adventure even then, in the late innings of my irresponsible life. "We'll build a bridge."

I began to haul deadwood over, levering it up into the air, and dropping it across the river between the gravel bar and the bank. I worried the splashes would wake up someone in the cabins. After a while the Professor joined in, hauling wood from the bank to build the bridge from his side.

It was a great bridge. We had four logs across the river, one of which, an aspen, had a branch we could use as a handrail.

It was time to test the bridge. An owl was hooting and nagging us from a cottonwood tree across the river. The main branch of the river shot past us to the west in the darkness on the other side of the gravel bar. I could make out the far bank rising darkly out of the water. I didn't want to be in that water. It was moving fast, and hummed the way rivers do, a noise so much a part of the place you only hear it if you think to listen.

The Professor went first. He's a natural athlete, nimble and quick, and I admired his progress. He was halfway when he stopped to balance. He moved ahead. Three-quarters. The water was deeper here. There were some branches on one of the logs requiring a brief plié. Now he had a foot on shore. He'd made it.

But then he slipped back, and one foot went in the river up to the ankle. He yowled. I jeered. No one said it wasn't competitive.

I'm stronger but less light-footed. I got a quarter of the way across. The bridge was four logs wide, but they were uneven, and crossing was tougher than it looked. Halfway, I was about to sidestep the brushy obstacle when I heard a lazy crack and our bridge collapsed. I was up to my knees in the Snake. I was out and across in no time, but not before the Professor was on his back, pounding the leaves. Now that I think of it, I hadn't heard him laugh like that in a long time.

The next night, driving home late, the Professor was rewinding a tape when I heard him say, "This guy's coming right at us." A car had swerved into our lane and was headed for my headlights. He was accelerating. I couldn't believe it at first, and then when he didn't move I swerved. The shoulder was narrow and sloped steeply away, and by the time I tried to turn back onto the road, my truck had somersaulted onto its side, the Professor's side.

Everything happened very slowly. There is that moment, when the ends of your life's elastic get pulled, and the threads spin furiously for an instant. That moment when the question pops up: Do I want to die? I asked my father about it once, and he said he wasn't afraid to die. He was seventy-five at the time. He liked his life, and feeling his muscles work, and sitting beside my mother at the movies, and spading his garden. He just wasn't afraid of going, or of what happened afterwards. He didn't see death as failure, as I did.

"Hang on," I said.

"Fuck, Ian," the Professor replied.

We came down on the side of the truck slowly. There was a shower of glass, as the Professor's window blew out. I heard metal squealing. The truck began heaving up onto its roof. We waited. We were looking at each other. Halfway up, the truck rocked back down on its side like a rough cradle.

Our seatbelts held us suspended horizontally in the air. I felt like an astronaut. Not that it was a new feeling.

I looked down at the Professor.

"Are you okay?" I said. I could smell beer. An unopened six pack had popped against the roof. The bottles weren't broken, but the tops were off. Terrific. Not to mention hundreds of cigarettes and packets of beef jerky and aspirin and coffee cups and Christ knows what else. Things did not look good. At that point I remembered there was a possibility of explosion.

"I'm fine," he said. "What is this, some new Canadian driving technique?"

"Man overboard," I said. "I told you these things tip easily."

Five faces appeared above me in my side window. "You guys okay?"

The tape, now rewound, blasted on. The song was "Funky Little Flower" by Loud Sugar. The Professor reached out to turn it down, turned the volume control the wrong way, and the noise quadrupled. It was a good way to impress the assembled multitudes of our seriousness.

We climbed out my window while the onlookers held the car stable. I checked to see if the Professor really was in one piece, but he was already riding me about overcompensating on the swerve. My driving was an ongoing joke between us, and he was not about to miss this prime opportunity. I wasn't sure how it would look, or if there had been any witnesses to attest to the oncoming car. I didn't want to spend the night in jail. I was glad the Professor was okay, but he was being alarmingly abstract. Whenever I said, "Is there anything in the car?" he said, "Never mind." It was a while before the police came and took a report, and implied that I had been drinking, and administered a breathalyzer, and discovered I was stone cold sober.

Gradually my paranoia gave way to a spotty dullness in my frontal lobes, as I thought about the actual size of the pain in the ass that now stood between Wyoming and home. I thought about eleven hundred miles with no side window in November. When the frustration wore off, we started laughing. It was a long time before the tow truck came and we hired a taxi back to our cabin. We stayed up drinking and thinking. We didn't talk much.

What I remember most clearly are the first still moments after hauling myself out of my sunken truck, standing by the side of that black wet highway, in the middle of goddamn black wet Wyoming, and looking south, toward L.A. I remember pulling out a packet of cigarettes and my lighter, and being told to stay away from the car, because of the gas. I remember thinking, Right, gas; be careful. Then I thought about all the stuff in the truck that I had bought with Johanna, that belonged to her, to me, to us, even stupid things like tire chains. I wanted the car to be the same as it had been when we had last driven it together.

I thought of our life together. I thought, ten yards later, twenty miles an hour faster, a car behind me, a drink in me, I'd be dead. In my mind I could see that other ending, the truck frame bent, wheels spinning in the air, blood inside the cab. I thought about some highway patrol sergeant calling my wife, saying there had been an accident; could see her bringing her hand to her mouth; could see her chest go down, could feel her heart spend itself in a single rush. I wanted to comfort her, tell her it would be fine, keep her company, soothe her fears, but I was dead. There was no solace for her. I thought of the baby in her, and how it might have had no father; how the child would be a reminder always to Johanna of my absence. Of my departure. That was when I wanted the miles between where I was and where she was to be gone, to be nothing but some grit in my pocket.

The Professor was smoking a few feet away. I watched him for a while. Headlights spun down on us every few minutes. Suddenly we seemed very foolish standing there, two men together on a highway in the middle of nowhere, as the red and blue police lights revolved, lighting us and shading us, revealing us and hiding us from others and ourselves. Suddenly we seemed out of place and pointless, like a couple of old mirrors someone found in a junk store, but that no one used any more. I don't suppose it was careless, really, but it seemed so. He knew it, and so did I. I wish it were more dramatic, or different from every other fool's story. Scared to death—that is the popular phrase, after all. But that's where we went over, and that's where I swam in the clear air, not knowing if I was laughing or crying, angry or sad, waving or drowning. That was where I thought, I want to go home now, to my wife and my child. I have to get home now. I have to stay alive.

16

Baby

Unexpected arrival of a climactic event – A man with a napkin on his head – Horrors and grossness – Fear and trembling – Darkness and light – Conclusion

I've been sleeping badly ever since I got back a couple of weeks ago. I lie awake for hours at a time, listening to my wife's steady, resilient breathing beside me. The time slides by slowly, like traffic on the freeways, inching its way along, with no discernible goal beyond the direction the highway is headed. I spool the nights together with worry.

Two nights ago was no different. At some hour of the streaked pre-dawn, I get out of bed to have a cigarette. I discover anew, for the thousandth time, that my wife is pregnant. Not only is she pregnant: the baby is now ten days late. Johanna is frantic, deeply insane. She looks up at me, eyes wild, her voice a bark.

"Are you glad we're having this baby?" Pause. "You can tell me the truth."

"Yes," I say.

"Why?"

"Because in the world I'm alone. You can never understand how anyone else feels, and they can't really understand how you feel. You can be in love or have sex and want to be the other person, but you never can be. The only time two people become one person is when they make a baby. It's the only time it happens."

All of this pours out of the night me, unpremeditated, as if I were a sugar dispenser.

When I wake up again, time has gone by. It's still early, but the sky is lighter. I can hear someone in my apartment.

Johanna is sitting in a rocking chair in the darkened living room. She looks like a large boulder, rolling back and forth. Something's different, and I watch for several minutes before I realize it's her concentration: she's a separate ship, on remote control, and I haven't a clue who's working the joystick.

"What's the matter?" I say. "Are you okay?"

She looks at me. "I think I'm in labor." She smiles.

I nod. I go into a daze. In the ensuing two hours, I assemble a baby swing that has been parked in its box in the dining room for the past three weeks, hang three pictures in the nursery, make eight phone calls, install the baby seat in the car, do a stack of Xeroxing, send three packages, and do two crossword puzzles. By then it's time for breakfast. I'm afraid to stop. Johanna catches me looking out the living room window. I'm thinking, everything's about to change.

"You know," she says, "I think I went into labor because of what you said last night. About two people becoming one. I suddenly knew it was okay to have this baby."

I smile at her. I look out the window. I think to myself, I hope I was telling the truth.

Later Johanna is in agony. She's in labor, has been for twelve hours. The contractions are now two minutes apart, and they make her jump and cry. The only way she can endure them is to lean over a chair, her forehead pressed hard against my forehead, and look at my shoes. "Your shoes," she whispers, her mouth clenched into a fist, "let me see your shoes."

When the pain finally becomes so great that it's disillusioning, when she realizes she has to do more than simply endure the pain, as if she were skiing, and instead transcend it, my wife has an epidural. One moment she's starring in a self-directed sequel, "The Exorcist Meets Alien," and then there is a small pop, a tiny gasp of pressure, as the needle enters a space between two vertebrae, and thirty seconds later she is behaving like a very satisfied opium addict. One minute she is screaming "Ooooooh no no Jesus shit no no no" and the next she's lounging on the birthing bed like Cleopatra on her barge, saying "Go for a walk, honey. Go and calm down. You need some rest."

The anesthesiologist, a hard-ass in his forties in green fatigues, has a balloon-print napkin on his head in some parody of the antiseptic and is wearing three days' growth and a diamond stud in his ear. "Are you a surfer?" I say.

"Triathlons," he says, not looking up from my wife's spine. He's known as the fastest, least talkative anesthesiologist in the hospital. "I did the Ironman."

He leaves. "My," the nurse says, "he really opened up to you."

My wife thinks he was God. Afterward, I hear her talking about him on the phone to a friend. "He had a good body," she says. "He was really cute."

Our obstetrician, the young genius named Katz, arrives. Soon to be a father himself, he's planning on delivering his own baby, he tells me. "I think it would be fun. But I don't think I'd do the episiotomy." He doesn't want to have to cut open his own wife's vulva. I laugh, as expected. I desperately want to be his friend.

What I'll never forget is Johanna's warbling cry when Katz does her episiotomy. The epidural has long since worn off. This is the worst shriek of all, as if she were on fire: a shrill loud narrow *ooooooo*, a tunnel of pain. I'm standing at her side, holding her legs back, counting out her pushes, and at the moment of that awful cry she seems like a girl. But I know she'll never be able to explain that pain. There is something unsayable between us now. She shrieks, I watch. I never expected to feel this lonely, not at the birth of my own child, but I do.

Everything becomes very detailed then and occurs in extreme close-up. Many things happen quickly and slowly at the same time. The details are like fractions that add up to a whole, but only very gradually.

At the peak of my wife's frenzy, for instance, the doctor casually but efficiently tells her to concentrate, as if they were studying for a math exam together. She hears him and she does so. The nurse, a woman from Mauritius whose face is beautiful and as black as ink, has an ancient, spiced accent like something you put on steak. "Poosh!" she commands. "Hawduh!" I notice all these details, one by one, and dwell on them, and yet when I return to the action in front of me no time seems to have passed. Everywhere blood is spilling and my wife is gasping and the doctor is moving swiftly and sweat is running down my back, and yet I remember these details: the curves of that accent, that old command, the calm of wisdom, damp flesh.

When it's time to push, I see someone in my wife I have never seen before: some *Ur-woman,* capable of tungsten focus and magnesium will, bearing down on her timeless purpose. Her red, blunt face, her lidded, grunting eyes. I think, She looks noble, like a woman in a painting by El Greco. Between pushes she flies off to the ceiling like some crazy wayward jet, and it is all I can do to haul her back for the next contraction; but my efforts are incidental. What matters is that when it matters, she knows what she has to do, and does it.

And then my daughter is out. She flies from the hole, blue and red and shiny, her head covered with blood, and sits in the doctor's hands, squalling and angry. I have a daughter.

I have a daughter.

The words don't mean anything yet. Her face is the only fact I've admitted to so far: her face, and the thin rubber membrane of her chest, her heart's curtain. I can't feel my way into her yet, because we share no history. But I think of her face, and I think of her tiny chest, and I think of her dying, and how unbearable the world would already be without her. This has all happened within a minute of her birth.

Then I know, birth is something I can't do, that no man could do. It is a contest too grown in the deep earth for mannish strength. I feel completely outclassed. I try to imagine passing a coconut through my penis, to see if I can imagine the pain, but my mind blanks out every time. This was the purpose my wife performed, and understood from within herself—a purpose that is hers and hers alone. Things have changed between us; she has reached some other plane I'll never know. My isolation filters down again, pervading the swank delivery room like a cool bank of weather. Johanna has grown and delivered a human being, and so that she will be willing to do it again, her body is already forgetting the details. I am left to see it all from a distance, with something that may or may not be a cooler eye, and to remember what I saw. Maybe that's my purpose as a man: I have to spray my seed, and then remember everything I notice.

I stand behind the doctor and watch as he stitches Johanna up. I stare for a long time at the bright red wound through which our child emerged. I thought I didn't want to look at this, but apparently I do: This was her most intimate place, a zone that in our past together only I was allowed to see. Everything, every moment, is fraught like this, swollen with import and crowding the room. The neighborhood between her legs looks like one of those corners in New York, Broadway and 54th, say, that are always under repair, the entrails of the city open for all the world to see, steam pouring from the sewer covers, MEN AT WORK signs. I think: This is the wound through which our daughter was born. Pretence strikes when you least expect it.

Then I remember I have a daughter. I turn around, and there she is, snipped and drained and wiped and watched, gasping for life on a tray of towels. I think I can hear fury in her scratchy, watery wails. She looks thoughtful, and angry, and urgent, as if right away, in her first few moments on earth, she knows all of life's pain. She looks into my eyes. I know she can't see, that it's an accident; but I look into hers as well, and there and then the strange flow begins, the tide of care between us. For a moment, all my fears run out of me, into her, and then away. She grounds me.

The doctor wants me to cut the cord. I do so. This is a symbolic moment, one of the events the books say I must solemnly remember. But what I remember without trying is my daughter on my wife's chest for the first time, and how I had to turn away, how my heart cracked. I don't know why. I don't know if what hurts me is joy or terror.

After all that throttle and pain, after Johanna struggles through tears to get the baby to accept her breast; after our hospital room begins to swim in my addled head; after I think to myself for the fiftieth time, We have to give the baby up, we'll never manage this, it's too big for us; and after, at long last, they both have fallen asleep, I sneak out of the room. I walk the corridors of the hospital, infinite tubes of life and death, until I find a way out, to the outside.

A smoky yellow night fog has covered all of Los Angeles. It's three a.m. I am terrified, a million times more terrified, for instance, than I have ever been on a remote glacier in a winter storm with no visible way off. What am I afraid of? Everything. I am afraid my daughter will die, that in my ineptitude I will fail her or that she will simply forget to live.

But I'm afraid of much more than that. Even on the first night of my daughter's life, her colonization of my mind is complete: I can go nowhere without thinking about her, worrying about her mother, and feeling guilty that they are there and I am here. It's the guilt that's the worst, I knew that was going to be the case, it was the guilt I was afraid of all along. The guilt seeps into everything. I have a new leader now, a new commander-in-chief. I knew I was susceptible to guilt, to bosses and commanders and all authority—but even in the form of my child, who is two hours old? I stayed aloof for so long in my life, stayed away from marriages and children and families and bonds, those ceremonies of love, because I knew love would make me a slave to my own guilt and pain, that it would destroy the pure selfish insensate energy within me. I never plugged into that pulse the way I wanted to; I never learned completely to break the back of my fear and my shame: which is to say, buck the bull, fuck the girl, ride the big wave, *be a man*. Instead, it's a definition I still learn every hour of the day. Had I been born in a different time, I might have learned it in the course of a cruel war, where the act of killing another human being would have taught me the meaninglessness of all things, and therefore the powerlessness of guilt. So I tell myself, anyway.

But there was no war—our fathers put that killing behind them—and we sons went away instead to our offices, supposedly to make the world a better, more domestic place. In a world of plenty, I lost my defensive, manly purpose. I found it again in being alone. But eventually everyone kind enough to want to civilize me persuaded me to give up solitary life, and I tried to find some love for myself by giving a woman what she wanted—a child. I never imagined I would love her this way. Now I have to pay for my satisfaction: the price is that I must relinquish control over, authority over, the rest of my life. I am afraid my life is over. I am afraid I have become one more member of the army of the dreary. I stand out in the night mist and I see nothing but worry and weight, claustrophobia and loneliness, disorder and fear, stretching out before me. I foresee my life, and I am afraid it looks like a wide thick carpet of conformity, broken by intermittent stains of terror. I stand on a street corner and I can't breathe.

I return to the hospital room and fall asleep. Some time passes. It always does. It's morning again, early enough that I know I have the jump on everyone. I wake up, shower, shave, dress in a clean green checked shirt (this detail seems important), and slip out of the hospital again before my wife and daughter come to. They, we, survived the night. We still have the drive home from the hospital ahead of us, which is daunting, because I now see there are psychopaths behind every wheel of every car on the street. Where the hell did they come from? They weren't there yesterday. Don't they realize I have a newborn daughter?

Outside it's a beautiful spring day, momentarily less daunting. March mist quietly washes the air. I can hear the city waking up again, for what hundred thousandth time. I wish I could tell you how much I love that noise, so full of metal. I know I sound like a fool, like every idiot born once more into the hangover of new fatherhood, that space of time where every note and package seems full of genius. That parking lot over there—brilliant! And those stop signs! What a great idea!

This epidural bliss will wear off too soon, but so far—so far—it's not a bad day. Maybe I needed the sleep. Everything seems new, ultra-real. Over there, on the steps of the hospital: a woman in her fifties, sucking down a cigarette in half the time it needs. Her face is a stone of worry. She's the mother of one of the women in labor on our ward. Her cheeks are ashen and cut out of her face, as if Cézanne were her plastic surgeon; she has blond hair and is wearing a red coat. Her cigarette smells fabulous. I want a cup of coffee. I want it bad, right now, here, in the present where I am, in the calm between each tick of time, here, and here, and here, and here. "You're in a new dimension" was how the lady on the elevator put it when she discovered I was a new father.

Stay here, I tell myself, over and over: stay right here. Today the light is wet and *zaftig*, and a green breeze rounds off every corner of the world. I have things to do, and a responsibility. I hope this cool weather lasts.